Introduction to Common Lisp

Introduction to Common Lisp

Taiichi Yuasa and Masami Hagiya
Research Institute for Mathematical Sciences
Kyoto University
Kyoto, Japan

Translated by
Richard Weyhrauch and Yasuko Kitajima

ACADEMIC PRESS, INC.
Harcourt Brace Jovanovich, Publishers

Boston   Orlando   San Diego
New York   Austin   London   Sydney
Tokyo   Toronto

ACADEMIC PRESS, INC.
Orlando, Florida 32887

United Kingdom Edition published by
ACADEMIC PRESS, INC. (London) Ltd.
24-28 Oval Road, London NW1 7DX

Library of Congress Cataloging-in-Publication Data

Yuasa, T. (Taiichi)
  Introduction to common lisp.

  Includes index.
  1. COMMON LISP (Computer program language) I. Hagiya,
Masami, 1957- . II. Title.
QA76.73.C28Y83 1987   005.13'3   87-1183
ISBN 0-12-774860-1

87 88 89 90   9 8 7 6 5 4 3 2 1
Printed in the United States of America

Contents

Preface

This book is both an introduction to Common Lisp and an introduction to Lisp explained using Common Lisp.

Lisp was first developed more than twenty years ago. The first widely used Lisp, the so-called Lisp 1.5, was developed in the late 1950s and early 1960s by a group of people led by John McCarthy at MIT. Since then, many versions of Lisp have been implemented. Just looking around the authors' office we can see the names of Lisps implemented in U.S. such as MacLisp, Interlisp, UCI Lisp, Portable Standard Lisp and Lisps implemented in Japan such as UTI Lisp and Lisp 1.9. All these Lisps are collectively called the Lisp system or simply Lisp.

The origin of the name Lisp is unclear; some people say it comes from List Programming and others say it comes from List Processor. What everyone agrees about is that it has something to do with lists. Lisp is good at processing lists which can be used to represent very complicated information efficiently if used correctly. Because of this list processing ability, Lisp has been used in the area of symbolic processing, especially for the following systems:

- Artificial Intelligence systems including Expert Systems
- Algebraic computation systems
- Theorem proving systems
- Machine translation systems

At the current time the situation is changing. Because of the high productivity of its programming environment, Lisp is now being used for more than list processing. Some of these new areas are:

- Numerical computation
- Graphics
- Text processing such as a text editor
- System programming

When programming, Lisp helps you prepare a program, test whether it works correctly, revise it if necessary, and then execute the program in a very efficient way. This is done by the programmer interacting with the system. Productivity when creating programs plays a critical role in the development of software. Thus it is natural that Lisp has started to be used over a wider application area.

The programmer using a Lisp system writes a program using the language called Lisp. The Lisp language is also used for interacting with the system. In other words, Lisp is the language designed to take advantage of all the abilities of the Lisp system. Just like other languages have dialects, the Lisp language has many dialects. It is said that there are as many Lisp dialects as Lisp systems since each different system has a different set of system functions. A program developed on one Lisp system usually requires some alteration in order to run on some other system. Many researchers have desired the definition and an implementation of a standard Lisp language.

The version of Lisp introduced in this book, namely Common Lisp, was designed by a group of Lisp researchers for the purpose of having a standardized language specification which was in the tradition of the MacLisp style of Lisp systems such as ZetaLisp, NIL, SPICE Lisp, and so on. However, Common Lisp has become the internationally standardized specification because of the following virtues:

- It has been designed by many researchers and system developers.
- Programs are highly transportable between systems.
- The specification of the language is independent of the hardware and the operating system.
- It has the extensive descriptive capability of the Lisp language.
- It can have an efficient executable system.
- A complete specification of the language exists.

Some Common Lisp systems have already been developed. Common Lisp systems will run on more and more computers in the future. Moreover, the International Organization for Standardization has been considering the adoption of Common Lisp as the standard Lisp language.

This book is designed to explain Common Lisp in a way that can be understood by beginners. It explains programming ideas such as list processing and symbolic processing using Common Lisp. We do not expect readers to know about the Lisp language or any other programming language. We do assume readers have some basic knowledge about computers, such as what a terminal and a keyboard look like and what an operating system is and a mathematical knowledge equivalent to the first year of high school.

The Common Lisp specification described in the manual called *Common Lisp: The Language* by Guy L. Steele (see [1] of Bibliography) is enormous and it is impossible for us to explain everything in that manual in this book. For this book, we selected the fundamental capabilities of Common Lisp and those capabilities that are critical for writing programs and are often used. Such selections were made based both on the experience of the authors and with the help of members of the Symbolic Manipulation Working Group of the Information Processing Society of Japan. The knowledge you will acquire from this book will be enough for you to write reasonable Lisp programs.

Lisp is an interactive system and it is best to learn Lisp by actually using the system. Although it is desirable for the readers to use the system while reading this book, we tried to include examples of the actual interaction with the system as much as possible for the reader who does not have access to a system. There is some variation in the way of starting up a system and error handling on different systems. The examples of interaction which appear in this book use Kyoto Common Lisp (see [2] of Bibliography). We have included some comments in those examples that might be different on different systems.

We would like to thank Professor Reiji Nakajima, Kyoto University, for his encouragement in writing this book. We also would like to thank students of Kyoto University, Takashi Suzuki, Hideki Tsuiki, Naoyuki Niide, and Akitoshi Morishima for their valuable comments from their actual learning experience with Common Lisp using this book.

Bibliography

[1] Steele, Guy Lewis Jr. *Common Lisp: The Language*. Digital Press, Burlington, MA., 1984.

[2] Yuasa, Taiichi, and Masami Hagiya. *Kyoto Common Lisp Report*. Teikoku Insatsu, Kyoto, 1985.

1   Basic Constructs

In this chapter we explain the basic constructs of Common Lisp. These include the notions of function, variable, and expression; the data structures called symbol and list; and the operations like function call and assignment. We also describe what a Common Lisp system is and how user interaction with the system works.

1-1 A Common Lisp System

In order to use a Common Lisp system, you need to get the system started. Different computers may use Common Lisp systems made by different research groups or companies. The way you start a Common Lisp system depends on which computer system you are using and what Common Lisp system is available on that system. Even the same Common Lisp system may have a different way of starting up when used with different operating systems. Throughout this book we will use Kyoto Common Lisp (KCL) running under UNIX for all our examples. If you are not using this system you must consult the Common Lisp users manual to find out how to start Common Lisp on your system. This is how you start up KCL:

```
% kcl
KCL (Kyoto Common Lisp)    April 1, 1986

>
```

The "%" has been typed by UNIX. The "kcl" on the first line is the command which is typed by you to ask UNIX to start up KCL. The next line is the message that is typed by the KCL system that you just started. The ">" on the last line is called the **Lisp Prompt**. When this prompt appears the Common Lisp system is ready to accept input. Just as starting up a Common Lisp system can be different for different versions of Common Lisp, the first message and the symbol used for a prompt depends on which Common Lisp system you are using. However, many Common Lisp systems use ">" as the prompt.

The main task of a Lisp system is to repeat the following work:

1. print the prompt
2. read and calculate the value of one expression
3. print the value of that expression

By the time you have started the system and it has printed the prompt sign, it already has done number one of the above list. Let's input a simple expression after the prompt sign:

```
>(+ 12 5)
17

>
```

"(+ 12 5)" is the Common Lisp expression which calculates $12 + 5$. To input this expression you first type "(", then you type "+", space, "1", "2", space, "5", then ")". Some systems require you to type different keys such as the return key or the line feed key to tell the system that you have finished inputing a line. Other systems do not require you to do that. In either case, the system will read the expression and then print 17. The system then prints another prompt as its way of telling you that it is finished and is waiting for your next expression.

Once you understand that (+ 12 5) is the expression used to calculate $12 + 5$, then it is easy to guess (* 3 4) is the expression for computing 3×4.

```
>(+ 12 5)
17

>(* 3 4)
12

>
```

As in these examples, a user inputs an expression and the system returns the value. By repeating this **interaction** with the system, a user can prepare a program, test it, and run it.

1-2 Functions

"(+ 12 5)" is the expression used to call the **function** named +. A function receives some data, works on it, and then returns some data. The function + receives some numbers and returns their sum. The data a function receives are called **arguments** and the data a function returns is called the **function value** or simply the **value**. When you give a function some arguments and let it do its job, we say that you **call** the function. If you call the function + with 12 and 5 as arguments, you get 17 as its value. 17 is the value of the expression (+ 12 5). The value of the expression which calls a function is the value of the function applied to its arguments.

Usually a function returns only one value like + did, however, there are some functions which return more than one value. An example is `floor` which does division. `floor` takes two numbers and returns the quotient and the remainder. For example,

```
>(floor 11 3)
3
2
```

The quotient of 11 and 3 is 3 and the remainder is 2, so the first value is 3 and the second value is 2.

The general expression for a function call is

$$(\langle\!\langle\text{function name}\rangle\!\rangle \quad \langle\!\langle\text{expression}_1\rangle\!\rangle \ldots \langle\!\langle\text{expression}_n\rangle\!\rangle)$$

In other words, a function call is a list consisting of a function name followed by some expressions surrounded by left and right parentheses. $\langle\!\langle\text{expression}_1\rangle\!\rangle \ldots \langle\!\langle\text{expression}_n\rangle\!\rangle$ specify the arguments to the function. The value of the ith expression $\langle\!\langle\text{expression}_i\rangle\!\rangle$ becomes the ith argument of the function. In the expression (+ 12 5), n is 2, $\langle\!\langle\text{expression}_1\rangle\!\rangle$ is 12, and $\langle\!\langle\text{expression}_2\rangle\!\rangle$ is 5. 12 and 5 are also expressions, so

```
>12
12
```

```
>5
5
```

Common Lisp systems view a number as a particular kind of expression which returns the number itself as its value. Let's look at another function call expression, (+ (* 3 4) 5) which also calls the function +. In this expression, $\langle\!\langle \text{expression}_1 \rangle\!\rangle$ is itself another function call expression (* 3 4) and $\langle\!\langle \text{expression}_2 \rangle\!\rangle$ is the expression 5. The value of (* 3 4) is 12 and the value of 5 is 5, so the value of the whole expression is 17.

```
>(+ (* 3 4) 5)
17
```

In other words, (+ (* 3 4) 5) is the expression to calculate $3 \times 4 + 5$, that is, it adds 5 to the product of 3 and 4. This illustrates that if any of $\langle\!\langle \text{expression}_1 \rangle\!\rangle \ldots \langle\!\langle \text{expression}_n \rangle\!\rangle$ is a function call expression, then the value of that expression becomes an argument. If a function returns more than two values, only the first value will be used as an argument. For example,

```
>(+ (* 3 4) (floor 11 3))
15
```

This expression is used for adding the product of 3 and 4 to the quotient of 11 divided by 3.

You cannot omit the left parenthesis or the right parenthesis. Even if the function has no arguments you need to put the function name inside parentheses.

The functions +, *, and floor are functions provided by every Common Lisp system. Such functions are called **System Functions**. A user can also **define** new functions. The way to call a function defined by a user is the same as the way a user calls a system function. Let's suppose you have defined a function named square which calculates the square of a number. You can use square in the following way:

```
>(square 8)
64

>(square (+ (square 2) 1))
25
```

1-3 Variables and Symbols

A **variable** can be thought of as a box for keeping data. You can put any data including numbers in a variable but only one piece of data can be kept in a variable at a time. The data in the variable is called the **value** of the variable and the process of putting data into a variable is called **assignment**. All variables have a name that can be used as an expression. When you give the system the name of a variable as an expression, it returns the value of that variable as the value of the expression. For example, suppose the value of variable x is 100, then

```
>x
100

>(+ x 5)
105
```

To assign a value to a variable, you type

```
>(setq  ⟨⟨variable name⟩⟩ ⟨⟨expression⟩⟩ )
```

The value of ⟨⟨expression⟩⟩ becomes a new value of the variable whose name is ⟨⟨variable name⟩⟩.

```
>(+ x 5)
105

>(setq x 10)
10

>(+ x 5)
15
```

As you can see from the above example, the expression for assignment, setq, also has a value like any other expressions. The value of this type of expression is the value that has been assigned to the variable. However, in the assignment expression, the act of assigning is more important than the value of the expression. In the above example, (setq x 10) has changed the value of x from 100 to 10. As a result, the value of (+ x 5) is different before and after the assignment. When you calculate (setq x 10), you get 10 as the value and at the same time, you change the value of variable x as a **side effect**. In our everyday life we use the word "side effect" when we mean unexpected effect or an effect which is not initially intended, like "I got hives as a side effect of the medicine I took." In computer science, we call any action other than that of getting the value of the expression a "side effect." When we say "calculate the expression," you might have an image of only getting the value of the expression, so we will say "evaluate the expression" from now on to remind us that side effects might be part of the process. We will say "When (setq x 10) is evaluated, the value of x becomes 10" or "When the system evaluates (+ (* 3 4) 5), (* 3 4) and 5 are evaluated first."

Since some expressions have such side effects, it is important to consider the order of evaluating expressions when you are using their value as an argument to a function. For example,

```
(floor (setq x (+ x 1)) (setq x (+ x 2)))
```

When evaluating the above function call expression, the value of the arguments to the function floor will be different depending on which assignment expression is evaluated first. Suppose an initial value of x is 10. If the left assignment expression is evaluated first, x will become 11 from the (+ x 1) and then 13 from (+ x 2). So, (floor 11 13) will be evaluated. If the right assignment expression is evaluated first, the value of x first becomes 12 and then 13. So, (floor 13 12) will be evaluated. To avoid this ambiguity Common Lisp systems evaluate expressions from left to right. Since most of us write from left to right, it is rather natural to do it from the left.

In one setq expression, you can assign many values by alternately listing the name of the variables and the values to be assigned. For example, if you want to assign 1, 2, and 3 to the variables x, y, and z, you type

```
(setq x 1 y 2 z 3)
```

The above expression does the same thing as the following expressions:

```
(setq x 1)
(setq y 2)
(setq z 3)
```

The setq expression computes each value to be assigned and then assigns that value to the corresponding variable from left to right. Each assignment causes a side effect, so the order of the assignments is important. Consider

```
(setq x 1 y (+ x 1))
```

When a Common Lisp system evaluates the above expression, no matter what value x had initially, the value of y after this assignment is always 2. This is because when the system evaluates the expression (+ x 1) to determine the value to be assigned to y, 1 had already been assigned to x. When using psetq (parallel setq), which is almost like setq, the assignments are done after all the values for the assignments have been computed.

```
(psetq x 1 y (+ x 1))
```

Here the value to be assigned to y is computed before the assignment to x. In the computation of (+ x 1), the value x which existed before the evaluation of the psetq expression is used. If the value of x before doing the psetq is 10, then the value of y after doing the psetq is 11.

The expression (setq x 10) looks like a function call expression, but it is not. The reason for this is not that its evaluation causes side effects. As you will see later in this book, some functions have side effects. The real problem is that the rules we stated for evaluating a function call expression require that if setq were a function then in the evaluation of the expression (setq x 10) the *value* of x should be the first argument to setq. For example, if the initial value of x is 100, both 100 and 10 should be given to setq. But 100 and 10 do not have the information about what variable to assign. It is meaningless to try to get the value of (setq x 10) by making x an expression that needs to be evaluated since the x in (setq x 10) is the name of a variable. In Common Lisp (setq x 10) is one of the expressions which are called **Special Forms**. "Form" is another way of saying "expression" in Lisp languages. The setq special form exhibits a special treatment for x by treating x as the name of a variable rather than evaluating it as you would in a function call.

There is a system function for assignment, which is called **set**. When we use set, the variable to be assigned is computed by an argument whose value is a symbol. Just like numbers, a **symbol** is a data structure in Common Lisp. Each symbol has a name.

```
(quote 《symbol name》 )
```

When a Common Lisp system evaluates the above expression, the value is 《symbol name》. For example, the value of the expression (quote x) is the symbol x. When the system prints a symbol, it uses the name of the symbol.

```
>(quote x)
x
```

(quote x) is also a special form for the same reason that (setq x 10) is
a special form. set takes a symbol and some data as an argument and
assigns that data to the variable whose name is the same as the name of
the given symbol. In order to assign 10 to the variable x, you would give
the symbol x and 10 to set.

```
>(+ x 5)
105

>(set (quote x) 10)
10

>(+ x 5)
15
```

As you can see, the name setq comes from a combination of this set and
the q in quote. The reason for having both the function set and special
form setq which do the same thing is that since set is a function, a program
can decide which variable will get a new value at the time the expression is
evaluated. Consider a function foo, whose value is a symbol. In a function
call expression (set (foo) 10), if the value of foo is the symbol x, the
value of variable x becomes 10. If the value of foo is y, then the value of
y becomes 10. In the setq statement, since the name of the variable is
specified, this behavior is impossible. Even so, setq is preferable when the
variable of the assignment will not change, since setq is short to input and
easy to read. (quote x) can be abbreviated to 'x using a quote mark. So,
instead of

```
(set (quote x) 10)
```

you can type

```
(set 'x 10)
```

which looks clearer. But this may be a matter of taste. Some tasks which
setq can do and which set cannot do will be explained later in this book.
    Since Common Lisp has a function which assigns a value to a variable,
it is natural to have a system function symbol-value which returns the
value of the variable with the same name when given a symbol. Of course,
this symbol is also used when first making the assignment to this variable.

```
>(setq x 10)
10

>(symbol-value 'x)
10
```

The difference between the (symbol-value 'x) expression and simply
the expression x is the same as the difference between (setq x 10) and
(set 'x 10).

Common Lisp has many names for variables. It even has a variable
whose name is the same as your name. Try to assign your age to a variable
with your name.

```
>(setq joe 31)
31

>joe
31
```

A Common Lisp system cannot keep around variables with every possible
name. The system stores only a few variables called **system variables**
and creates a box for storing data as part of a new symbol whenever a
new variable is required. It is fine to think that there are boxes for every
name of a variable in the system. However, you should remember the boxes
for every name except system variables are empty before they are assigned
something and you will get an **error** message if you try to get the value of
an empty box. Each system has slightly different error messages. In KCL,
the error message looks like the following and you type :q to recover from
the error.

```
>jennifer

Error: The variable JENNIFER is unbound.
Error signaled by SYSTEM:TOP-LEVEL.

>>:q

>
```

Some system variables cannot be assigned. Their values are already given
and cannot be changed. Such variables have a constant value and are called
constants. In Chapter 9 we will explain ways to make variables other than
system variables into constants. pi, nil, t are examples of constants.

```
>pi
3.141592653589793    ; the value of the constant pi is an
                     ; approximate value of the ratio of the
                     ; circumference of a circle to its diameter

>nil
nil                  ; the value of the constant nil is the
                     ; symbol nil

>t
t                    ; the value of the constant t is a symbol t
```

(The remarks after the ";"s are user comments.) As you will see later in this book, nil is used very frequently. By having the constant nil, you do not have to type the quote mark in front of nil ('nil) to get nil as a value. The constant t is made for the same reason. nil and t are the only two system constants which were made for this reason. Other system constants such as pi are useful because they represent a special numeric value.

```
>(* pi (expt 5 2))    ; the area of a circle with the radius of 5
78.53981633974482     ; (expt 5 2) is a square of 5
```

1-4 Lists

You now know Common Lisp can use both numbers and symbols as data. There are other kinds of data in Common Lisp. In this section we will explain one of them—the data structure **list**.

A list is an ordered row of data. The system function list has a list as its value. The function list can have any number of any kind of data elements as arguments. The row of data becomes the value of this function.

```
>(list 1 2 3 4 5 6 7 8 9 10)
(1 2 3 4 5 6 7 8 9 10)

>(list 'we 'eat 'rice)
(we eat rice)
```

The value of the first expression is a list of numbers 1 ... 10 and the value of the second expression is a list of three symbols, we, eat, rice. The data objects that make up a list are called **elements** of the list. The system prints the elements of a list from left to right. Each element of a list can be a different kind of data and it can even be another list.

```
>(list 10 (list 'little 'indian 'boys))
(10 (little indian boys))
```

(10 (little indian boys)) is a list made of two elements. The first element is the number 10 and the second element is a list of three symbols, little, indian, boys. The function length will tell you the number of the elements in a list.

```
>(length
    (list 10 (list 'little 'indian 'boys)))
2
```

(One expression can be written on multiple lines. Indenting slightly after the first line makes it easier to read. The system ignores white spaces. Carriage return and line feed characters are treated as white spaces.) Since a list is a data object, it can be given to a function as an argument and can be assigned to a variable.

```
>(setq noun-phrase
        (list 'little 'indian 'boys))
(little indian boys)

>(list 10 noun-phrase)
(10 (little indian boys))
```

You can make a list of data by giving elements as arguments to list. If you already know what elements the list is to have, it may be more useful to type (quote ⟨⟨list declared⟩⟩).

```
>(quote (10 (little indian boys)))
(10 (little indian boys))
```

Just as we could write 'we for (quote we), we can use the quote mark to write

```
>'(we eat rice)
(we eat rice)
```

```
>(setq noun-phrase
       '(10 (little indian boys)))
(10 (little indian boys))
```

A list is a different kind of data from numbers and symbols with one exception. A list without any elements, the **empty list**, is the same as the symbol nil. Since the system prints the name of a symbol when it prints a symbol, it will print nil for the empty list.

```
>(list)
nil

>'( )
nil
```

The fact that the empty list and the symbol nil are the same may sound strange but this fact is very useful in Lisp and you will find out why later.

The functions car, cdr, cons are the most basic functions for operating on lists. car (pronounced as if you were talking about an automobile) takes a list as an argument and returns the first element of the list as its value. cdr (pronounced "coulder") also takes a list as an argument and returns all the elements of the list except the first as its value.

```
>(car '(we eat rice))
we

>(cdr '(we eat rice))
(eat rice)

>(cdr (cdr '(we eat rice)))
(rice)

>(cdr (cdr (cdr '(we eat rice))))
nil
```

When given an empty list as an argument, car and cdr return nil.

```
>(car nil)
nil

>(cdr nil)
nil
```

The word car comes from Content of Address part of Register and cdr
comes from Content of Decremental part of Register which were assembler
instructions for the IBM 704, but it is not necessary to remember this.

The function cons, the abbreviation of constructor, is a function which
adds one data item to the front of a list. Its first argument is the data to
be added and its second argument is the initial list.

```
>(cons 'we '(eat rice))
(we eat rice)

>(cons 'they (cdr '(we eat rice)))
(they eat rice)

>(cons 'never (cdr '(we eat rice)))
(never eat rice)
```

If you add an element to the front of the empty list, you will get a list
consisting of one element.

```
>(cons 'single nil)
(single)

>(cons nil nil)
(nil)
```

The second expression makes a list with the empty list as its only element.

The following functions are made by combining car and cdr:

caar	cadr	cdar	cddr
caaar	caadr	cadar	caddr
cdaar	cdadr	cddar	cdddr
caaaar	caaadr	caadar	caaddr
cadaar	cadadr	caddar	cadddr
cdaaar	cdaadr	cdadar	cdaddr
cddaar	cddadr	cdddar	cddddr

The names of all of the above functions start with "c" and end with "r".
The combination of a and d shows the combination of car and cdr which
this function computes. In order to get the third element of a list, you type

```
>(car (cdr (cdr '(1 2 3 4))))
3
```

Taking "a", "d", and "d", caddr can be used.

```
>(caddr '(1 2 3 4))
3
```

The use of `caddr` is compact and efficient because only one function is called rather than the three that are called in the first expression. The function

    (cddadr x)

has the same value of the following expression

    (cdr (cdr (car (cdr x))))

1-5 Evaluation and Forms

In Lisp, why do we write (+ 12 5) rather than 12+5 to calculate $12 + 5$? Doesn't (+ 12 5) look like a list with three elements, +, 12, 5? Well, (+ 12 5) is actually a list of data.

At the beginning of this chapter, we looked at the example,

    >(+ 12 5)
    17

Here the system reads (+ 12 5) and prints 17 as its value. More precisely, during the process of reading, the system changed a row of characters into data. "To read (+ 12 5)" means that a row of the following characters are changed into a list data structure consisting of the symbol +, the number 12 and the number 5.

    left parenthesis
    +
    white space
    1
    2
    white space
    5
    right parenthesis

By typing at the keyboard on the terminal, a user was sending a list to the system. The system processes this list and returns 17 as its value. The value of a list (+ 12 5) is 17. In other words, the system evaluates the list, not a row of letters.

A system function `eval` comes from the word "evaluation" and is used to evaluate data. The function `car` returns the symbol + when it receives the list (+ 12 5). The function `eval` returns the value of the list after evaluating the list.

```
>(car '(+ 12 5))
+

>(eval '(+ 12 5))
17
```

The function `car` looks at a list as a piece of data from which it can extract its first element while the function `eval` looks at a list as an expression which it can try to evaluate. When you give (+ 12 5) to the system, you should think of it as a function call expression, but when the system returns the list (+ 12 5) to you as a value, you should think it is a list of data.

```
>(+ 12 5)
17

>(cons '+ '(12 5))
(+ 12 5)
```

The same thing can be said for variables.

```
>x
100

>(eval 'x)
100

>(cadddr '(the value of x is 100))
x
```

Giving a variable named x to the system means giving it a symbol named x. We sometimes consider the symbol x as the name of a variable.

You already know that 'x and '(we eat rice) are the abbreviations of (quote x) and (quote (we eat rice)), respectively. Both of them are lists where the symbol `quote` is the first element, x and (we eat rice) are the second elements, respectively. In a list (quote ⟨⟨data⟩⟩), the value of the list is its second element. The value of 'x is the symbol x and the value of '(we eat rice) is the list (we eat rice). In Common Lisp every form can be looked at as a piece of data. This is a characteristic of all Lisp languages. But, this does not mean all data can be considered as an expression. As we said above, an expression is called a "form" in the Lisp language. A form is a data structure which is considered to be an expression.

Let us sum up a form and its value. All the data except lists and symbols are forms for which the data itself is the value of the form. An example of this kind of form is a number. All symbols are also forms and the value of a variable with the same name as the symbol is the value of this form. A list can be one of three different kinds of form.

1. **Function Call Form**: A list in which the first element is a symbol which names a function and in which all the rest of the elements are forms. The function specified by the first element is called with the values of the rest of the elements as arguments and the value returned by the function is the value of the form. The lambda expression, which will be explained in Chapter 6, can be used instead of the function name in a function call form.

2. **Special Form**: A list which has one of the following names as a first element:

```
block                 macrolet
catch                 multiple-value-call
compiler-let          multiple-value-prog1
declare               progn
eval-when             progv
flet                  quote
function              return-from
go                    setq
if                    tagbody
labels                the
let                   throw
let*                  unwind-protect
```

Each list with one of the above symbols as its first element has different kinds of data for the rest of the elements and has a different way of evaluating the special form and getting the value. We have already explained `setq` and `quote`. Other special forms will be explained later.

3. **Macro form**: A list whose first element is the name of a macro.

Lists which do not belong to any one of these three classes are not forms. For example, (1 2 3 4) is not a form and cannot be evaluated.

The macro form will be explained in detail in Chapter 7. In this chapter we will just give you an idea of what it is. You should think of a macro form as an abbreviated version of some other form. For example, Common Lisp systems have a macro called incf and its macro form (incf x) can be thought of as an abbreviation of the form (setq x (1+ x)). This form has the effect of adding 1 to the value of variable x. (1+ is the system function which takes a number and adds one to it.)

```
>x
100

>(incf x)
101

>x
101
```

You can use macroexpand to find out what underlying form a macro form abbreviates. If the argument to macroexpand is a macro form, it returns the expanded version of its argument as its first value and t as its second value. If the argument is not a macro form, macroexpand returns the form itself as its first value and nil as its second value. In this way you can tell if a form is a macro form or not by looking at the second value.

```
>(macroexpand '(incf x))
(setq x (1+ x))
t

>(macroexpand '(setq x (1+ x)))
(setq x (1+ x))
nil
```

In this book, we will describe many macro forms, but we will not explain the forms they abbreviate unless it is necessary for the reader to understand them. You can always find out what the underlying form is by calling macroexpand. One important thing to remember is that the form which is the value of macroexpand may be different in different Common Lisp systems because there may be more than one form which does the same job. For example, (setq x (1+ x)) and (setq x (+ x 1)) perform the same action so some Common Lisp systems may show (setq x (+ x 1)) as the value of (macroexpand '(incf x)). Please remember that the programs shown by macroexpand in this book are just typical examples.

2   Function Definitions

By this time you already know enough about Common Lisp to use the system quite a lot. You have learned how to use any system function once you know what it does and you have also learned how to get the system to remember the value of a function and how to use this value later. You can also construct complicated expressions by combining simpler expressions.

In this chapter, we will explain how to write a program. When we say "write a program," we mean "define a function of your own." It is much easier to define and call a function to evaluate an expression many times than to type the same expressions over and over again. When an expression is big and complicated it is much easier to remember the meaning of the expression if it is replaced by a single function definition. Once you define a function, even if you forget the details of *how* it computes its value, you can use it as long as you remember *what* the function is for.

2-1 How to Define a Function

To define a function, you use `defun`. For example, to define the function `square` which multiplies a number by itself, you type:

```
(defun square (x) (* x x))
```

The general form of `defun` is made up of three parts: the name of the function you want to define, a parameter list, and the body of the function.

In the above example, the name of a function is **square**, the parameter list is **(x)** and the body is **(* x x)**. The parameter list **(x)** specifies that the variable **x** is to be used as a parameter. A **parameter** is a variable which is used to initially store an argument to a function. When you call **square**, the parameter **x** is first set to the argument of **square**, the body **(* x x)** is evaluated and its value is returned as the value of the function. In other words, the value of the **square** function is the value of **(* x x)** where **x** is its argument.

Once you evaluate a **defun** expression, you can call the function defined by the **defun** expression.

```
>(defun square (x) (* x x))
square

>(square 4)
16

>(square -2)
4
```

As you can see from the above example, the name of the function to be defined is returned as the value of a **defun** expression.

Let's look at another example:

```
>(defun who-eats-what (who what)
    (list who 'eat what))
who-eats-what

>(who-eats-what 'we 'rice)
(we eat rice)
```

The function **who-eats-what** takes two arguments and returns a list made of the first argument of **who-eats-what**, the symbol **eat**, and the second argument of **who-eats-what**. The parameters of this function are **who** and **what**. When the system calls **who-eats-what**, the first argument is set to **who** and the second argument is set to **what**. If a function has more than two parameters, the arguments are set to the parameters one by one; the first argument is set to the first parameter, the second argument is set to the second parameter, and so on.

You can redefine a function by using **defun** in exactly the same way as you do when you define a function.

```
>(defun who-eats-what (who what)
   (list who 'eat what))
who-eats-what

>(who-eats-what 'we 'rice)
(we eat rice)

>(defun who-eats-what (what)
   (list 'who 'eats what '?))
who-eats-what

>(who-eats-what 'rice)
(who eats rice ?)
```

You cannot define a function which has the same name as one of the special forms. For example, you will get an error message if you try to define **setq**. You should avoid defining functions which have the same name as system functions or macros since the system may be using such functions. In order to discourage the redefinition of such functions, KCL prints a warning if a user tries to redefine a system function.

```
>(defun car (x) (* x x))
Warning: CAR is being redefined.

car

>
```

If you have redefined a function by mistake, you should exit the system and start again. Each system has a different way of exiting. In KCL, the function **bye** will get you out of the system.

```
>(bye)
```

When you restart the system, it will have forgotten about any definitions in the previous sessions. In KCL, the function **by** is also available to get you out of the system just in case **bye** has been redefined.

Generally, the body of a function is made up of multiple expressions.

(**defun** ⟨⟨function name⟩⟩   ⟨⟨parameter list⟩⟩
   ⟨⟨expression$_1$⟩⟩ ... ⟨⟨expression$_n$⟩⟩)

When you call a defined function, the system evaluates ⟨⟨expression$_1$⟩⟩ ... ⟨⟨expression$_n$⟩⟩ one by one and the value of the function is the value of the last expression. The values of all the expressions except the last one will not be used, therefore, they exist only for side effects.

```
>(defun foo (x y)
   (print x) (print y) (+ x y))
foo

>(foo 1 2)

1
2
3

>
```

The body of the above function **foo** is made up of three expressions. The first expression prints the first argument and the second expression prints the second argument, both as side effects. The third expression actually produces the value of the function. As you can see from the above example, the system prints 1 and 2, and then prints 3, the value of the function.

2-2 Local Variables

In the definition of the function **square**

```
(defun square (x) (* x x))
```

the parameter x is a variable which is valid only locally in the body of **square**.

When you type

```
(square 4)
```

the system creates a new box named x and puts 4 inside this box. This process is called "**binding** the variable x to 4." After this is done we say "x is **bound** to 4." The x in the body of the function **square**, (* x x), refers to this new box. That is why the value of the **square** function is the square of its argument.

Binding is different from assignment. While assignment replaces the content of the existing box, binding makes a new box and sets up an initial value for this box. Binding does not change the value of any existing box.

```
>(setq x '(a b))
(a b)

>(square 4)
16
```

In this example before the system calls **square**, a box for x has already been created. The binding of x in **square** does not affect the content of this box. So, if you type

```
>x
```

the system prints the value of x before **square** was called. The system will print

```
>x
(a b)
```

This shows that the x in the body of **square**, i.e., (* x x), is looked up in a different box than the x below:

```
>x
```

These two x's are different variables. Also, an x which is used as a parameter in another function is different from the x which is used as a parameter in **square**.

```
(defun add1 (x) (1+ x))
```

The above x has the same name as the x in **square**, but they are two different variables.

The fact that the parameter x is only valid inside of the body of **square** means that the **scope** of the variable x is the body of **square**.

scope of x

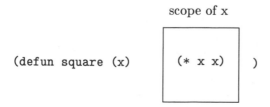

(defun square (x)   (* x x)   )

The scope of a variable is the extent of the places where it makes sense to refer to that variable (places you can either get its value or assign it a new value). Outside of this scope, the value of the variable cannot be gotten and the variable cannot be assigned a value. The parameter of **square** can be referenced only inside the body of **square**.

(defun ⟨⟨function name⟩⟩ (⟨⟨variable₁⟩⟩ ... ⟨⟨variableₘ⟩⟩)
    ⟨⟨expression₁⟩⟩ ... ⟨⟨expressionₙ⟩⟩)

The scope of the variables ⟨⟨variable₁⟩⟩ ... ⟨⟨variableₘ⟩⟩, thought of as the parameters of a function, is just the body of the function, that is, ⟨⟨expression₁⟩⟩ ... ⟨⟨expressionₙ⟩⟩ and these parameters cannot be referenced anywhere else. A variable whose scope is limited, like the parameter x in **square**, is called a **local variable**. Other variables are called **global variable**s. For example, in the above example

>(setq x '(a b))

the variable x is a global variable and can be referenced anywhere. By typing

>(setq x ⟨⟨statement⟩⟩)

you can assign a value to this global variable anytime you want and by typing

>x

you can get its value. If a variable, say x, can be referenced outside of the scope of any local variable x, then that variable is global. For example,

>(defun foo () (setq count (1+ count)))
foo

The variable **count** is referenced in the body of the above example, but because **foo** has no parameters, the body of **foo** is not part of the scope of any local variable. Therefore, **count** is a global variable and the global value of **count** increases by 1 every time **foo** is called.

>(setq count 0)
0

>(foo)
1

```
>(foo)
2

>count
2
```

The same thing will happen even when **foo** is called in the following way:

```
>(defun bar (count) (foo))
bar
```

In this case the only parameter of **bar** is **count**. The scope of the parameter **count** is the body of **bar** but the body of **foo** is not considered part of the body of **bar** and so is outside of its scope.

```
>count
2

>(bar 200)
3

>count
3
```

The parameter of **bar** is never referenced in its body and can not be used at all since it cannot be referenced outside the body of **bar**.

The system function **symbol-value** which gets the value of a variable and which was described in the previous chapter always returns the value of the global variable which is named by its argument.

```
>(defun foo (x) (* (symbol-value 'x) x))
```

Even if **symbol-value** is called inside of the scope of a local variable x, it returns the value of the global variable x. In the above expression, the function **foo** will return the value of its argument multiplied by the value of the global variable x. The assignment function **set** works in the same way. On the other hand if a **setq** expression (which is a special form)

```
(setq x 2)
```

is inside of the scope of local variable x, the evaluation of this form will result in an assignment to the local variable x. If it is outside such a scope, the value will be assigned to the global variable x. An expression which calls the function set

```
(set 'x 1)
```

always assigns to the global variable x even if it is inside of the scope of a local variable x. For example,

```
>(defun bar (x)
   (set 'x 2)
   (setq x 3)
   (* (symbol-value 'x) x))
bar

>(bar 0)
6
```

After the above example, the value of the global variable x is 2. The local variable is used both as a parameter which receives the argument of bar and as a temporary storage place for the data. You can store the value of an expression in a local variable and use it without calculating it over again. You can also keep the value and use it after other calculations.

There are many other ways to make a local variable besides as a parameter. Consider the special form let. The general form of let is

$$(\text{let } ((\ \langle\langle\text{variable}_1\rangle\rangle\ \langle\langle\text{initial value}_1\rangle\rangle\ )$$
$$\cdots$$
$$(\ \langle\langle\text{variable}_m\rangle\rangle\ \langle\langle\text{initial value}_m\rangle\rangle\ ))$$
$$\langle\langle\text{expression}_1\rangle\rangle$$
$$\cdots$$
$$\langle\langle\text{expression}_n\rangle\rangle\ )$$

$\langle\langle\text{variable}_1\rangle\rangle \ldots \langle\langle\text{variable}_m\rangle\rangle$ are the names of local variables. First, $\langle\langle\text{initial value}_1\rangle\rangle \ldots \langle\langle\text{initial value}_m\rangle\rangle$ are evaluated and the variables are bound to the corresponding initial values. Then the expressions in the body of the let expression, $\langle\langle\text{expression}_1\rangle\rangle \ldots \langle\langle\text{expression}_n\rangle\rangle$, are evaluated one by one. The value of the let expression is the value of $\langle\langle\text{expression}_n\rangle\rangle$. The scope of the variables $\langle\langle\text{variable}_1\rangle\rangle \ldots \langle\langle\text{variable}_m\rangle\rangle$ is the body of the let expression.

For example,

```
(defun square-square (x)
   (let ((y (* x x)))
      (* y y)))
```

`square-square` is a function for raising a number to the fourth power. The system first calculates the square of the argument and then it calculates the square of that value. By keeping the value of the first square in the local variable y, the system avoids computing the square of x more than once.

The expression

```
(defun square-square (x) (* (* x x) (* x x)))
```

requires three multiplications and is therefore less efficient. You can also write

```
(defun square-square (x) (* x x x x))
```

but this expression also requires performing three multiplications. The first example requires multiplying only twice.

You can omit ⟨⟨initial value⟩⟩ in the

```
( ⟨⟨variable⟩⟩ ⟨⟨initial value⟩⟩ )
```

part of a let expression. If the ⟨⟨initial value⟩⟩ is omitted the system assumes its value is `nil`.

```
>(let (x (y 1)) (list x y))
(nil 1)
```

The scope of a variable can extend into a let expression.

```
(defun to-the-fifth (x)
  (let ((y (* x x)))
    (* y y x)))
```

The scope of the parameter x extends throughout the body of the function which includes the body of the let, (* y y x). The x in (* y y x) is the parameter x. Many of the kinds of expressions which are explained later in this book, like the let expression, will not affect the scope of a variable. (There are some exceptions, but they are very rare.)

```
(defun ⟨⟨function name⟩⟩ (x)
  . . .
  (. . . (. . . ⟨⟨expression⟩⟩ . . .) . . .)
    . . .)
```

The above ⟪expression⟫ is usually within the scope of the parameter x no matter what other expressions exist around it.

```
(let ((x 1))
      . . .
  (. . . (. . . ⟪expression⟫ . . .) . . .)
      . . .)
```

In all cases, ⟪expression⟫ is within the scope of the local variable x. This does not necessarily mean, however, that an x that appears in ⟪expression⟫ is the x that was bound to 1 when entering the let, because ⟪expression⟫ may belong to the scope of more than one variable x.

```
(let ((x 2))
  (let ((x 3)) (* x x)))
```

Here (* x x) belongs not only to the scope of the x which is bound by the outer let but also to the scope of the x which is bound by inner let. In such cases the innermost scope takes precedence. In other words, the system refers to the variable which is bound by the innermost expression if there is more than one scope for a local variable. In the above example, the value of (* x x) is 9, not 4, since the x in (* x x) is bound by the inner let expression.

```
>(defun ⟪function name⟫ (x)
  (let ((x 3)) (* x x)))
```

In the above expression, the value of x in (* x x) is 9 independent of the value of the argument. This is because the x is bound by the let expression.

Another special form is let*. If you replace let with let* in the general let expression, you get the general expression for let*.

```
(let* (( ⟪variable₁⟫ ⟪initial value₁⟫ )
        . . .
       ( ⟪variableₘ⟫ ⟪initial valueₘ⟫ ))
  ⟪expression₁⟫
      . . .
  ⟪expressionₙ⟫ )
```

The let* expression does the same thing as the let expression except that the scope of a variable which the let* expression binds not only contains the body of the let* but also contains the rest of the variable specifications.

```
(let* ((x 3) (y (* x x)))
  (* x y y))
```

Unlike the case of `let`, the variable specification (y (* x x)) belongs to the scope of the x which is bound by the `let*` expression. The `let*` expression first binds x to 3, evaluates (* x x) with that binding, and then binds y to the value of (* x x). In other words, the `let*` expression makes the variable bindings one at a time while the `let` expression does all of the variable bindings at one time.

```
(let ((x 3) (y (* x x)))
  (* x y y))
```

In the above `let` expression, the system gets the initial values of the two variables for binding first, and then does the binding simultaneously. When (* x x) is evaluated, the x in (* x x) has not been bound by the `let`. This x would either be a local variable bound outside this expression or the global variable. The scope of the variable x is within the body of the `let` expression and does not extend to (* x x). The x in (* x x) is not the variable bound by the `let` expression.

The name `let*` comes from `let` since `let*` works the same as `let` except for the above-mentioned difference.

2-3 Predicates and True-False Values

It sometimes becomes necessary to test a condition in a function. Suppose you are trying to define a function that computes the absolute value of a number. The absolute value of a positive number is the number itself, the absolute value of a negative number is the number after reversing its sign. Let's use x as a parameter. We can use the system function "-" to reverse the sign of a number. The function for the absolute value should be defined to return the value of (- x) if it is a negative number and return the value of x if it is a positive number. This example shows that what to do next sometimes depends on whether some condition is true or false.

Although there are no special data structures for true or false, Lisp treats "true" (correct) and "false" (incorrect) as data. In addition to having itself as its fixed value and its use as the empty list, Lisp uses `nil` to mean false. Any data other than `nil` is interpreted to mean true. In the Lisp world anything which is not false is considered to be true.

We call a function used for determining whether a condition is true or false a **predicate**. Such functions return `nil` if the condition is not true and return something other than `nil` if the condition is true. A function for comparing the size of two numerical values is also a predicate. The

system function < takes two numbers and returns t if the first argument
is smaller than the second argument and returns nil otherwise. In other
words, < is the function which can be used to test if its first argument is
smaller than its second. It is usual for predicates like < to return t when
the condition is true. t stands for the "t" in "true."

```
>(< 1 2)
t

>(< 2 1)
nil

>(< 2 2)
nil
```

The following is the list of predicates for comparing the relative sizes of
numbers. All of them return t if the argument is correct and nil otherwise.

Function name	Meaning
>	greater than
=	equal
/=	not equal
<=	less than or equal
>=	greater than or equal
plusp	bigger than 0, positive
zerop	0
minusp	smaller than 0, negative
evenp	even number
oddp	odd number

The "p" at the end of the predicate stands for **predicate** and is pronounced
like the letter "p." You might imagine the p is a question mark and think
zero? instead of zerop.

The function for computing the absolute value can be defined as follows:

```
>(defun my-abs (x)
    (if (minusp x) (- x) x))
my-abs
```

We call this function my-abs rather than abs in order not to confuse it
with the system function called abs. The body of my-abs has the value of
"(- x) if x is less than 0" or "x if x is not less than 0." An if expression
is a special form.

(if 《condition》 《expression₁》 《expression₂》)

When an if expression is evaluated, the 《condition》 is evaluated first. If the value is not nil, 《expression₁》 is evaluated and its value becomes the value of the if expression. In this case, 《expression₂》 is not evaluated. If the value of 《condition》 is nil, the 《expression₂》 is evaluated and its value is returned as the value of the if expression. An if expression can also be written without an 《expression₂》.

(if 《condition》 《expression₁》)

If the 《condition》 evaluates to true then the above expression returns the value of 《expression₁》, otherwise it returns nil. It does exactly the same thing as the expression

(if 《condition》 《expression₁》 nil)

An expression whose action depends on whether a condition is true or false is called a **conditional expression**. In a conditional expression, the condition to test is represented by a **logical expression**. It is even possible for (+ x y) to be a logical expression.

```
>(if (+ x y) 'always   'never )
always
```

The value of (+ x y) is numerical and can never have the value nil. For this reason it would be rather strange to use (+ x y) as a logical expression. The above expression always has the value always no matter what the value of x and y are.

2-4 Elements of Logical Expressions

The function not and the macros and and or are used to combine logical expressions and build up more complicated logical expressions from simpler ones. The function not returns t if its argument is nil, otherwise it returns nil.

(not 《condition》)

If the 《condition》 is true, it returns false and if the 《condition》 is false, it returns true. not is the function for reversing true or false. Using not, the definition for my-abs can be rewritten as:

```
>(defun my-abs (x)
   (if (not (minusp x)) x (- x)))
my-abs
```

This expression can be read "if x is not negative, then return x, otherwise, return (- x)."

The system function null works exactly like not. As we mentioned above, nil also is used for the empty list. null is normally used as a predicate for determining if a list is the empty list.

```
>x
(single)

>(null x)
nil

>(null (cdr x))
t
```

You can also type (not (cdr x)) instead of (null (cdr x)), but we use null because the word null is more related to the empty list. You can type (null (minusp x)) instead of (not (minusp x)), but we use the word not because it is more related to nesting predicates.

$$(\text{and} \ \langle\!\langle \text{condition}_1 \rangle\!\rangle \ldots \langle\!\langle \text{condition}_n \rangle\!\rangle \ )$$

The and expression is used for checking whether a collection of conditions are all true. If any one of the conditions returns nil, the value of an and expression becomes nil. If not, the value of the last condition $\langle\!\langle \text{condition}_n \rangle\!\rangle$ (which should not be nil) is returned as the value of the and expression. A predicate for determining whether a number is greater than 0 and less than 100 is defined by:

```
>(defun percent-p (x)
   (if (and (>= x 0) (<= x 100)) t nil))
percent-p
```

Since both t and nil always evaluate to themselves, you do not need a " ' " in front of them. The if in the above expression can be omitted since the following and expression will return either nil or t as a value.

```
>(defun percent-p (x)
   (and (>= x 0) (<= x 100)))
percent-p
```

The ⟨⟨condition⟩⟩s in an **and** expression are evaluated from left to right. When any ⟨⟨condition⟩⟩ returns **nil**, the system stops the evaluation and does not evaluate the rest of the ⟨⟨condition⟩⟩s. The order in which the ⟨⟨condition⟩⟩s are evaluated is important in an **and** expression. The above expression is based on the assumption that **percent-p** will only get a number as an argument. If it is given an argument which is not a number, the system will print an error message when it calls the predicate >=. The above example should be rewritten so that **percent-p** returns **nil** when it is given an argument that is not a number.

```
>(defun percent-p (x)
    (and (numberp x) (>= x 0) (<= x 100)))
percent-p
```

numberp is the system predicate for determining whether a data structure is a number or not. Since the ⟨⟨condition⟩⟩s are evaluated from left to right in an **and** expression, if the argument is not a number, **(numberp x)** will return **nil** and the evaluation will stop. In this case the predicate >= will not be called. If you rewrite the above expression as

```
(and (>= x 0) (numberp x) (<= x 100))
```

or

```
(and (>= x 0) (<=x 100) (numberp x))
```

the predicate >= will be called first. In the case when the argument is not a number, the system will print an error message.

The expression starting with **or**

```
(or ⟨⟨condition₁⟩⟩ ... ⟨⟨conditionₙ⟩⟩ )
```

checks whether any one of a set of conditions is true and informally it means ⟨⟨condition$_1$⟩⟩ or ... or ⟨⟨condition$_n$⟩⟩. The value of an **or** expression is the value of the leftmost condition whose value is not **nil**. If all the conditions evaluate to **nil** then the value of the **or** expression is also **nil**. We can define **my-abs** using **or**.

```
>(defun my-abs (x)
    (if (or (plusp x) (zerop x)) x (- x)))
my-abs
```

Like the **and** expression, the conditions in an **or** expression are evaluated from left to right. As soon as one condition returns a value other than **nil**, the evaluation is terminated without evaluating the rest of the conditions.

There is no limit on the number of conditions in an **and** or an **or** expression. If there are no conditions, the value of an **and** expression is **t** since no condition means no false condition, and the value of an **or** expression is **nil** since no condition means no true condition.

Unlike **not**, **and** and **or** are macros. For your reference, the original expressions for **and** and **or** are:

```
>(macroexpand '(and x y z))
(if x (if y z))
t

>(macroexpand '(and x y))
(if x y)
t

>(macroexpand '(and x))
x
t

>(macroexpand '(and))
t
t

<(macroexpand '(or x y))
(let ((#:g817 x)) (If #:g817 #:g817 y))
t

>(macroexpand '(or x))
x
t

>(macroexpand '(or))
nil
t
```

#:g817 is a random symbol that the system uses as a temporary variable to keep the value of **x**. This symbol was created using the system function **gensym** which will be explained in Chapter 4.

2-5 Conditional Expressions

An expression whose action is determined by whether a condition is true or false is called a conditional expression. The if expression we described in the previous section is one kind of conditional expression. In this section we will talk about four basic kinds of conditional expressions: when, unless, cond, and case.

Before talking about these expressions, we look at the special form progn.

$$(\text{progn } \langle\!\langle\text{expression}_1\rangle\!\rangle \ldots \langle\!\langle\text{expression}_n\rangle\!\rangle \text{)}$$

In a progn, the expressions $\langle\!\langle\text{expression}_1\rangle\!\rangle$ ... $\langle\!\langle\text{expression}_n\rangle\!\rangle$ are evaluated from left to right and the value of $\langle\!\langle\text{expression}_n\rangle\!\rangle$ is returned as the value of the progn expression. The values of the rest of the expressions are not used, so usually these expressions are there only for the side effects. If a progn expression has only one expression, the value of the progn expression

$$(\text{progn } \langle\!\langle\text{expression}\rangle\!\rangle \text{)}$$

is the value of that expression

$$\langle\!\langle\text{expression}\rangle\!\rangle$$

The two expressions above have the same value. As a special case, if the progn does not have an expression, the value of progn is nil.

The conditional expression when

$$(\text{when } \langle\!\langle\text{condition}\rangle\!\rangle \ \langle\!\langle\text{expression}_1\rangle\!\rangle \ldots \langle\!\langle\text{expression}_n\rangle\!\rangle \text{)}$$

works just like

$$(\text{if } \langle\!\langle\text{condition}\rangle\!\rangle \ (\text{progn } \langle\!\langle\text{expression}_1\rangle\!\rangle \ldots \langle\!\langle\text{expression}_n\rangle\!\rangle \text{))}$$

When the $\langle\!\langle\text{condition}\rangle\!\rangle$ is true, $\langle\!\langle\text{expression}_1\rangle\!\rangle$ ... $\langle\!\langle\text{expression}_n\rangle\!\rangle$ is evaluated from left to right and the value of $\langle\!\langle\text{expression}_n\rangle\!\rangle$ is returned as the value of the when expression. If the $\langle\!\langle\text{condition}\rangle\!\rangle$ is false, the value of the when expression is nil. If you want to evaluate expressions only when a $\langle\!\langle\text{condition}\rangle\!\rangle$ is false, you can type

$$(\text{when } (\text{not } \langle\!\langle\text{condition}\rangle\!\rangle \text{) } \langle\!\langle\text{expression}_1\rangle\!\rangle \ldots \langle\!\langle\text{expression}_n\rangle\!\rangle \text{)}$$

The following expression using **unless** looks better. The general form of **unless** is

$$(\text{unless } \langle\!\langle condition \rangle\!\rangle \ \langle\!\langle expression_1 \rangle\!\rangle \ldots \langle\!\langle expression_n \rangle\!\rangle \ )$$

If you want to have several conditions and do different things for each condition, you can use nested **if** expressions, but it may be hard to read the resulting program because it contains too many **if**s.

```
>(defun goose (x)
      (if (= x 1) 'one
          (if (= x 2) 'two
              (if (= x 3) 'three
                  (if (= x 4) 'four
                  'many)))))
goose
```

The above program takes the numbers, 1, 2, 3, or 4, and returns **one**, **two**, **three**, or **four**, respectively. If the number is any other number, it returns **many**. As you can see, the program is very hard to read because the **if**s are scattered. The same program using the conditional expression **cond** is much easier to read.

```
>(defun goose (x)
    (cond ((= x 1) 'one)
          ((= x 2) 'two)
          ((= x 3) 'three)
          ((= x 4) 'four)
          (t 'many)))
goose
```

The general form of a **cond** is made of several lists. The first element of each list is a condition and the rest of the elements in the list are the expressions which will be evaluated when the condition is true.

$$(\text{cond } (\ \langle\!\langle condition_1 \rangle\!\rangle \ \langle\!\langle expression \rangle\!\rangle \ldots \langle\!\langle expression \rangle\!\rangle \ )$$
$$(\ \langle\!\langle condition_2 \rangle\!\rangle \ \langle\!\langle expression \rangle\!\rangle \ldots \langle\!\langle expression \rangle\!\rangle \ )$$
$$\ldots$$
$$(\ \langle\!\langle condition_n \rangle\!\rangle \ \langle\!\langle expression \rangle\!\rangle \ldots \langle\!\langle expression \rangle\!\rangle \ ))$$

First, $\langle\!\langle condition_1 \rangle\!\rangle$ is evaluated. If its value is **nil**, the $\langle\!\langle condition_2 \rangle\!\rangle$ is evaluated. This process is repeated until some condition has a value which is not **nil**. When this happens the expressions after this condition will be evaluated from left to right and the value of the right most expression becomes the value of the cond. The rest of the conditions and their associated expressions will not be evaluated. In the above example, suppose the argument to goose is 3. First (= x 1) is evaluated. Since its value is nil, the second condition (= x 2) is evaluated. This value is also nil, so the third condition (= x 3) is evaluated. The value of this condition is t and the expression 'three is evaluated and its value is returned as the value of the cond expression.

If all the conditions evaluate to nil, the value of the cond is nil. In this case, none of the expressions after the conditions will be evaluated. In the above example, the last condition is the expression t. Since the value of t is t itself and will never be nil, we know that 'many will be evaluated if the four previous conditions have returned nil. In this case t can be interpreted as "otherwise." Any expressions other than nil can be used as "otherwise," but we recommend using t because it is easiest and it is the custom in Lisp programming.

Consider the following function definition using cond.

```
>(defun what-is-this (x)
    (cond ((numberp x)
            (cons x '(is a number)))
          ((symbolp x)
            (cons x '(is a symbol)))
          (t '(i dont know))))
what-is-this

>(what-is-this 'emblem)
(emblem is a symbol)

>(what-is-this '(may be you dont know))
(i dont know)
```

You can use a case expression if you just want to make a choice based on previously enumerated data.

```
>(defun goose (x)
    (case x
        (1 'one)
        (2 'two)
        (3 'three)
        (4 'four)
        (otherwise 'many)))
goose
```

The general form of a **case** expression is

```
(case ⟨⟨key⟩⟩
    (⟨⟨list₁⟩⟩ ⟨⟨expression⟩⟩...⟨⟨expression⟩⟩ )
    (⟨⟨list₂⟩⟩ ⟨⟨expression⟩⟩...⟨⟨expression⟩⟩ )
    . . .
    (⟨⟨listₙ⟩⟩ ⟨⟨expression⟩⟩...⟨⟨expression⟩⟩ ) )
```

⟨⟨list₁⟩⟩ ... ⟨⟨listₙ⟩⟩ are the lists of choices in this expression. They are not evaluated but are used directly. If there is only one element in the list, the list can be replaced by that element. In the above example **goose, 1** and **2** are abbreviations for **(1)** and **(2)**. The **case** expression starts by the evaluation of the ⟨⟨key⟩⟩. The value of the ⟨⟨key⟩⟩ is called the **key value**. If a key value matches with any one of the elements of a list, the system evaluates the expressions associated with that list in left to right order and the value of the final expression is returned as the value of the **case** expression. If it does not match any element of any ⟨⟨list⟩⟩, the value of the **case** expression is **nil**. There is one exception when the last ⟨⟨listₙ⟩⟩ is **otherwise** or **t**. **otherwise** and **t** are not the abbreviation of **(otherwise)** or **(t)**, but they should be interpreted as what to do "if the key value does not match an element of any of the above lists," and in this case the system will evaluate the expressions which follow ⟨⟨listₙ⟩⟩ and the value of the last expression will be returned as the value of the **case** expression. Next, we would like to give some advice for using the **case** expression.

```
>(defun nonsense (x)
   (case x
      ((a b 3) 1)
      (c 2)
      ((otherwise) 3)
      ((t) 4)
      (nil 5)
      ((nil) 6)
      (t 7)))
nonsense
```

If the argument of **nonsense** is either **a**, **b**, or **3**, the value is **1**. If the argument is the symbol **c**, the value is **2**. **((otherwise) 3)** yields **3** as a value when the key value is the symbol **otherwise**. You should not write **(otherwise 3)** instead of **((otherwise) 3)**, because this is confusing and some systems may return **3** for any argument other than **a**, **b**, **3**, or **c**. The same thing can be said about **((t) t)**. If the argument to **nonsense** is the symbol **nil**, **6**, and not **5** will be returned. This is because **(nil 5)** is the

same as (() 5) and no key value can be in this list, so (nil 5) might as
well be deleted. In order to say "if the key value is nil," you should write
((nil) 6). (t 7) is the same as (otherwise 7). If the argument is not
a, b, c, otherwise, t, nil, or 3, nonsense returns the value 7.

2-6 Multiple-Valued Functions

The usual kind of function returns one value when it is called. A function
which returns more than one value is called a **multiple-valued function**.
A multiple-valued function may return multiple values in some cases and
one value in others. A function which does not return any value is also
called a multiple-valued function for convenience.

Two of the typical multiple-valued functions are the system functions
values and values-list. values gets some number of arguments and
returns these arguments themselves as its values. The first argument becomes the first value and the second argument becomes the second value,
etc. If there are no arguments, it will return without any values.

```
>(values)

>(values 1)
1

>(values 1 2)
1
2
```

values-list takes a list and returns all the elements of that list as its
values.

```
>(values-list '(a b c))
a
b
c
```

In the defun expression

$$(\text{defun } \langle\!\langle \text{function name}\rangle\!\rangle \ \langle\!\langle \text{parameter list}\rangle\!\rangle$$
$$\langle\!\langle \text{expression}_1\rangle\!\rangle \ldots \langle\!\langle \text{expression}_n\rangle\!\rangle \ )$$

if the last $\langle\langle$expression$_n\rangle\rangle$ calls **values**, the function to be defined returns the values which **values** returns. If **values** returns two values, the function returns two values. Generally speaking, the value of the last expression becomes the value of its function.

```
>(defun plus-minus (x y)
    (values (+ x y) (- x y)))
plus-minus

>(plus-minus 6 4)
10
2

>(defun cannot-help (x y) (plus-minus x y))
cannot-help

>(cannot-help 6 4)
10
2
```

As we said in Chapter 1, when the values of an expression are used as an argument to a function, only the first value is used. If the expression does not have any value, **nil** will be used as an argument to the function.

```
>(list (values 1 2) (values 3) (values))
(1 3 nil)
```

To make effective use of multiple values, you should use the special forms or the system macros which all start with the word "**multiple-value**".

```
multiple-value-setq
multiple-value-bind
multiple-value-list
multiple-value-prog1
multiple-value-call
```

multiple-value-setq assigns the values of an expression to a list of variables one by one.

```
(multiple-value-setq (x y) (floor 7 3))
```

The above expression assigns the first value of **floor** to a variable x and the second value to y. After the execution of this expression, the value of x will be 2 and the value of y will be 1 (7 divided by 3 is 2 plus 1). The general form of `multiple-value-setq` is

```
(multiple-value-setq
  ( ⟪variable₁⟫...⟪variableₙ⟫ )
  ⟪expression⟫ )
```

The system evaluates ⟪expression⟫ and assigns its first value to ⟪variable₁⟫ and its second value to ⟪variable₂⟫, etc. If there are not as many values of ⟪expression⟫ as there are variables, `nil` will be assigned to the extra variables. An excess number of values will be discarded. ⟪expression⟫ can have multiple values or it can have only one value. If ⟪expression⟫ has only one value, `nil` will be assigned to the rest of the variables. In the general `setq` expression

```
(setq ⟪variable⟫ ⟪expression⟫ )
```

if ⟪expression⟫ has two or more values, the first value will be assigned to ⟪variable⟫. If the ⟪expression⟫ does not have any values, `nil` will be assigned to ⟪variable⟫. A `multiple-value-setq` expression with one variable

```
(multiple-value-setq ( ⟪variable⟫ ) ⟪expression⟫ )
```

is exactly the same as

```
(setq ⟪variable⟫ ⟪expression⟫ )
```

We can say `multiple-value-setq` is the generalized form of `setq` or we can say `setq` is a special version of `multiple-value-setq`.

The generalized form of the `let` expression is `multiple-value-bind`. The general form is

```
(multiple-value-bind
  ( ⟪variable₁⟫...⟪variableₘ⟫ ) ⟪expression⟫
  ⟪expression₁⟫...⟪expressionₙ⟫ )
```

Each variable is bound to the corresponding value of the expression, then the body ⟪expression₁⟫ ... ⟪expressionₙ⟫ is executed, and the value of ⟪expressionₙ⟫ will be returned as the value of the `multiple-value-bind` expression. `multiple-value-bind` treats an excess or a deficiency of values in exactly the same way as in the `multiple-value-setq` form. For example,

```
>(multiple-value-bind (x) (floor 7 3)
    (list x))
(2)

>(multiple-value-bind (x y) (floor 7 3)
    (list x y))
(2 1)

>(multiple-value-bind (x y z) (floor 7 3)
    (list x y z))
(2 1 nil)
```

A `multiple-value-bind` expression with only one variable

(multiple-value-bind (⟪variable⟫) ⟪expression⟫
   ⟪expression$_1$⟫ ... ⟪expression$_n$⟫)

is the same as the `let` expression

(let ((⟪variable⟫ ⟪expression⟫))
   ⟪expression$_1$⟫ ... ⟪expression$_n$⟫)

The `multiple-value-list` expression returns a list of values which the system gets by evaluating the expressions. In other words, it does the operation exactly the opposite of `values-list`.

```
>(multiple-value-list (floor 7 3))
(2 1)
```

`multiple-value-prog1` and `multiple-value-call` are the special forms for the multiple-valued functions.

(multiple-value-prog1 ⟪expression$_1$⟫ ... ⟪expression$_n$⟫)

The above expression evaluates ⟪expression$_1$⟫ ... ⟪expression$_n$⟫ one by one and returns all the values of ⟪expression$_1$⟫ as its values. If ⟪expression$_1$⟫ has two values such as the two values of `floor`, `multiple-value-prog1` returns both. There is a system macro called `prog1`

(prog1 ⟪expression$_1$⟫ ... ⟪expression$_n$⟫)

The difference from `multiple-value-prog1` is that `prog1` returns only the first value as its value even if ⟨⟨expression₁⟩⟩ has more than one value. We will talk about `multiple-value-call` in Chapter 6.

Special forms and system macros other than the above-mentioned special forms and macros do one of two things to the values of an expression:

A. Use only one value. If the expression has more than one value, it uses the first one. If the expression does not have a value, it uses `nil`.

B. Use all the values.

Generally, when a special form or a system macro does some tasks using the value of an expression, it does A. Only when it returns the value of an expression as its own value, it does B. For example,

        (setq ⟨⟨variable⟩⟩ ⟨⟨expression⟩⟩)

does A, because the value of ⟨⟨expression⟩⟩ is used to change a value of the ⟨⟨variable⟩⟩. If ⟨⟨expression⟩⟩ returns more than one value, all the values except the first one will be ignored. When ⟨⟨expression⟩⟩ does not return a value, `nil` will be used as the value of ⟨⟨expression⟩⟩. Although the `setq` expression returns the value of ⟨⟨expression⟩⟩ as its own value, ⟨⟨expression⟩⟩ will be treated as A, so `setq` will have only one value. Also,

        (prog1 ⟨⟨expression⟩⟩ ...)

needs to keep the value of ⟨⟨expression⟩⟩ for a while, so it works like A.

        (setq ⟨⟨variable⟩⟩ ⟨⟨expression⟩⟩ ... ⟨⟨variable⟩⟩ ⟨⟨expression⟩⟩)
        (psetq ⟨⟨variable⟩⟩ ⟨⟨expression⟩⟩ ... ⟨⟨variable⟩⟩ ⟨⟨expression⟩⟩)
        (let ((⟨⟨variable⟩⟩ ⟨⟨expression⟩⟩)) ...)
        (let* ((⟨⟨variable⟩⟩ ⟨⟨expression⟩⟩)) ...)
        (case ⟨⟨expression⟩⟩ ...)
        (if ⟨⟨condition⟩⟩ ...)
        (when ⟨⟨condition⟩⟩ ...)
        (unless ⟨⟨condition⟩⟩ ...)
        (cond ((⟨⟨condition⟩⟩ ...))
                   ...
              ((⟨⟨condition⟩⟩ ...)))

The above ⟨⟨expression⟩⟩s and ⟨⟨condition⟩⟩s also work as A. We said that `nil` as the value of a ⟨⟨condition⟩⟩ means "false"; that is, when ⟨⟨condition⟩⟩ does not return any value, ⟨⟨condition⟩⟩ will be interpreted to be false. For example,

        (if (values) 'never 'always)

The value of the above condition will always be **always**. The **progn** expression

(**progn** $\langle\!\langle$expression$_1\rangle\!\rangle$ ... $\langle\!\langle$expression$_n\rangle\!\rangle$)

will return the value of $\langle\!\langle$expression$_n\rangle\!\rangle$. Therefore, $\langle\!\langle$expression$_n\rangle\!\rangle$ is treated according to B. No matter how many values $\langle\!\langle$expression$_n\rangle\!\rangle$ has, all of them will become the values of the **progn** expression.

```
(let  (...)  ...〈〈expression〉〉 )
(let* (...)  ...〈〈expression〉〉 )
(if 〈〈condition〉〉 〈〈expression〉〉 〈〈expression〉〉 )
(when 〈〈condition〉〉...〈〈expression〉〉 )
(unless 〈〈condition〉〉...〈〈expression〉〉 )
(cond (( 〈〈condition〉〉...〈〈expression〉〉 ))
         ...
       (( 〈〈condition〉〉...〈〈expression〉〉 )))
(case 〈〈key〉〉
  ( 〈〈list〉〉...〈〈expression〉〉 )
      ...
  ( 〈〈list〉〉...〈〈expression〉〉 ))
```

The $\langle\!\langle$expression$\rangle\!\rangle$s in the above will be treated as B. The **and** expression

(**and** $\langle\!\langle$condition$_1\rangle\!\rangle$ $\langle\!\langle$condition$_2\rangle\!\rangle$ $\langle\!\langle$condition$_3\rangle\!\rangle$)

and

(**if** $\langle\!\langle$condition$_1\rangle\!\rangle$ (**if** $\langle\!\langle$condition$_2\rangle\!\rangle$ $\langle\!\langle$condition$_3\rangle\!\rangle$)

have the same value. $\langle\!\langle$condition$_1\rangle\!\rangle$ and $\langle\!\langle$condition$_2\rangle\!\rangle$ will be treated as A and $\langle\!\langle$condition$_3\rangle\!\rangle$ will be treated as B.

(**or** $\langle\!\langle$condition$_1\rangle\!\rangle$ $\langle\!\langle$condition$_2\rangle\!\rangle$ $\langle\!\langle$condition$_3\rangle\!\rangle$)

$\langle\!\langle$condition$_1\rangle\!\rangle$ and $\langle\!\langle$condition$_2\rangle\!\rangle$ in the above expression will be treated as B and $\langle\!\langle$condition$_3\rangle\!\rangle$ will be treated as B.

We end this chapter by showing you the function which solves the quadratic equation, $x^2 + bx + c = 0$.

```
>(defun quadratic-equation (b c)
     (let ((root (sqrt (- (* b b)
                          (* 4 c)))))
        (if (zerop root)
            (/ (- b) 2)
            (values (/ (+ (- b) root) 2)
                    (/ (- (- b) root) 2)))))
quadratic-equation

>(quadratic-equation 2 1)
-1

>(quadratic-equation -3 2)
2.0
1.0
```

If there are two solutions, the two of them are returned as the value of
quadratic-equation. The function values returns two values. These two
values automatically become the values of the if expression, and finally
become the values of the function quadratic-equation.

3   Control Structure

Now you can define very simple functions, combine system functions and new functions which you have defined, and control the program by using conditional expressions. However, you need to know more advanced program controls in order to make more powerful and useful programs. For example, when you want to write a simple predicate for determining whether elements in a list are all numbers or not, you need to have repetitive control to repeat the decision for each element in a list. In this chapter, we will explain the basic technique of program controls. The techniques are all basic and other more advanced controls are just the combinations of the basic controls. Moreover, these basic techniques are enough to control actual programming.

3-1 Recursive Call

When you define more than one function, the order in which the functions are defined is not important. Even if one function calls another function, there is no rule about which function of the two has to be defined first. Consider the definition of the two functions foo and bar.

```
(defun foo (x) (+ (bar x) x))

(defun bar (x) (* x x))
```

foo calls bar, but it does not matter whether bar has already been defined. The important thing is that bar needs to be defined at the time when foo is actually called. When foo is defined, the system only remembers its

definition and it does not check which functions are called in the body.
The system only finds out about `bar` when `foo` is called and its body is
executed and it actually tries to call `bar`. If you redefine `bar` after you have
defined `foo`, the system uses the most recent definition.

```
>(defun foo (x) (+ (bar x) x))
foo

>(defun bar (x) (* x x))
bar

>(foo 2)
6

>(defun bar (x) (* x x x))
bar

>(foo 2)
10
```

If the system does not call a function `g` while executing the body of `f`, `g`
does not have to be defined even if the function `f` contains a call to the
function `g`.

```
>(defun f (x)
    (if (numberp x) (g x) 'not-a-number))
f

>(f 'pumpkin)
not-a-number
```

In the above example, `g` is called only when the argument to `f` is a number.
This means that `g` does not have to be defined as long as numbers are not
used as an argument to `f`.

It is possible for a function to call itself. Consider the following function
which expects a list of numbers as its argument.

```
>(defun list-add1 (x)
    (if (null x)
        nil
        (cons (1+ (car x))
              (list-add1 (cdr x)))))
list-add1
```

If the argument is the empty list, (null x) is true and list-add1 returns nil which is the empty list.

```
>(list-add1 nil)
nil
```

If the argument is a list of length one, for example, (8), then (null x) is false, so the system evaluates

```
(cons (1+ (car x)) (list-add1 (cdr x)))
```

First,

```
(1+ (car x))
```

is evaluated and the system gets 9 for the first argument of cons. Next,

```
(list-add1 (cdr x))
```

is evaluated. That is, while list-add1 is being executed, list-add1 has also been called. Since the value of (cdr x) is the empty list, list-add1 will be called with the empty list as an argument and will return the empty list. This value becomes the second argument to cons and the value of the cons expression becomes the pair of 9 and the empty list, (9).

```
>(list-add1 '(8))
(9)
```

When you **trace** a function, the system prints the function name and the value of its arguments whenever the function is called. If you trace list-add1, you can see how list-add1 is called.

```
>(trace list-add1)
(list-add1)

>(list-add1 '(8))
   1> (list-add1 (8))      ; first called with argument (8)
     2> (list-add1 nil)    ; next called with argument nil
     <2 (list-add1 nil)    ; its value is nil
   <1 (list-add1 (9))      ; value of first call is (9)
(9)
```

You can stop tracing by typing `untrace`. Let's keep tracing to see what happens when a longer list of numbers is given to `list-add1`.

```
>(list-add1 '(7 2 3 8))
   1> (list-add1 (7 2 3 8))
     2> (list-add1 (2 3 8))
       3> (list-add1 (3 8))
         4> (list-add1 (8))
           5> (list-add1 nil)
           <5 (list-add1 nil)
         <4 (list-add1 (9))
       <3 (list-add1 (4 9))
     <2 (list-add1 (3 4 9))
   <1 (list-add1 (8 3 4 9))
(8 3 4 9)
```

When `list-add1` gets (7 2 3 8) as an argument, it calls itself with the `cdr` of (7 2 3 8), namely (2 3 8), as an argument and returns the value (8 3 4 9), which is the `cons` of 7+1=8 and (3 4 9). When `list-add1` receives (2 3 8) as an argument and it calls itself with (3 8) as an argument, it returns (3 4 9) as its value which is the `cons` of 2+1=3 and (4 9). When `list-add1` gets (3 8) as an argument, it calls itself with (8) as an argument and returns the value (4 9) which is the `cons` of 3+1=4 and (9). When `list-add1` receives (8) it returns (9) as a value.

As you may have noticed, `list-add1` is a function which returns a list with each element increased by 1. The definition of `list-add1` can be described as: "as long as the argument list is not the empty list, the value of `list-add1` is the `cons` of the value of `list-add1` for all the elements except the first one in the list and the first element plus 1. If the argument is the empty list, then the value of `list-add1` is the empty list."

A call of a function from inside itself is said to be a **recursive call** (sometimes if `f` is calling `g` and `g` is calling `f`, this is also called a recursive call.) A function which does a recursive call is said to be **defined recursively**. The above function `list-add1` is defined recursively and it calls itself recursively when it is given a list of numbers as an argument.

The value of a local variable does not change because of a recursive call to a function. Consider the binding of a variable. If you type

```
>(list-add1 nil)
```

the parameter `x` of `list-add1` is bound to `nil`. In other words, on entry to the function a new box is created for `x` and `nil` is put in this box. The same thing happens again when `list-add1` is called recursively.

```
>(list-add1 '(8))
```

First, (8) is put in a new box created for x. While the body is being executed, `list-add1` is called recursively and `nil` is put into a second box for x. The content of the first box does not change before or after the recursive call. In order to verify this, let's look at another example. Since `list-add1` does not use the parameter x after the recursive call, we will use a new function for the next example.

```
>(defun list-sum (x)
   (if (null x)
       0
       (+ (list-sum (cdr x)) (car x))))
list-sum
```

When we evaluate

```
>(list-sum '(8))
```

this function calls itself recursively with `nil` as an argument. After this recursive call, `list-sum` looks for the first element of the parameter x. Since the value of x has not been influenced by the recursive call, x still has (8) as a value and 0+8, i.e., 8 becomes the value of `list-sum`.

```
>(list-sum '(8))
8
```

As another example of a recursive definition, let us define a function for factorial. The factorial of a positive integer is the product of all the integers from 1 through n, $1 \times 2 \times \cdots \times (n-1) \times n$. The factorial of $n-1$ is the product of all the integers from 1 through $n-1$. This means that the factorial of n would be the factorial of $n-1$ multiplied by n. For the special case of 0, factorial of 0 is 1. So, a function `fact` for factorial can be defined as:

```
>(defun fact (n)
   (if (zerop n)
       1
       (* n (fact (1- n)))))
fact

>(trace fact)
(fact)
```

```
>(fact 3)
   1> (fact 3)
     2> (fact 2)
       3> (fact 1)
          4> (fact 0)
          <4 (fact 1)
       <3 (fact 1)
     <2 (fact 2)
   <1 (fact 6)
6

>(untrace fact)
(fact)

>(fact 40)
8159152832478977343456112695961158942720
00000000
```

3-2 Block Structure

Usually a **progn** expression

$$(\text{progn} \ \langle\!\langle \text{expression}_1 \rangle\!\rangle \dots \langle\!\langle \text{expression}_n \rangle\!\rangle \ )$$

evaluates each $\langle\!\langle \text{expression}_1 \rangle\!\rangle \ \dots \ \langle\!\langle \text{expression}_n \rangle\!\rangle$, but there are exceptions to this rule. The mechanism called **non-local exit** can terminate the execution of a **progn** in the middle of the evaluation of any expression. In this section, we will talk about block structure which defines the scope of non-local exit.

Block Structure makes use of the combination of two special forms, **block** and **return-from**. The general form of the **block** expression

$$(\text{block} \ \langle\!\langle \text{block name} \rangle\!\rangle \ \langle\!\langle \text{expression}_1 \rangle\!\rangle \dots \langle\!\langle \text{expression}_n \rangle\!\rangle \ )$$

takes the body of the **block** expression, $\langle\!\langle \text{expression}_1 \rangle\!\rangle \ \dots \ \langle\!\langle \text{expression}_n \rangle\!\rangle$, as one **block** and calls it $\langle\!\langle \text{block name} \rangle\!\rangle$. In **block** expressions, each of the expressions in the body are evaluated one by one. If a **return-from** expression,

$$(\text{return-from} \ \langle\!\langle \text{block name} \rangle\!\rangle \ \langle\!\langle \text{block value} \rangle\!\rangle \ )$$

which uses the same ⟨⟨block name⟩⟩ is evaluated in the body, the execution of that block is terminated and the value of ⟨⟨block value⟩⟩ is returned as the value of block expression. If the last ⟨⟨expression$_n$⟩⟩ is evaluated, the value of ⟨⟨expression$_n$⟩⟩ becomes the value of block expression. For example,

```
(block there
   (print x)
   (when (numberp x)
      (return-from there (1+ x)))
   (print 'not-a-number)
   (list x x))
```

The system first prints the value of the variable x. If this value is a number, the execution of the block expression is stopped and it returns (1+ x) as its value. If the value of x is not a number, the system prints the symbol not-a-number and finishes the execution of the block expression by returning the value of (list x x).

The ⟨⟨block name⟩⟩ in a block expression and a return-from expression should be a symbol and it is not evaluated. The ⟨⟨block name⟩⟩ is not an expression whose value is a symbol. A block can be given any name. Any symbol which is given as the ⟨⟨block name⟩⟩ becomes the name of that block. Each block name can be referred to anywhere inside of that block, but not outside of the block. In other words,

```
(return-from ⟨⟨block name⟩⟩   ⟨⟨block value⟩⟩ )
```

only makes sense as long as it is inside a block with the same ⟨⟨block name⟩⟩. Like variables, the places where a block can be referred to is called the scope of the block name. Unlike variables, there is no block which is global.

The scope of one block expression is not affected by any other block expression.

```
(block outside
   ...
   (block inside
      ...
      (case x
         (1 (return-from outside '(a b c)))
         (2 (return-from inside  '(1 2 3))) )
       ...)
    ...)
```

The above `case` expression belongs to the scope of the `inside` block as well as to the scope of the `outside` block. Therefore, when the `case` expression is executed, if the value of the `x` is 1, the `outside` block stops its execution. If the value of a variable `x` is 2, the `inside` block stops its execution.

If two blocks with the same name exist, the inner block overrides the outer block.

```
(block foo
   (f1)
   (block foo
     (f2)
     (return-from foo nil)
     (f3))
   (f4))
```

In the above example, the symbol `foo` in the `return-from` expression refers to the inner block. This means that the functions are called in the order `f1`, `f2`, and `f4`. The ⟪value⟫ in a `return-from` expression can be omitted.

    (return-from ⟪block name⟫)

has the same value of

    (return-from ⟪block name⟫ nil)

There is one kind of block which the system sets up automatically. We can imagine that the body of a function defined as

    (defun ⟪function name⟫ ...)

is a block whose name is the same as the ⟪function name⟫. When the following expression

    (return-from ⟪function name⟫ ⟪function value⟫)

is evaluated inside the body of this function, the execution of the function stops and the value of ⟪function value⟫ is returned as the value of the function. For example,

```
(defun foo (x)
  (unless (symbolp x)
    (return-from foo 'not-a-symbol))
  ...)
```

The function **foo** stops its execution as soon as the argument is not a symbol and returns the symbol **not-a-symbol** as its value. There are also some system macros which automatically construct a block named **nil**. **loop** is one of these.

$$(\text{loop } \langle\!\langle \text{expression}_1 \rangle\!\rangle \dots \langle\!\langle \text{expression}_n \rangle\!\rangle \text{ })$$

The above expression evaluates $\langle\!\langle \text{expression}_1 \rangle\!\rangle$ through $\langle\!\langle \text{expression}_n \rangle\!\rangle$. After it finishes one iteration, it repeats the same operation again and again. A **return-from** expression specifying **nil** as its block name

$$(\text{return-from nil } \langle\!\langle \text{value} \rangle\!\rangle \text{ })$$

or the macro expression with the same value

$$(\text{return } \langle\!\langle \text{value} \rangle\!\rangle \text{ })$$

will stop this infinite loop. When it stops, the value of **loop** will be $\langle\!\langle \text{value} \rangle\!\rangle$. If you don't need the value of the **loop** expression, you simply can type

```
(return)
```

or the following expressions which have the same value:

```
(return-from nil nil)
```

```
(return nil)
```

In addition to **loop**, the system macros **prog**, **prog***, **do**, **do***, **dolist**, and **dotimes** automatically create blocks called **nil**. We describe these macros in the next section. The only blocks which the system creates by itself are those which surround the body of a function and which have the same name as the function, and the blocks named **nil** which are created by the macros mentioned above.

3-3 Program Structure

The `tagbody` and `go` are special forms for so-called jumping.

```
(tagbody
    (when (some-condition) (go a))
    (f1)
 a  (f2)
    (f3))
```

During the execution of the above program, when `(some-condition)` is true, the system jumps over `(f1)` and evaluates only `(f2)` and `(f3)`. A **tag** called a exists between `(f1)` and `(f2)` and the system jumps to this tag when it evaluates `(go a)` and continues its evaluation from the tag. If `(some-condition)` is false, `(go a)` will not be executed, so the system evaluates `(f1)`, ignores the tag a, and evaluates `(f2)` and `(f3)`.

The general form of a `tagbody` is

```
(tagbody
    ⟨⟨tag name or tag expression⟩⟩ . . .
        ⟨⟨tag name or tag expression⟩⟩  )
```

Any list is considered to be a tag expression and anything except a list is considered to be a tag name, but usually symbols are used as tag names. `tagbody` evaluates each expression in ⟨⟨tag name or tag expression⟩⟩ in turn and stops when it reaches the last expression. It jumps to a tag when it executes a `go` expression and restarts the evaluation with the expression which appears immediately after the tag. If there is no expression after the tag the execution is stopped. The value of a `tagbody` is always `nil`. A `tagbody` cannot have two tags with the same name since two tags with the same name will make it ambiguous where to go.

The `go` expression

```
(go ⟨⟨tag name⟩⟩  )
```

does not evaluate the ⟨⟨tag name⟩⟩ but uses the tag name (usually a symbol) itself. This expression does not provide for a so-called "computed goto." For example,

```
(go (if (zerop x) a b))
```

The system interprets the above expression as the order to jump to the tag (if (zerop x) a b). However, a list can never be a tag name. If the system tries to execute this expression, it will print an error message. If you want to compute where to jump to, you should write

```
(if (zerop x) (go a) (go b))
```

The scope of a tag is the whole body of the tagbody expression which contains this tag.

```
(tagbody (...) boo (...) (...) foo (...) woo)
```

The three tags, boo, foo, and woo, can be used only within this tagbody expression. The system cannot jump into a tagbody expression using a go from outside of the tagbody.

```
(tagbody ... (foo) the-end)
```

In the same way, the system cannot jump to the tag the-end from the body of the function foo, since the body of foo is outside of the scope of the tag the-end. Like variables and blocks, if two tags with the same name exist, only the inner tag is used and the outer tag is hidden.

```
(tagbody
    (tagbody
        (go there)
        (f1)
    there
        (f2))
    (f3)
  there
    (f4))
```

When the system executes the above program, it jumps to the there which belongs to the inner tagbody, and it will execute (f2), (f3), and (f4) consecutively.

The loop expression which we explained in a previous section,

$$(\texttt{loop } \langle\!\langle \text{expression}_1 \rangle\!\rangle \ldots \langle\!\langle \text{expression}_n \rangle\!\rangle \ )$$

has the same value of the following expression using tag and block:

```
(block nil
  (tagbody
   temp
     (progn ⟪expression₁⟫...⟪expressionₙ⟫ )
     (go temp)))
```

We are assuming that $\langle\langle expression_1 \rangle\rangle$ ... $\langle\langle expression_n \rangle\rangle$ do not contain a
(go temp) expression.

Next, we will explain the system macros called prog and prog*. These
macros work like tagbody and in addition bind variables and set up blocks.
The general form of prog is

$$(\text{prog } ((\ \langle\langle variable_1 \rangle\rangle\quad \langle\langle initial\ value_1 \rangle\rangle\ )$$

$$\ldots$$

$$(\ \langle\langle variable_m \rangle\rangle\quad \langle\langle initial\ value_m \rangle\rangle\ ))$$
$$\langle\langle expression_1 \rangle\rangle \ldots \langle\langle expression_n \rangle\rangle\ )$$

This is equivalent to the following expression:

$$(\text{block nil}$$
$$(\text{let } ((\ \langle\langle variable_1 \rangle\rangle\qquad \langle\langle initial\ value_1 \rangle\rangle\ )$$

$$\ldots$$

$$(\ \langle\langle variable_m \rangle\rangle\qquad \langle\langle initial\ value_m \rangle\rangle\ ))$$
$$(\text{tagbody } \langle\langle expression_1 \rangle\rangle \ldots \langle\langle expression_n \rangle\rangle\ )))$$

If you replace prog with prog*, then you get the general form of a prog*.
prog* differs from prog only in that prog* uses let* instead of let.

3-4 Macros for Iteration Constracts

The system macros do and do* are the most general and the most powerful
macros for iteration.
The general form of do is

$$(\text{do } ((\ \langle\langle variable_1 \rangle\rangle\ \langle\langle initial\ value_1 \rangle\rangle\ \langle\langle step_1 \rangle\rangle\ )$$

$$\ldots$$

$$(\ \langle\langle variable_m \rangle\rangle\ \langle\langle initial\ value_m \rangle\rangle\ \langle\langle step_m \rangle\rangle\ ))$$
$$(\ \langle\langle end\ condition \rangle\rangle\ \langle\langle expression \rangle\rangle\ \ldots\ \langle\langle expression \rangle\rangle\ )$$
$$\langle\langle expression_1 \rangle\rangle$$

$$\ldots$$

$$\langle\langle expression_n \rangle\rangle\ )$$

Broadly speaking, the do expression repeats the execution of the body of the do expression, $\langle\langle\text{expression}_1\rangle\rangle$ ... $\langle\langle\text{expression}_n\rangle\rangle$, using $\langle\langle\text{variable}_1\rangle\rangle$ ... $\langle\langle\text{variable}_m\rangle\rangle$ as local variables. It continues to repeat this until $\langle\langle\text{end condition}\rangle\rangle$ becomes true. The variables $\langle\langle\text{variable}_1\rangle\rangle$ ... $\langle\langle\text{variable}_n\rangle\rangle$ can be used locally in the do expression. When the system evaluates a do expression, it first evaluates $\langle\langle\text{initial value}_1\rangle\rangle$ ... $\langle\langle\text{initial value}_n\rangle\rangle$ and binds these values to each local variable. It then evaluates the $\langle\langle\text{end condition}\rangle\rangle$. If its value is nil, the system executes the body. It then prepares to loop evaluating $\langle\langle\text{step}_1\rangle\rangle$ ... $\langle\langle\text{step}_m\rangle\rangle$, assigning these values to the local variables, and evaluating the $\langle\langle\text{end condition}\rangle\rangle$ again. The system repeats this process until the value of $\langle\langle\text{end condition}\rangle\rangle$ evaluated to true. It then evaluates the expressions which are found after the $\langle\langle\text{end condition}\rangle\rangle$ without executing the body. The value of the last expression in this list is returned as the value of the do expression. Another way of writing the general do expression is:

```
(block nil
    (let (( ⟨⟨variable₁⟩⟩ ⟨⟨initial value₁⟩⟩ )
            . . .
         ( ⟨⟨variableₘ⟩⟩ ⟨⟨initial valueₘ⟩⟩ ))
      (tagbody
       loop
         (when ⟨⟨ending condition⟩⟩
             (return (progn ⟨⟨expression⟩⟩...⟨⟨expression⟩⟩ )))
           ⟨⟨expression₁⟩⟩
             . . .
           ⟨⟨expressionₙ⟩⟩
           (psetq ⟨⟨variable₁⟩⟩ ⟨⟨step₁⟩⟩
                    . . .
                  ⟨⟨variableₘ⟩⟩ ⟨⟨stepₘ⟩⟩ )
         (go loop))))
```

Here we assume that the tag called loop is not used anywhere else. Consider the following example program using do.

```
>(defun sublists (list)
    (let ((y nil))
      (do ((x list (cdr x)))
          ((endp x) y)
        (setq y (cons x y)))))
sublists
```

```
>(sublists '(a b c d))
((d) (c d) (b c d) (a b c d))
```

endp is a predicate that checks for the end of the list. If its argument is the empty list, it returns **t**. If the argument is a list other than an empty list, it returns **nil**. If the argument is not a list, the system returns an error message.

In the list for specifying the local variables in a **do** expression,

$$(\ \langle\!\langle \text{variable} \rangle\!\rangle \ \langle\!\langle \text{initial value} \rangle\!\rangle \ \langle\!\langle \text{step} \rangle\!\rangle \ )$$

$\langle\!\langle \text{step} \rangle\!\rangle$ can be omitted. If $\langle\!\langle \text{step} \rangle\!\rangle$ is omitted, the local variables will not be recomputed after each iteration. If $\langle\!\langle \text{step} \rangle\!\rangle$ and $\langle\!\langle \text{initial value} \rangle\!\rangle$ are omitted, the local variables will be assigned the initial value **nil** and will keep this value throughout the evaluation of the **do**. If there are no $\langle\!\langle \text{expression} \rangle\!\rangle$s after the $\langle\!\langle \text{end condition} \rangle\!\rangle$, the system finishes the **do** expression as soon as the $\langle\!\langle \text{end condition} \rangle\!\rangle$ becomes true and it returns the value **nil**. A **do** expression does not need to have any expression in its body. For example, **sublists** in the above example can be defined as follows:

```
>(defun sublists (list)
   (do ((x list (cdr x))
        (y nil (cons x y)))
       ((endp x) y)))
sublists

>(sublists '(a b c d))
((d) (c d) (b c d) (a b c d))
```

If you replace **do** with **do*** in the general **do** expression, you get the general **do*** expression. The differences between **do** and **do*** are the way the local variables are initialized and the method of updating their values each time through the loop. As you can see from the above expression, the **do** expression initializes its local variables by using **let** and binds the local variables to the initial values after all the initial values are calculated. In a **do** expression the initial values for the local variables are all evaluated before any local variable is bound. This means that even if some expression which is used to compute the initial value of a local variable contains a variable with the same name as a local variable, the values of these variables are independent of one another. Also, **do** uses **psetq** when assigning new values to the local variables. The replacements are all done at the same time after $\langle\!\langle \text{step}_1 \rangle\!\rangle \ \ldots \ \langle\!\langle \text{step}_n \rangle\!\rangle$ are calculated using the old values of the local variables. As opposed to **do**, **do*** uses **let*** instead of **let** and **setq** instead of **psetq**. The general form of a **do*** expression is equivalent to the following expression:

```
(block nil
   (let* (( 《variable₁》 《initial value₁》 )
              . . .
          ( 《variableₘ》 《initial valueₘ》 ))
      (tagbody
       loop
         (when 《ending condition》
               (return (progn 《expression》 . . . 《expression》 )))
         《expression₁》
             . . .
         《expressionₙ》
         (setq 《variable₁》 《step₁》
                   . . .
                 《variableₘ》 《stepₘ》 )
         (go loop))))
```

The initialization and recomputation of each local variable are done one after another. The value of any local variable which has already been bound can be used in the calculation of the rest of the initial values. The value of a local variable which has already been calculated can be used whenever some other local variables are recomputed.

In order to see the difference between **do** and **do***, let's replace **do** with **do*** in the above definition of **sublists**:

```
>(defun sublists (list)
   (do* ((x list (cdr x))
         (y nil (cons x y)))
        ((endp x) y)))
sublists

>(sublists '(a b c d))
(nil (d) (c d) (b c d))
```

The initial values of the local variables, x and y, have the same value as in the **do** expression, but they will change after each time around the loop. First, the **cdr** of a list x becomes the new value of x and then the new value of x is added to the list y. As a result, the value of **sublists** is not the same as the value of **sublists** using **do** expression.

dolist and **dotimes** are also macros for iteration. You can use **do** and **do*** to get the same effect, but it is useful to know these macros as they can be used often.

`dolist` repeats a set of operations for as many times as there are entries in a list. The general form is

```
(dolist ( ⟨⟨variable⟩⟩ ⟨⟨list expression⟩⟩ ⟨⟨value⟩⟩ )
        ⟨⟨expression₁⟩⟩ ... ⟨⟨expressionₙ⟩⟩ )
```

This is equivalent to the following expression:

```
(do* ((temp ⟨⟨list expression⟩⟩ (cdr temp))
      ( ⟨⟨variable⟩⟩ (car temp) (car temp)))
     ((endp temp) ⟨⟨value⟩⟩ )
   ⟨⟨expression₁⟩⟩
      ...
   ⟨⟨expressionₙ⟩⟩ )
```

First, the system evaluates ⟨⟨list expression⟩⟩ and its value must be a list. In turn it binds ⟨⟨variable⟩⟩ to each element of the list and evaluates the body of `dolist`, that is, ⟨⟨expression₁⟩⟩ ... ⟨⟨expressionₙ⟩⟩. When the system has repeated this process for all the elements of the list, it evaluates ⟨⟨value⟩⟩ and this ends the execution of the `dolist`. This ⟨⟨value⟩⟩ is returned as the value of the `dolist`. If ⟨⟨value⟩⟩ is omitted, `dolist` returns `nil`. In the next example we define a function, using `dolist`, which returns the elements of a list in reverse order.

```
>(defun list-reverse (list)
   (let ((y nil))
      (dolist (x list y)
         (setq y (cons x y)))))
list-reverse

>(list-reverse '(a b c))
(c b a)
```

Even though ⟨⟨value⟩⟩ is within the scope of ⟨⟨variable⟩⟩ it always has the value `nil` at the time the system evaluates ⟨⟨value⟩⟩.

`dotimes` repeats an evaluation as many times as it is requested. Its general form is

```
(dotimes ( ⟨⟨variable⟩⟩ ⟨⟨integer expression⟩⟩ ⟨⟨value⟩⟩ )
         ⟨⟨expression₁⟩⟩ ... ⟨⟨expressionₙ⟩⟩ )
```

and has the same value of the following expression:

```
(do* ((temp ⟨⟨integer expression⟩⟩ )
      ( ⟨⟨variable⟩⟩ 0 (1+ ⟨⟨variable⟩⟩ )))
     ((>= ⟨⟨variable⟩⟩ temp) ⟨⟨value⟩⟩ )
     ⟨⟨expression₁⟩⟩
       ...
     ⟨⟨expressionₙ⟩⟩ )
```

The system first evaluates ⟨⟨integer expression⟩⟩ and its value must be an integer. If its value is n, the system successively binds ⟨⟨variable⟩⟩ to the integers $0 \ldots n-1$ and for each value of ⟨⟨variable⟩⟩ it evaluates ⟨⟨expression₁⟩⟩ ... ⟨⟨expressionₙ⟩⟩, which is the body of the dotimes expression. In other words, the system repeats the evaluation of the body n times. Finally, it evaluates ⟨⟨value⟩⟩ and returns this value as the value of the dotimes. If ⟨⟨value⟩⟩ is omitted, the value of the dotimes is nil. For example,

```
>(let ((y nil))
    (dotimes (x 10 y)
       (setq y (cons x y))))
(9 8 7 6 5 4 3 2 1 0)
```

⟨⟨value⟩⟩ is within the scope of ⟨⟨variable⟩⟩ and when ⟨⟨value⟩⟩ is evaluated the value of ⟨⟨variable⟩⟩ should be the same as the value of ⟨⟨integer expression⟩⟩ if the value is positive. (If the value of ⟨⟨variable⟩⟩ is negative, it will be 0.)

3-5 catch and throw

While block and return-from give what is called a **static** non-local exit, catch and throw provide the user with the ability to do **dynamic** non-local exits. The block expression corresponding to each return-from expression can be determined by looking at the entire expression which contains the return-from, because a return-from expression always exits from its surrounding block expression and the block expression and return-from expression both explicitly mention the name of the block. The block expression that corresponds to a throw can never change as the result of a computation. On the other hand, the relationship between a catch expression and a throw expression usually cannot be decided until they are actually evaluated, even though there are a few cases where this relationship can be determined. A `throw` expression is not necessarily found inside a `catch` expression since the **catch tag** which associates a `throw` expression to a `catch` expression is only determined at the time of the evaluation.

The `catch` expression

(catch ⟨⟨catch tag⟩⟩ ⟨⟨expression₁⟩⟩ ... ⟨⟨expressionₙ⟩⟩)

first evaluates the ⟨⟨catch tag⟩⟩ and then evaluates each expression in the body, ⟨⟨expression₁⟩⟩ ... ⟨⟨expressionₙ⟩⟩. The value of ⟨⟨expressionₙ⟩⟩ is returned as the value of a `catch`. However, if ever a `throw` expression

(throw ⟨⟨catch tag⟩⟩ ⟨⟨value⟩⟩)

is evaluated in the process of evaluating one of these expressions and the value of the ⟨⟨catch tag⟩⟩ in the `throw` expression is the same as the value of the ⟨⟨catch tag⟩⟩ in the `catch` expression, the evaluation of the `catch` expression stops and it returns as its value the ⟨⟨value⟩⟩ computed in the `throw` expression. The `throw` expression can be anywhere. It can be directly inside the scope of the `catch` expression or it can be in a function called during the evaluation of a `catch`. At the time of evaluation of the `throw` expression, the system stops the evaluation of the `catch` expression with the same catch tag.

```
(defun willie-mays (x)
   (if (numberp x) x (throw 'ball 1)))
```

The above expression terminates the evaluation of any `catch` expression which has the symbol called `ball` as its catch tag if the argument of `willie-mays` is not a number. Since the expression for the catch tag is always evaluated, `ball` needs to be quoted.

```
(defun 3times (x) (catch 'ball (* (willie-mays x) 3)))
```

When the above expression is called, `willie-mays` is called in the middle of the evaluation of `catch` expression whose catch tag is `ball`. If the value of `x` is a number, say 5, the value of `willie-mays` is 5 and the value of (* (willie-mays x) 3) becomes 15. So, the value of the `catch` expression is 15 and the value of 3times is 15.

```
>(3times 5)
15
```

If the value of x is not a number, the system terminates the execution of catch expression in the middle of the execution of the body of willie-mays and the value of catch becomes 1 which is computed by the throw expression.

```
>(3times 'giants)
1
```

If the system calls the function willie-mays from a different function

```
(defun 4times (x) (catch 'ball (* (willie-mays x) 4)))
```

The value of the catch expression in this function can also be computed by the throw expression which is in the body of willie-mays.

```
>(4times 'giants)
1
```

Any data structure can be used as catch tag, but usually symbols are used. There is a reason for this. When the system executes a throw expression it looks for the catch expression which corresponds to it. That is, the one which has the "same" catch tag as the one in the throw expression. By the "same," we mean that the two data structures must return true when they are given to the eq predicate, which is explained in Chapter 5. Some data structures are not the "same" even if they look like the same. Symbols do not have this strange behavior. For example, in

```
(catch '(a b) (throw '(a b) nil))
```

catch and throw can never correspond to each other. In

```
(catch 'a (throw 'a nil))
```

they will always correspond. To make the matter more complicated, in

```
(catch 100000 (throw 100000 nil))
```

whether the catch and throw correspond or not might depend on which computer system you are using. So, unless there is a special reason for

using a data structure other than a symbol, it is better to use a symbol for
a catch tag.

The system produces an error message if a **throw** expression does not
have a corresponding **catch** expression. If there are two or more **catch**
expressions with the same catch tag, the expression which started to be
executed last is the one that stops its execution.

```
>(defun f1 () (catch 'me (cons 1 (f2))))
f1

>(defun f2 () (catch 'me (cons 2 (f3))))
f2

>(defun f3 () (throw 'me (list 3)))
f3
```

After typing the above definitions, if you call **f1**, both the **catch** expression
in **f1** and the **catch** expression in **f2** have the catch tag **me** active when
the system starts to execute the **throw** expression in **f3**. Since the **catch**
expression for **f2** started its execution later than **catch** expression for **f1**,
it terminates its execution and the function **f2** returns the list (3) as a
value. Therefore,

```
>(f1)
(1 3)
```

Consider the following strange function using **catch** and **throw**.

```
(defun where-in-the-list (x tags)
   (if (null tags)
       (throw x 0)
       (1+ (catch (car tags)
             (where-in-the-list x (cdr tags)))))))
```

This is a function for figuring out where a symbol is located in a list, using
catch and **throw**.

```
>(where-in-the-list 'b '(a b c d))
2
```

Let's trace the above function since it is defined recursively.

```
>(trace where-in-the-list)
(where-in-the-list)
```

```
>(where-in-the-list 'b '(a b c d))
    1> (where-in-the-list b (a b c d))
      2> (where-in-the-list b (b c d))
        3> (where-in-the-list b (c d))
          4> (where-in-the-list b (d))
            5> (where-in-the-list b nil)
        <2 (where-in-the-list 1)
      <1 (where-in-the-list 2)
  2
```

The system stopped the execution of the catch expression for the second call in the middle of the fifth call. If you give where-in-the-list a symbol which does not exist in the list, you will get an error message.

```
(where-in-the-list '? '(a b c d))
```

The reason for this error is left to the reader to figure out.

The next special form we will look at is unwind-protect.

$$(\text{unwind-protect}\ \langle\!\langle expression\rangle\!\rangle\ \langle\!\langle expression_1\rangle\!\rangle \dots \langle\!\langle expression_n\rangle\!\rangle\ )$$

The above form first evaluates $\langle\!\langle expression\rangle\!\rangle$. When the evaluation of $\langle\!\langle expression\rangle\!\rangle$ stops, either normally or by some form of non-local exit, it evaluates $\langle\!\langle expression_1\rangle\!\rangle \dots \langle\!\langle expression_n\rangle\!\rangle$. For example, in

```
(let ((x 4))
   (unwind-protect
      《expression》
      (print x)))
```

when the evaluation of $\langle\!\langle expression\rangle\!\rangle$ stops for any reason it prints the value of x at that time. If the evaluation of $\langle\!\langle expression\rangle\!\rangle$ ends normally the value of $\langle\!\langle expression\rangle\!\rangle$ becomes the value of unwind-protect.

```
>(let ((x 4))
   (unwind-protect
      (progn (setq x (1+ x)) (* x x))
      (print x)))
5
25
```

Here we look at a sample program in which the evaluation of ⟨⟨expression⟩⟩ does not end normally.

```
>(block foo
    (let ((x 4))
       (unwind-protect
           (return-from foo (* x x))
           (print x))))
4
16

>(tagbody
      (let ((x 4))
         (unwind-protect
             (progn (setq x (1+ x))
                    (go the-end))
             (print x)))
         the-end)
5
nil

>(catch 'ball
    (let ((x 4))
       (unwind-protect
           (progn (setq x 0) (willie-mays 'giants))
           (print x))))
0
1
```

The `willie-mays` in the above expression is the function which we described at the beginning of this section.

4   Symbols and Packages

The expressions `nil` for an empty list, `car` and `cdr` for function names, `if` and `block` for special forms are all examples of the symbol data type. We type the name of the symbol when we want to refer to it. Every symbol data structure has a name. This sounds natural, but the fact that a thing has a name means that there exists some mechanism for associating a name with the symbol it names. The existence of this association makes it possible for the system to produce the same symbol `nil` every time you input the word "nil". In this chapter, we will talk about this mechanism.

4-1 Symbol Name and Print Name

When the system reads a symbol, it does not distinguish capital and lower case. We input `nil` for the empty list or false, but you can also use any one of the following:

nil	niL	nIl	nIL
Nil	NiL	NIl	NIL

to get the same result.

```
>'(nil niL nIl nIL Nil NiL NIl NIL)
(nil nil nil nil nil nil nil nil)
```

Also, in the form

```
>(defun square (x) (* x x))
```

four symbols, `defun`, `square`, x, and * are used. The result will be the
same when you input them in capital letters. You can also type

```
>(SQUARE 4)
```

or

```
>(SqUaRe 4)
```

because the system reads both of them as `square`. If you distinguish upper
case and low case, each symbol will be said to have several symbol names.
For example, `nil` will have eight symbol names as listed above and `square`
will have 64 symbol names (the 6th power of 2) and any symbol name for
`square` will denote `square`.

   The system does not remember all of a symbol's names, but it rather
remembers one of them which we call the **print name**. The print name
of a symbol is a data structure called a character string. We will talk
about a character string in Chapter 10. In this section, let's just assume a
character string is a simple array of characters. A character string is input
and output using double quotes.

```
>"This is a string."
"This is a string."
```

If the system evaluates a character string as a form, the string itself is
returned as the value. We use a system function called `symbol-name` to
get the print name of a symbol. For example, the print names of `nil` and
`square` are

```
>(symbol-name nil)
"NIL"

>(symbol-name 'square)
"SQUARE"
```

As you can see from the above example, the print name usually consists
entirely of capital letters. When the system reads a symbol, it first changes
any lower case letters to upper case ones and then looks for a symbol with

the same print name. If there is one, the system returns that one. If not, the system creates a new one.

On the other hand, when the system prints a symbol, the method for printing depends on the value of a global variable called *print-case*. Throughout this book we are imagining that the value of *print-case* is set to use lower case. This causes the system to change upper case characters in the print name to lower case characters and to output the print name in lower case. Thus nil is printed as "nil" and square is printed as "square". However, many systems print upper case as the standard. Whether or not to use upper case or lower case is a matter of taste and you can change the value of *print-name* if you prefer otherwise. Details of this will be explained in Chapter 11.

You can create a symbol whose print name has upper and lower case characters using a vertical bar "|". For example,

```
|AbC|
```

makes a symbol whose print name is "AbC".

```
>(symbol-name '|AbC|)
"AbC"
```

This symbol is different from a symbol whose print name is "ABC". This is natural since every symbol has only one print name. To check whether two data structures are the same symbols, you can use a predicate eq, which will be explained in the next chapter. If the data structures are the same, eq returns t. If they are different, it returns nil.

```
>(eq 'AbC 'abc)
t

>(eq '|AbC| 'abc)
nil
```

A symbol referred to using lower case is usually distinguished from the symbol created using a vertical bar.

```
>'(abc AbC |AbC|)
(abc abc |AbC|)
```

|AbC| works exactly in the same way as other symbols without vertical bars. You can define a function called |AbC| and use a function called |AbC|.

```
>(defun |AbC| (x) (* x x))
|AbC|

>(|AbC| 4)
16

>(setq |AbC| '(a b c))
(a b c)

>|AbC|
(a b c)
```

A vertical bar is also used to express a special symbol. For example,

```
|(a b c)|
```

is not a list, but a symbol with a print name "(a b c)".

```
|123|
```

is not a number, but a symbol whose print name is "123". You can also use a backslash "\" instead of a vertical bar. The character right after a backslash will always become part of the print name.

```
>'(a\bc \(a\ b\ c\) \123)
(|AbC| |(a b c)| |123|)
```

There are a few characters which are treated specially in Common Lisp, but the following characters can be used in a print name without using backslashes.

!	$	%	&	@
~	{	}	<	>
[	]	*	/	-
∧	?			

Also, the following characters do not require backslashes if they will not be confused with a number.

```
                +       -
```

For example, if we write

```
1+
```

a backslash is not necessary in front of the "+".

4-2 Packages

The mechanism for combining the name of a symbol with a symbol itself is called a **package**. A package is like a dictionary for symbols. If you look up a print name in a package, you can get the symbol corresponding to that print name. The system always looks in a package when it reads data or a form.

A package is also a kind of data. The fact that a package is data means that more than one package can exist in the system at the same time just like an entry for a word can appear in more than one dictionary or in different languages.

Every Common Lisp system has the following four packages:

* `user` package
* `lisp` package
* `keyword` package
* `system` package

Some systems have additional packages and a user can also create new packages.

Let's look at an example. Suppose you type

```
>'has-not-yet-seen-this-symbol
```

Probably the system does not have a symbol with this name. So, the system creates a new symbol whose print name is

```
"HAS-NOT-YET-SEEN-THIS-SYMBOL"
```

and this symbol is registered in the `user` package. This allows the system to find this symbol when `has-not-yet-seen-this-symbol` is input.

A Common Lisp system always has a global variable called `*package*` which has a package data structure as its value. The package kept in `*package*` is called the **current package**, which is the actual package currently being used. When the system is started, the current package is the `user` package and remains to be so unless another package is assigned. The `user` package is the usual package which a user uses for his work. When the system reads a symbol, it refers to the current package and thus new symbols are made in the current package. The above-mentioned symbol, `has-not-yet-seen-this-symbol`, is registered in the `user` package because the current package is the `user` package.

If you return a package as a value, it is output in the following way:

```
#<...>
```

where "..." is different depending on the system. KCL prints

```
>*package*
#<"USER" package>
```

However, you cannot input a package by typing this. You have to use a name in order to input a package and you can get the package from a package name using a function called `find-package`. The argument to `find-package` is either a symbol or an array of letters.

```
>(find-package 'user)
#<"USER" package>
```

If you change the global value of `*package*`, the current package changes. For example, by evaluating

```
>(setq *package* (find-package 'lisp))
```

the current package becomes the `lisp` package.

As in the above example, you can change the current package by directly changing the value of the variable `*package*`, however, there is a system function called `in-package` which is more often used for this purpose.

```
>(in-package 'new-york)
```

The current package is now a package called `new-york`. If there is no package called `new-york`, a new package called `new-york` will be created. In KCL, when the current package becomes the package called `new-york`, the prompt also becomes

```
NEW-YORK>
```

If the current package is other than the package `user`, the prompt will be

⟪package name⟫ >

Let's look at an example in KCL.

Suppose the current package is `new-york`,

```
NEW-YORK>'office
office
```

The symbol called `office` will be registered in the `new-york` package. If you then type

```
NEW-YORK>(in-package 'los-angeles)
```

which changes the current package to `los-angeles`, and then type

```
LOS-ANGELES>'office
office
```

Another symbol called `office` is created and is registered in the `los-angeles` package. `office` in the `new-york` package and `office` in the `los-angeles` package are two different symbols.

4-3 Internal Symbols and External Symbols

Packages have been developed in order to avoid confusion during the implementation of a giant program consisting of function names and variable names created over a long period of time by different people. A big program is usually created in units called modules. During the development of a big program, it is useful to decide which packages should be assigned for use in which modules. In the `new-york` package and in the `los-angeles` package, some symbols with the same name, for example, `office`, can be defined and used as long as they are defined in different packages. This means that different development groups do not need to worry about conflicts in the symbols they use locally in their part of a project.

```
LOS-ANGELES>(defun office (...) ...)
```

and

```
NEW-YORK>(defun office (...) ...)
```

have the same symbol name but they are different symbols. So, if you type

```
LOS-ANGELES>(office ...)
```

the function `office` defined in the `los-angeles` package will be called. If you type

```
NEW-YORK>(office ...)
```

the function called `office` defined in the `new-york` package will be called. So, if you define local symbols in a module using different packages, you do not have to worry about functions being the same name. The same thing can be said about variables, especially, global variables. If you type,

```
LOS-ANGELES>(setq office 1)
```

and then you type

```
NEW-YORK>(setq office '(a b c))
```

you will get

```
LOS-ANGELES>office
1
```

and

```
NEW-YORK>office
(a b c)
```

Other functions of packages will be discussed later in this section. You should understand them from the point of view of developing programs and you will see why it is important to have such functions.

When a new symbol is created and registered in a package, the symbol works as an **internal symbol**. For example, in the previous section, we showed

```
LOS-ANGELES>'office
office
```

Here, `office` is an internal symbol of the `los-angeles` package. The fact that a symbol is an internal symbol of a package means that the symbol is a local symbol in the package and it cannot be referred from any other package. In order to be able to refer a symbol from some other packages, the internal symbol has to be converted to an **external symbol**.

We use the system function `export` to convert internal symbols to external symbols. When you type

```
LOS-ANGELES>(export 'office)
```

`office` becomes an external symbol of the `los-angeles` package. External symbols can be referred from other packages by typing

《package name》 : 《symbol name》

For example,

```
NEW-YORK>'los-angeles:office
los-angeles:office
```

Notice that output also has the package name as part of what is printed.

An external symbol of a package can be **import**ed to another package. In other words, an external symbol can be registered in another package. For example, if you type

```
LOS-ANGELES>(in-package 'chicago)
```

and then you type

```
CHICAGO>(import 'los-angeles:office)
```

a symbol `office` which is in the `los-angeles` package is now registered also in the `chicago` package and becomes an internal symbol of the `chicago` package. At this point, a symbol called `office` of the `los-angeles` package belongs to both the `los-angeles` and the `chicago` packages. In this case

```
CHICAGO>'office
office
```

and

```
LOS-ANGELES>'office
office
```

are returning the same symbol. Therefore,

```
CHICAGO>(eq 'office 'los-angeles:office)
t
```

As opposed to this,

```
NEW-YORK>'office
```

is a different symbol.

```
NEW-YORK>(eq 'office 'los-angeles:office)
nil
```

The functions export and import can take a list of symbols as an argument instead of just one symbol, and all the symbols in a list are exported or imported. Also, export and import can take a package as a second argument. In that case, the symbols will be exported from or imported to the mentioned package, not to the current package.

Rather than importing external symbols one by one from some other package, you can also make the system see all the external symbols of some other package without moving them. The function use-package performs this task. If you type

```
LOS-ANGELES>(in-package 'boston)
```

and then

```
BOSTON>(use-package 'los-angeles)
```

the system can see all the external symbols in los-angeles package from the boston package; "the boston package uses the los-angeles package." For example,

```
BOSTON>'office
office
```

The system returns the symbol office which comes from the los-angeles package. Unlike importing to the chicago package in the above, the symbol office from the los-angeles package is not registered in the boston package. The reason for being able to access the symbol office from the los-angeles package while in the boston package is that the boston package is 'using' the los-angeles package.

use-package can also take a package as a second argument. In this case, the package which appears as the second argument is 'using' the package which appears as the first.

The symbols which the system has when it starts, such as nil, car, and cons, are registered as external symbols in the lisp package. Other packages can always 'use' the lisp package without mentioning it. If you type

```
BOSTON>'cons
cons
```

the system returns the cons from the lisp package. This accounts for our ability to say

```
BOSTON>(car '(1 2))
1
```

Each symbol has a record of the package where it was initially registered and this package is called its **home package**. For example, in the above example, there is a symbol `office` which is registered in both the `los-angeles` package and the `chicago` package, but the home package of `office` is the `los-angeles` package. To get the symbol's home package, a function `symbol-package` is used.

```
CHICAGO>(symbol-package 'office)
#<"LOS-ANGELES" package>
```

When you want to do a certain operation globally to all the symbols in a package, you can use the macro `do-symbols` which has the general form

(do-symbols (⟨⟨variable⟩⟩ ⟨⟨package expression⟩⟩ ⟨⟨value⟩⟩)
    ⟨⟨expression$_1$⟩⟩ ... ⟨⟨expression$_n$⟩⟩)

First, the system evaluates the ⟨⟨package expression⟩⟩. Its value has to be a package. Then, the system binds ⟨⟨variable⟩⟩ to all the symbols of the assigned package one by one, then evaluates ⟨⟨expression$_1$⟩⟩ ... ⟨⟨expression$_n$⟩⟩ for each symbol. Finally, the system evaluates ⟨⟨value⟩⟩ and its value is returned as the value of the `do-symbols` expression. ⟨⟨value⟩⟩ can be omitted and in this case, the value of `do-symbols` is `nil`. For example, if you type

```
>(let ((x nil))
   (do-symbols (s (find-package 'lisp) x)
     (setq x (cons s x))))
```

the system returns a list of all the symbols in the `lisp` package. The order in which the system binds the symbols is not uniform. If you use `do-external-symbols` rather than `do-symbols`, the system binds only the external symbols. If you use `do-all-symbols`, the system binds all the symbols registered in the system and you do not need to specify a package.

You can use the function `list-all-packages` to get a list of the packages existing in the system. `list-all-packages` does not require arguments.

4-4 Interning

The operation of getting a symbol from a print name and a current package is called **interning**. Interning is done using the following procedure:

1. If a symbol with the given print name is registered in the current package, the system returns that symbol. If not, go to 2.
2. If a symbol with the given print name is an external symbol of the package which the current package is using, the system returns that symbol. If not, go to 3.
3. The system creates a new symbol with the given print name, registers it as an internal symbol in the current package, and returns the new symbol.

Interning is being done when the system reads a form or some data, but it can also be done using the function `intern`. By evaluating

    (intern ⟪character string⟫)

the system interns ⟪character string⟫ as the print name of a symbol and returns the symbol as a result. `intern` can also take a second argument.

    (intern ⟪character string⟫ ⟪package⟫)

In this case the system interns ⟪character string⟫ in the package given as the second argument and returns the symbol which it gets as a result. In other words, the system does the above-mentioned operations 1–3 using its second argument instead of the current package.

    `intern` is a multiple-valued function which returns two values. The first value is the symbol which you wanted. The second value is one of the following:

`:internal`	(if it has been registered as an internal symbol)
`:external`	(if it has been registered as an external symbol)
`:inherited`	(if it has been registered as an external symbol of the package used)
`nil`	(if newly created)

The first two symbols are called keywords and their use will be explained later. For example,

```
>(intern "NIL")
nil
:inherited

>(intern "NEW-SYMBOL")
new-symbol
nil
```

```
>(in-package 'new-york)
#<("NEW-YORK" package>

NEW-YORK>(intern "OFFICE")
office
:internal

>(in-package 'los-angeles)
#<"LOS-ANGELES" package>

LOS-ANGELES>(intern "OFFICE")
office
:external

>(in-package 'chicago)
#<"CHICAGO" package>

CHICAGO>(intern "OFFICE")
office
:internal

>(in-package 'boston)
#<"BOSTON" package>

BOSTON>(intern "OFFICE")
office
:inherited
```

The function find-symbol works similarly as intern, but it does not create
the new symbol specified by operation 3. This function returns nil as a
first value when the system cannot find a symbol with the given print name.
For example,

```
>(find-symbol "NEW-SYMBOL")
nil
nil
```

In general the system cannot see internal symbols of other packages, but
if you are strongly motivated you can do a sneaky thing to see them. By
typing:

⟪package name⟫ : : ⟪symbol name⟫

between the ⟪package name⟫ and the ⟪symbol name⟫ you can get the same effect as

```
(intern ⟪symbol name⟫ ⟪package⟫ )
```

For example, if you type

```
LOS-ANGELES>'new-york::office
```

the system can refer an internal symbol `office` in the `new-york` package from the `los-angeles` package. However, if you type

```
LOS-ANGELES>'new-york:office
```

the `office` in the `new-york` package is not an external symbol, and the system gives an error message. Also, `office` in the `los-angeles` package is an external symbol, so

```
NEW-YORK>'los-angeles::office
```

and

```
NEW-YORK>'los-angeles:office
```

are the same thing.

Naturally, when you output a symbol it is relative to the current package; that is, it is output so that the symbol is returned to its original package if it is reread without changing a current package. This means that a symbol may be output in a different way from the way in which it was input. For example,

```
CHICAGO>'los-angeles:office
office
```

In the above case, since `los-angeles:office` is already imported in the `chicago` package, the system will return `los-angeles:office` even if it reads `office` in the `chicago` package. That is to say, the system outputs symbols in the simplest form.

```
NEW-YORK>(intern "OFFICE" 'los-angeles)
los-angeles:office
:external

NEW-YORK>(intern "OFFICE" 'chicago)
chicago::office
:internal
```

4-5 Predefined Packages

Symbols which the system provides such as `nil`, `car`, `cons`, etc, are registered as external symbols of the `lisp` package. Any packages which are not the `lisp` package or the `keyword` package use the `lisp` package unless another package is specified, even if they are created using `in-package`.

The `keyword` package is a special package for registering **keywords**. The symbols of the `keyword` package can be referenced using

    keyword:⟨⟨symbol name⟩⟩

or

    keyword::⟨⟨symbol name⟩⟩

but by convention you can also use

    :⟨⟨symbol name⟩⟩

Unlike other packages, when the system registers a new symbol in the `keyword` package, the keyword is registered as an external symbol in the `keyword` package and becomes a variable with a constant value which is the symbol itself. In other words, if the system evaluates this keyword, it gets the keyword itself.

    >:this-is-a-keyword
    :this-is-a-keyword

Keywords, which will be discussed in Chapter 6, are often used for specifying parameters for a system function or a user defined function.

Beside the `keyword` package and the `user` package, the `system` package is a predefined package.

4-6 Shadowing

Let us suppose you want to define a function called `if` even if a special form like `if` is not allowed to be redefined. In such a case, if you type

    >(shadow 'if)

If the current package does not have such symbol, a new symbol `if` will be
registered in a current package. If the current package has such symbol,
nothing happens. Since `if` is usually an external symbol of the `lisp` package and it is not registered in the `user` package, a new symbol `if` which
is different from the `if` in the `lisp` package will be registered in the `user`
package. If you input `if` in the `user` package, the new symbol will be referred. In such a case, the `if` in the `lisp` package is said to be shadowed
by the `shadow` function. After this we could define

```
>(defun if (x)
   (cond ((zerop x) 1)
         (t (* x (if (1- x)))))))
```

After that, if you want to refer the `if` in the `lisp` package, you can use
`lisp:if`. For example,

```
>(defun if (x)
    (lisp:if (zerop x)
             1
             (* x (if (1- x))))))
```

The `shadow` function can take a list of symbols as an argument instead
of a single symbol. In this case, each symbol in a list will be `shadowed`.
Also, you can specify a package using a second argument to `shadow`.

4-7 Functions for Making Symbols

During list processing, sometimes it becomes necessary to create new symbols. If the name is not important and the symbol does not have to belong
to any particular package, you can use a function called `gensym`. This
function

```
>(gensym)
```

returns the symbol `g0` and its print name is `"G0"`. This symbol is not
registered in any package and, as a result, does not have a home package.
A symbol created by `gensym` is printed as

```
#:⟨⟨symbol name⟩⟩
```

So,

```
>(gensym)
#:g0
```

Each time you call **gensym**, the number which appears as part of the print name of this symbol increases by one.

```
>(gensym)
#:g1

>(gensym)
#:g2
```

If you type (**gensym** 0), the number of the symbol goes back to 0.

```
>(gensym 0)
#:g0
```

However, the symbol returned here is not the same symbol as the symbol #:g0 which was created initially. **gensym** creates and returns a new symbol every time you execute it. If you give a character string to **gensym**, the print name will then start with that character string.

```
>(gensym "FOO-")
#:foo-1

>(gensym)
#:foo-2
```

As we said before, a symbol created by **gensym** does not have a home package. Thus

```
>(symbol-package (gensym))
nil
```

If you want to return a new symbol and register it in a package, you can use **gentemp** instead of **gensym**. When you type

```
>(gentemp)
```

a new symbol whose print name is "t0" is created and registered in the current package if 1) the print name "T0" is not registered in the current package and 2) it is not registered as an external symbol of the package which the current package uses.   Otherwise, the system checks a symbol t1.

```
>(gentemp)
t1
```

Next time gentemp is called, the system checks the symbol t2.

gentemp can take up to two arguments. The first argument is a character string which specifies the print name for gentemp just like gensym. The second argument is a package. If the second argument is given, a new symbol is registered in that package rather than in the current package.

5   List Structure

In this chapter, we will talk about how list structure is represented inside the system. So far, we have only looked at a list of data as a simple array of data. However, some functions of the system cannot be understood without knowledge of how lists are represented. Such functions are also explained in this chapter.

5-1 cons Cells

A list is represented using a box called a **cons cell**. In one cons cell, there are two places to keep data. One place is called the **car** part and the other is called the **cdr** part. The first element of a list is in the car part and the rest of the list is stored in the **cdr** part. In the list (we eat rice), the first element is the symbol we and the rest of the list is the list (eat rice). So, this list is represented using a cons cell in which the car part contains the symbol we and the **cdr** part contains the list (eat rice). This can be illustrated as

The box

shows a cons cell and the left side of the box is the `car` part and right side is the `cdr` part. The content of the `car` part and the `cdr` part can be written inside the square if it fits. If not, you can use an arrow to indicate the content. Now, (eat rice) in the `cdr` part of the cons cell is itself a list, so it can also be expressed as a cons cell.

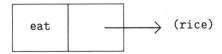

The first element of (rice) is `rice` and the rest of this list is the empty list. The empty list is represented using the symbol `nil`, so (rice) is represented as

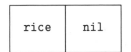

In this way, (we eat rice) is expressed using three cons cells.

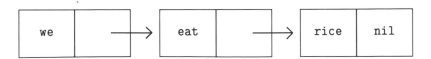

As we already said, the `car` of (we eat rice) is the symbol `we` and the `cdr` is a list (eat rice). The functions `car` and `cdr` are the functions which take a cons cell and simply return either the `car` part or the `cdr` part. The function `cons` creates a cons cell and puts its first argument in the `car` part and its second argument in the `cdr` part. As a result, if the first argument is the symbol `we` and the second argument is the list (eat rice), the list (we eat rice) is created and this becomes the value of the function `cons`.

```
>(cons 'we '(eat rice))
(we eat rice)
```

The important thing to remember here is that `cons` will not change the already existing content of a cons cell. It creates a new list with the list given as its second argument. Let's look at an example:

```
>(setq x '(we eat rice))
(we eat rice)

>(setq y (cons 'they (cdr x)))
(they eat rice)
```

The first `setq` expression assigns the list (we eat rice) to the variable x. This state can be illustrated as follows:

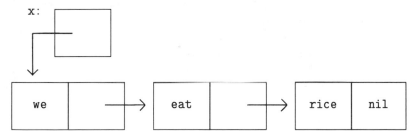

In the second `setq` expression, `cons` creates a new cons cell. The original list (we eat rice) stays the same.

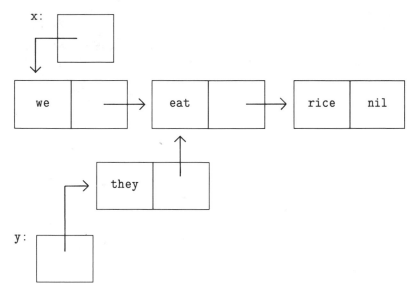

After the evaluation of the second `setq` expression, the value of the variable x remains unchanged.

In the above example, the list (eat rice) is part of two boxes at the same time. It is hard to imagine, in everyday life, that one thing can be in two boxes at the same time, so let us try to explain this more carefully. Each cons cell or data structure such as a symbol is hidden somewhere in the memory of the computer. Every such place in the memory has an address and one thing the system can do is to get the data from one particular address (a fixed piece of data will not move to another address). The actual thing stored in the box (for variables and for the car part or the cdr part of a cons cell) is not the data itself, but rather the address where such data is kept. In the above example, precisely speaking, the address of the cell representing (eat rice) is kept in the cdr part of the cell for (we eat rice). We can translate "The address for A is kept in B" to "B points at A." That is why the boxes contain arrows.

The second argument to the function cons does not necessarily have to be a list. The system creates a new cons cell and puts the second argument in the cdr part whether or not it is a list. As a result, if the first argument is the symbol a and the second argument is the symbol b, the following new structure is created and this becomes the value of the cons.

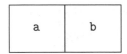

If the cdr part of a cons cell is not a list, the data structure of such a cons cell is called a **dotted pair**. The reason for this name is that the system inserts a dot "." between the data in the car part and the data in the cdr part when it displays such data. Also, you need to insert a dot between the car part and the cdr part when you input a dotted pair to the system.

```
>(cons 'a 'b)
(a . b)

>(car '(a . b))
a

>(cdr '(a . b))
b
```

When the system prints (⟨⟨data₁⟩⟩ . ⟨⟨data₂⟩⟩) it means a cons cell with ⟨⟨data₁⟩⟩ as the car part and ⟨⟨data₂⟩⟩ as the cdr part. If ⟨⟨data₂⟩⟩ is a list, the display shows a list rather than a pair.

```
>'(d . nil)
(d)
```

```
>'(a . (b c d))
(a b c d)
```

In other words,

$$(\langle\!\langle\text{data}\rangle\!\rangle \ . \ (\ \dots \ ))$$

is the same as

$$(\langle\!\langle\text{data}\rangle\!\rangle \ \dots \ )$$

and

$$(\langle\!\langle\text{data}\rangle\!\rangle \ . \ \texttt{nil})$$

is the same as

$$(\langle\!\langle\text{data}\rangle\!\rangle \ )$$

For example,

```
(a . (b . nil))
```

is the same as

```
(a . (b))
```

and it is also the same as

```
(a b)
```

which is just the list consisting of a and b.

```
>(a . (b . nil))
(a b)
```

If we replace nil with a symbol c

```
(a . (b . c))
```

This is the same as

```
(a b . c)
```

The data for both of them are illustrated as follows.

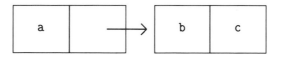

The system uses the latter form to display this data since it is clearer.

```
>(cons 'a (cons 'b 'c))
(a b . c)

>'(a . (b . c))
(a b . c)

>'(a b . c)
(a b . c)
```

The above data is called a **dotted list**, because, although it is not a list, it looks like a list and the last cell is a dotted pair. The system function list* takes the cons of its last argument with the ones that come before it and returns the result as its value. If the last argument is a list, the value of list* becomes a list, if not, the value is a dotted pair or a dotted list.

```
>(list* 'a 'b '(c d e))
(a b c d e)

>(list* '(c d e))
(c d e)

>(list* 'a 'b)
(a . b)

>(list* 'a 'b 'end)
(a b . end)
```

You need some empty space (or a line feed or a tab which will be treated as empty space) around the dot when you input a dotted pair or a dotted list. If you forget the empty space around the dot, the following will happen.

```
>(car '(a.b))
a.b                    ; the symbol a.b

>(car '(a. b))
a.                     ; the symbol a.

>(cdr '(a .b))
(.b)                   ; the list (.b)
```

Each cons cell is a single data structure and is called a **cons**.

```
>(setq x '(we eat rice))
```

The value of the variable x is the list (we eat rice). However, it can also be viewed as a cons whose car part is the symbol we and whose cdr part is the list (eat rice). 'List' and 'dotted list' are always the result of the combination of cons. A dotted pair can be interpreted as a cons in which the cdr part is not nil or another cons. Precisely speaking, the functions car and cdr receive a cons or nil as their arguments. The value of the function cons is always a cons. In Lisp terminology 'dotted pair' is sometimes used to mean cons data, but in this book, whenever we use 'dotted pair' we mean only the case mentioned above. The system predicate consp checks whether a data structure is a cons or not.

```
>(consp '(a . b))
t

>(consp 'a)
nil

>(consp '( ))
nil
```

The empty list is the same as the symbol nil, therefore, it is not a cons. There is a predicate called listp for deciding whether a data structure is a cons or an empty list. Because of this confusing name, please do not misunderstand that this predicate is for deciding whether a data structure is a list or not.

```
>(listp '(a . b))
t

>(listp 'a)
nil
```

```
>(listp '( ))
t
```

All data except a cons are called **atom**s. There is a predicate called `atom`

```
(atom x)
```

which has the same value as

```
(not (consp x))
```

5-2 Destructive List Operations

The system functions called `rplaca` and `rplacd` are used for changing the content of a cons cell. `rplaca` is for replacing the `car` part and is pronounced as re-plack-a. `rplacd` is for replacing the `cdr` part and is pronounced as re-plack-dee. The first argument of both functions is a cons and these functions put the second argument in the `car` part or the `cdr` part of this cons, respectively. Consider the following examples.

```
>(setq x '(we eat rice))
(we eat rice)

>(setq y (cons 'now x))
(now we eat rice)

>(rplaca x 'they)
(they eat rice)

>x
(they eat rice)

>y
(now they eat rice)
```

The state after the evaluation of the two **setq** expressions is illustrated as follows:

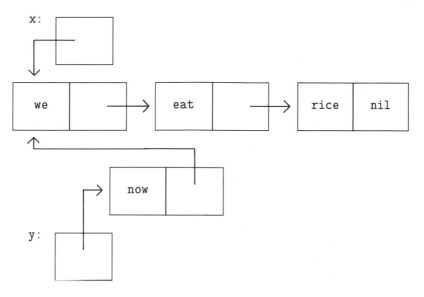

After **rplaca** gets the cons stored in a variable x and replaces its **car** part with **they**, the result is that the value of a variable x changes to (they eat rice) from (we eat rice). The value of the variable y changes from (now we eat rice) to (now they eat rice).

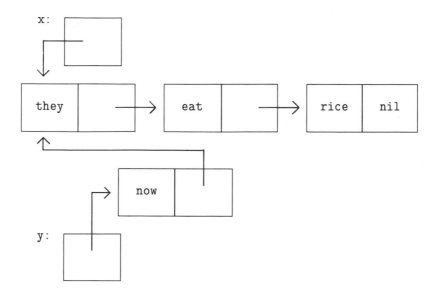

By using **rplaca** and **rplacd**, you can create a so-called **circular list**. A circular list is a data structure which points back into itself when you

follow the `car` part or the `cdr` part of the cell. Suppose the value of `x` is
(`eat rice`).

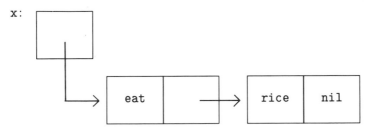

If you type

```
>(rplacd x x)
```

the system puts the address of the cell which is pointed to by `x` into the
`cdr` part of the cons cell. In other words, this cell now points to itself.

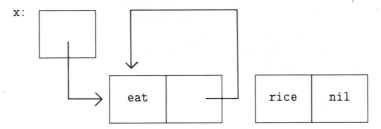

As a result, when the system tries to print the value of this `rplacd` expression, the symbol `eat` will appear infinitely often.

```
>(setq x '(eat rice))
(eat rice)

>(rplacd x x)
(eat eat eat eat eat eat eat eat eat eat
 eat eat eat eat eat eat eat eat eat eat
 eat eat eat eat eat eat eat eat eat eat
 eat eat eat eat eat eat eat eat eat eat
 eat eat eat eat eat eat eat eat eat eat
 ...
```

In the above case, the system has a method for forcing such a computation
to stop. Each system has its own method, so please find out about the
method before trying the above example.

Using `rplaca` and `rplacd` gives you complete control over manipulating lists, but on the other hand, there are possibilities for causing side effects which you did not expect to happen. Also, there is the danger of making an endless list. This means that you should use these functions very carefully and try to avoid using them if possible. For example, if you simply want to change the value of a variable x to (they eat rice), you can type

```
(setq x (cons 'they (cdr x)))
```

By doing this, there is no danger of changing the value of the variable y by mistake.

Both system functions `append` and `nconc` take some lists as arguments and return the list of all the elements in all the lists as their value.

```
>(append '(a (b c)) '(1 2) '(z))
(a (b c) 1 2 z)

>(nconc '(a (b c)) '(1 2) '(z))
(a (b c) 1 2 z)
```

`append` creates a new list using elements in each list. `nconc` "destructively" operates the lists received as arguments. `nconc` connects two lists by moving the next list in its argument list into the `cdr` part of the last cell in each previous list. Since `nconc` does not use any new cells at all, `nconc` does the job faster than `append`. You should be aware that some unexpected side effects might happen when the lists given to `nconc` are already in use. Consider the following examples.

```
>(setq x '(1 2))
(1 2)

>(nconc x '(3 4 5))
(1 2 3 4 5)

>x
(1 2 3 4 5)
```

Since the system connects a list (3 4 5) directly to the end of the list which is in the variable x, the value of the variable x changes. If you use `append` which makes a new list, rather than `nconc`, the value of x will be unchanged.

5-3 Equality

We already know the function = for deciding the equality of numbers, i.e., whether two numbers are equal or not. In this section, we will talk about three system functions eq, eql, and equal for deciding the equality of data. These functions take two data objects and return t if they are equal and return nil if not. However, the meaning of equality is slightly different in these three functions. The meaning becomes "broader" as you use eq, eql, equal. If two data objects are equal by eq, then they are equal by eql. If two data objects are equal by eql, then they are equal by equal. Conversely, if they are not equal by equal, then they will not be equal by eq nor eql. If they are not equal by eql, they will not be equal by eq.

When two data objects are of a different kind, the value of these functions is nil. If one argument is a number and the other is a symbol, the value of these functions is nil. If the two arguments are a number and a list or a symbol and a list, the value will be nil.

```
>(equal 1 'one)
nil

>(equal 1 '(o n e))
nil

>(equal 'one '(o n e))
nil
```

The above example will have the same result if equal is replaced with eq or eql. If the data objects are the same, these functions will all have t as a value. Let's look at a variable x.

```
>(eq x x)
t

>x
(a b c)

>(setq y (cdr x))
(b c)

>(eq (cdr x) y)
t
```

The last example has the value t because the two arguments of eq are the
cdr part of the list in the variable x. The value will be t even when eq
is replaced by eql or equal. As we said in the previous chapter, only one
symbol of each name exists in a package. For example, if you type

```
>(setq x 'atcholi)
atcholi

>(setq y 'atcholi)
atcholi
```

a variable x and a variable y are assigned with exactly the same symbol.
So, you will get

```
>(eq x y)
t
```

and

```
>(eq x 'atcholi)
t

>(eq 'atcholi 'atcholi)
t
```

The above form will give the same results when eq is replaced by eql or
equal.

Before explaining the difference among eq, eql, and equal, we will show
you that two data objects which look the same can actually be different.
For example, in

```
>(setq x (list 'a 'b) y (list 'a 'b))
(a b)
```

the values of x and y are the list of a and b.

```
>x
(a b)

>y
(a b)
```

However, the value of **x** and the value of **y** are different lists, because each
time

```
(list 'a 'b)
```

is evaluated, new cons cells are created.

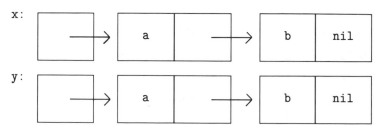

When you type

```
>(cons '(a b) '(a b))
```

the system will do the following as it reads the above form,

```
(list 'cons
        (list 'quote (list 'a 'b))
        (list 'quote (list 'a 'b)))
```

As you can see the system makes a list of **a** and **b** twice. Therefore, even
though the arguments to `cons` are both lists consisting of **a** and **b**, they are
not the same data objects.

The same thing happens for the numbers. Each system represents numbers slightly differently, but usually the system uses a box for a number
(a number cell) just like a list. For example, when reading

```
>(setq x 10)
```

the system prepares a number cell for the number **10** and then puts this
number cell in **x**, rather than put **10** directly in **x**.

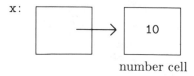

number cell

Whether this number cell is a new one or an already existing box with **10**
in it depends on the system. For example, if the value of the variable **y** is
10 before this assignment, **x** and **y** may have the same cell

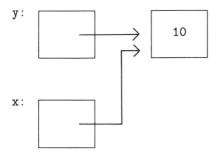

or x and y may have different number cells.

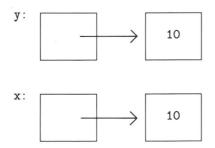

Unlike a cons cell, the contents of a number cell cannot be changed directly.

```
>(1+ x)
```

In this case the system creates a new number box for 11. On some systems it may use an already existing number cell for 11, but it never replaces the content of the number cell for 10 with 11. Therefore, you do not have to worry about whether the system uses the old number box or creates a new number box, but you should just remember that the numbers with the same value might be different data objects.

eq returns t when two data are literally the same data object. In other cases it returns nil.

```
>(eq '(a b) '(a b))
```

Since the above two arguments are not the same data, the value of eq would be nil.

```
>(eq '(a b) '(a b))
nil
```

The value of

```
>(eq 10 10)
```

depends on the Common Lisp system you are using. The value may be **t** or **nil**.

eql returns **t** when two data objects are exactly the same, when two data objects are numbers with the same value, or when two data objects are the character data for the same character. In other cases, it returns **nil**. We will talk about character data in Chapter 10.

```
>(eql 10 10)
t

>(eql 2432902008176640000
      2432902008176640000)
t
```

equal, broadly speaking, returns **t** when two data are displayed the same. Otherwise, it returns **nil**. It returns **t** for two different data objects whenever they are numbers with the same value.

```
>(equal 2432902008176640000
        2432902008176640000)
t
```

Two lists whose elements are the same are equal when tested by **equal**, since they will be displayed in the same way.

```
>(eql '(a b) '(a b))
nil

>(equal '(a b) '(a b))
t

>(equal '(a b)
        (cons 'a (cdr (list 1 'b))))
t
```

More precisely, **equal** applied to two lists returns **t** when the lengths of two lists are the same and when **equal** is applied to each pair of corresponding elements of these lists.

```
>(equal '(10 (little indians))
        '(10 (little indians)))
t
```

In the above example, since the first elements in two lists are both 10 and the second elements in two lists are both (little indians), all the elements in two lists are equal from the point of view of equal, therefore, the two lists are equal from the point of view of equal.

Generally, the time required for computing the comparison gets longer in the order eq, eql, equal. eq checks whether two data objects are the same or not but does not check what kind of data they are. eql checks whether two data objects are the same or not. If they are not the same, eql checks whether both data objects are numbers or characters. If they are numbers, eql checks whether they have the same value. If they are characters, eql checks whether they are the same character. Thus it requires more time for the comparison. equal further checks whether two data objects are lists or not. If so, it checks whether the corresponding elements in the lists are equal or not. For this reason it requires more time for the comparison than eql. Data objects which are equal from the eq or eql point of view are already equal from the point of view of equal. Since it takes the longest time to compare using equal, it would be better to use eql or eq if they will be sufficient. When you know that two data objects are symbols, you should use eq. When you also need to compare numbers, you should use eql. If you need to compare only numbers, it would be better to use = than using eql since it is more efficient. By using =, you can also avoid comparing any data other than numbers since = only compares numbers and it will give you an error message when you try to compare data of any other type. If the data for comparison are always characters, it would be better to use the system function char= than using eql for the same reason as using = for numbers.

5-4 Garbage Collection

As you use the system, some cells become unused. In the following example, the list (we eat rice) is assigned to the variable x, but right after that another data object is assigned to x. Consequently, the list (we eat rice) cannot be used again and the three cons cells for this list cannot be used.

```
>(setq x '(we eat rice))
(we eat rice)
```

```
>(setq x '(but we dont))
(but we dont)
```

Most systems reuse cells that are no longer being used by recycling. If the system keeps making new `cons` and `list`s the system will eventually reach the point where it no longer has any room left to make a new cell. In this case, the system needs to recycle the old cells.

There are several ways to recycle the old cells, but the most popular way is by **garbage collection**. Garbage collection is done by first making marks on all the data being used at the time the system goes beyond the limit. The system then puts marks on each cons cell of any list that it has already marked. The system notes the cells without marks as the cells for recycling. It recycles such cells and will put marks back on them. When the system needs to use the cells noted for recycling, such cells are made available for use. When the number of cells for recycling becomes very small, another garbage collection will be done. The system repeats this as necessary.

The time required for garbage collection is different for different systems. It usually takes several seconds to tens of seconds depending on the amount of data being used. Usually, the system stops the execution of the expression input by a user and concentrates on the garbage collection. This sometimes gives you the impression that the system stops and then starts to work again.

6   Functions

In the previous chapters, we explained that binding arguments to their corresponding parameters was one method of transferring arguments to functions. In Common Lisp, there are other methods of transferring the arguments. We will talk about them in this chapter. Also in the previous chapters, we described system functions and functions defined by `defun`. In this chapter, we describe functions without names, functions which are used only inside of a certain form, and functions that call other functions. In other words, we will explain everything about functions in Common Lisp.

6-1 Lambda Expressions

A lambda expression is a list for defining a function and always starts with the symbol `lambda`.

```
(lambda (x) (* x x))
```

The above expression is a lambda expression which defines a function which squares a number. `x` is a parameter of this function and its body is (`* x x`). If the first element of a list form is a lambda expression, the function defined by the lambda expression will be called. The system treats

the arguments exactly in the same way as a function call which starts with
a function name.

```
>((lambda (x) (* x x)) 3)
9
```

A function definition using `defun`

```
(defun square (x) (* x x))
```

is actually used to associate the name **square** with the function defined by
the lambda expression

```
(lambda (x) (* x x))
```

If you give a name to this function instead of writing

```
((lambda (x) (* x x)) 3)
```

using a lambda expression, you can simply write

```
(square 3)
```

In the above example, the same thing happens if you call **square** or if
you directly use the lambda expression which defines **square**. Generally,
there is a slightly different result between calling functions defined by a
defun expression and using a lambda expression for defining a function.
The reasons for this difference are 1) the scope of a variable or a block
will not be influenced by a lambda expression and 2) the system does not
automatically define a block around a lambda expression. In

```
>(defun foo () (setq count (1+ count)))
foo
```

`count` is a global variable. Even if this function is called from inside of the
scope of a local variable such as `count`

```
>(let ((count 0))
   (foo)
   count)
0
```

it does not affect the local variable. However, if you replace the call to `foo`
with the corresponding lambda expression, the variable `count` in the body

of the lambda expression will refer to the local variable count since the
lambda expression belongs to its scope.

```
>(let ((count 0))
   ((lambda () (setq count (1+ count))))
   count)
1
```

Also, in

```
>(block bar
    (1+ ((lambda ()
             (return-from bar 0)))))
0
```

the bar in the return-from is the same as the bar in the block expression.
But in the definition

```
>(defun bar () (return-from bar 0))
bar
```

the bar in the return-from refers to the new block which the system
automatically creates when this function is called. Therefore,

```
>(block bar
    (1+ (bar)))
1
```

A lambda expression is not a form, so it cannot be evaluated. If you type

```
>(lambda (x) (* x x))
```

the system will think you are trying to call a function named lambda. There
is no system function called lambda. Even if there were, the system would
think that this function is to be applied to the values of (x) and (* x x)
as arguments and would do a meaningless evaluation.

The general form of a lambda expression has a parameter list right after
the lambda and can have several expressions in the body.

(lambda ⟨⟨lambda list⟩⟩ ⟨⟨expression₁⟩⟩ . . . ⟨⟨expressionₙ⟩⟩)

When the system calls a function defined by a lambda expression, it evaluates each expression in the body and returns the value of ⟨⟨expressionₙ⟩⟩

as a value. A **lambda list** means "a list which specifies the parameters of
a function defined by a lambda expression." Since functions which can be
defined by `defun` can also be defined by a lambda expression, we will call
its ⟨⟨parameter list⟩⟩ a ⟨⟨lambda list⟩⟩ from now on. The general form of a
`defun` expression is

> (defun ⟨⟨function name⟩⟩ ⟨⟨lambda list⟩⟩
> ⟨⟨expression$_1$⟩⟩ ... ⟨⟨expression$_n$⟩⟩)

The general form of a lambda list is

> (⟨⟨variable⟩⟩ *
> [&optional ⟨⟨optional parameter specification⟩⟩ *]
> [&rest ⟨⟨variable⟩⟩]
> [&key ⟨⟨keyword parameter specification⟩⟩ *
>   [&allow-other-keys]]
> [&aux ⟨⟨auxiliary variable specification⟩⟩ *]
>)

The things inside the "[ ]" can be omitted and "⟨⟨ ⟩⟩*" means that a
sequence of zero or more of these things must be present. &optional,
&rest, &key, &allow-other-keys, and &aux are special symbols that can
appear in a lambda list and are called **lambda-list-keywords**. These
symbols are not symbols in the keyword package even though they are
called "keywords," but are simply ordinary symbols starting with "&".

Variables which appear before any lambda-list-keywords are called
required parameters and when a function is called it must have arguments which correspond to these parameters. Each required parameter
is bound to its corresponding argument—the first required parameter is
bound to the first argument, the second required parameter is bound to
the second argument, etc. Each corresponding argument becomes the initial value of such a required parameter. When a lambda-list does not have
any lambda-list keywords, all of the parameters can be said to be required
parameters. All the lambda-lists (parameter-lists) we have mentioned so
far consist entirely of required parameters. In such a list the number of arguments given to a function should be the same as the number of required
parameters.

> (lambda (x y) ...)

When you call the above function, you have to give it two arguments.

You can specify some **optional parameters** using the lambda-list-
keyword &option. Optional parameters do not have to have corresponding

arguments when a function is called. Arguments which are not associated with a required parameter will then be associated with the optional parameters. For example, in

```
((lambda (x y &optional ...) ...)
   1 2 3 4 ...)
```

the arguments 1 and 2 will be bound to the required parameters x and y, the argument 3 will be bound to the first optional parameter, and the argument 4 will be bound to the second optional parameter. The rest of the arguments will be bound to their corresponding parameters. An optional parameter takes its corresponding argument, if any, as an initial value. If there are no such arguments, it will take a value specified in the lambda-list called its **default value** as an initial value. The general form of an optional parameter specification is a list made up of three elements.

(⟨⟨variable⟩⟩ ⟨⟨expression⟩⟩ ⟨⟨supplied-p variable⟩⟩)

⟨⟨variable⟩⟩ is the name of the local variable to be used as the optional parameter, ⟨⟨expression⟩⟩ is the expression to be used for computing the default value, and ⟨⟨supplied-p variable⟩⟩ is the name of a local variable to be used for checking whether the corresponding argument exists or not. If there is a corresponding argument, the supplied-p variable is bound to t, if not, it is bound to nil.

```
>((lambda (a &optional (b 3 c))
     (list a b c))
   1 2)
(1 2 t)

>((lambda (a &optional (b 3 c))
     (list a b c))
   1)
(1 3 nil)
```

In the above example, a is a required parameter, b is an optional parameter, and c is a supplied-p variable for the optional parameter b. In the first call, since 2 is the argument associated with b, b is bound to 2 and c is bound to t. The expression 3 which provides the default value of b will not be evaluated. In next call, since there is no argument which corresponds to b, the value 3 becomes the initial value of b and the value of c becomes nil.

If the supplied-p variable is not going to be used, the ⟪supplied-p⟫ part of the specification of an optional parameter can be omitted.

(⟪variable⟫ ⟪expression⟫)

If a default value does not need to be specified, this can be contracted to

(⟪variable⟫)

in which case it does not have to be a list, so you can simply use

⟪variable⟫

In these cases, `nil` is used as the default value.

```
(lambda (&optional x (y) (z nil)) ... )
```

The above three optional parameters all have `nil` as their default value and this specification has the same effect as

```
(lambda (&optional x y z) ... )
```

A local variable called a **rest parameter** can be specified right after the lambda-list-keyword **&rest**. The arguments of a function that remain unaccounted for after binding the required and optional parameters are put together to make a list and this list is bound to the rest parameter.

```
>((lambda (a &optional b &rest c)
    (list a b c))
   1 2 3 4)
(1 2 (3 4))

>((lambda (a &optional b &rest c)
    (list a b c))
   1 2)
(1 2 nil)

>((lambda (a &optional b &rest c)
    (list a b c))
   1)
(1 nil nil)
```

The previous examples show that if there are no arguments which are bound to an optional parameter, the rest parameter is bound to `nil`. Now let's define the system function called `list`.

```
>(defun list (&rest x) x)
```

The above expression is sufficient since all the arguments are bound to the parameter x as one list.

Parameters called **keyword parameters** can be specified right after the lambda-list-keyword &key. Just like the optional parameters, a keyword parameter is optional and does not need to have a corresponding argument. Consider the following function using keyword parameters:

```
>(defun cons* (&key ((:car x) 1)
                    ((:cdr y) 2))
    (cons x y))
cons*
```

`((:car x) 1)` and `((:cdr y) 2)` are specifications of keyword parameters. The variables x and y are keyword parameters. 1 and 2 are the default values of each keyword parameter. Since `:car` and `:cdr` both start with a colon ":", they are both symbols in the keyword package, i.e., they are keywords. If the keyword `:car` exists as an argument to `cons*`, then the next argument becomes an initial value of x and if the keyword `:cdr` exists as an argument, then the next argument becomes the initial value of y. For example, if you type

```
(cons* :cdr 4)
```

the initial value of the keyword parameter y is 4 and the initial value of x is the default value 1.

```
>(cons* :cdr 4)
(1 . 4)
```

Since `cons*` is a function, the system always evaluates an expression which is given as an argument. In the above example, `:cdr` and 4 are evaluated. Since `:cdr` is a keyword, the value of `:cdr` is `:cdr` itself. Of course, in the call to `cons*` above, even if `:cdr` is replaced with an expression whose value is `:cdr`, the result would be the same.

```
(cons* (car '(:cdr :cddr)) 4)
```

```
(cons* ':cdr 4)
```

Both expressions will make `:cdr` the first argument to `cons*` and the value of the expression will be `(1 . 4)`. Other calls to `cons*` will produce

```
>(cons* :car 3 :cdr 4)
(3 . 4)

>(cons* :cdr 4 :car 3)
(3 . 4)

>(cons* :car 3)
(3 . 2)

>(cons*)
(1 . 2)
```

The specification of each keyword parameter is done using the following form:

((⟨⟨keyword⟩⟩ ⟨⟨variable⟩⟩) ⟨⟨expression⟩⟩ ⟨⟨supplied-p variable⟩⟩)

The ⟨⟨supplied-p variable⟩⟩ acts just like the supplied-p variable for an optional parameter. It is bound to `t` if there is an argument to the function which is the initial value of keyword parameter when it is called and is bound to `nil` if not. If it is not used, the ⟨⟨supplied-p variable⟩⟩ can be omitted. The ⟨⟨expression⟩⟩ which defines the default value will be evaluated only when the call to the function does not supply an initial value for the keyword parameter. If ⟨⟨expression⟩⟩ is omitted the default value becomes `nil`.

((⟨⟨keyword⟩⟩ ⟨⟨variable⟩⟩))

is equivalent to

((⟨⟨keyword⟩⟩ ⟨⟨variable⟩⟩) nil)

If the ⟨⟨keyword⟩⟩ and ⟨⟨variable⟩⟩ are replaced by just ⟨⟨variable⟩⟩ then the system assumes that the variable name is the same as the name of the keyword parameter.

(x ⟨⟨expression⟩⟩)

is equivalent to

((:x x) ⟨⟨expression⟩⟩)

With this in mind, the above `cons*` can be defined as

```
>(defun cons* (&key (car 1) (cdr 2))
   (cons car cdr))
```

Naturally, as a keyword specification

(x)

is equivalent to

((:x x)) or ((:x x) nil)

and can simply be rewritten as

x

Any argument to a function that is not associated with a required parameter or an optional parameter will give an initial value to a keyword parameter.

```
(lambda (a b &optional c d
             &key ...)
  ...)
```

The first four arguments will be associated either with a required parameter or with an optional parameter. From the fifth on they will provide initial values to keyword parameters. Therefore, starting with the fifth argument, a keyword and a value have to be specified alternately, even when a rest parameter is specified.

```
(lambda (a b &optional c d
             &rest e
             &key ...)
  ...)
```

In the above example, 1) a list made of all the arguments starting with the fifth is bound to the rest parameter e and 2) at the same time, these arguments will provide initial values of any keyword parameters which appear in that list.

You will get an error message if an argument has a keyword which was not specified in the lambda list.

```
(cons* :vehicle 3 :cdr 4)
```

The above produces an error since the keyword :vehicle has not been specified in the lambda list of cons*. However, there is an exception. When a keyword called :allow-other-keys appears as an argument and the next argument is anything but nil, you will not get an error message. :allow-other-key can be anywhere in the place of a keyword.

```
(cons* :allow-other-keys t
       :vehicle 3 :cdr 4)

(cons* :vehicle 3
       :allow-other-keys 100 :cdr 4)

(cons* :vehicle 3 :cdr 4
       :allow-other-keys '(a b c))
```

The above expressions will not cause an error and each of their values is (1 . 4). Also, if a lambda-list-keyword called &allow-other-keys appears right after the keyword specifications in a lambda list, you will not get an error message. For example,

```
>((lambda (&key (car 1) (cdr 2)
                &allow-other-keys)
    (cons car cdr))
  :vehicle 3 :cdr 4)
(1 . 4)
```

After the lambda-list-keyword &aux, you can specify **auxiliary variables**. An auxiliary variable is a variable used locally inside of a function and does not relate to the arguments of a function. Local variables can also be declared using special forms such as let and let*, however, a declaration using the lambda-list-keyword &aux is simpler. For example,

```
(lambda (a b) (let* ((c 1) (d 2)) ...))
```

can be rewritten using &aux as

```
(lambda (a b &aux (c 1) (c 2)) ...)
```

An auxiliary variable is specified by a list made up of a variable name and
its initial value.

(《variable》 《expression》)

When the 《expression》 is nil, this can be abbreviated as

(《variable》)

or simply

《variable》

Inside an 《expression》 for computing the default value of either an optional
parameter or a keyword parameter or inside an 《expression》 for computing
the initial value of an auxiliary variable you are allowed to refer those parameters or supplied-p variables which have already been computed before
the current parameter specification. For example,

```
(lambda (r1 r2
         &optional (op1 r1 s1)
                   (op2 (if s1 op1 r2))
         &key (k (list r1 r2 op1 op2) s2)
         &aux (a (and s1 s2)))
  ...)
```

When no argument corresponds to op1 (in other words, if only two arguments exist), the first argument becomes the initial value of op1 and the
second argument becomes the initial value of op2. If there are three arguments, the third argument corresponding to op1 becomes the default value
of op2. The value of the auxiliary variable a becomes t only when the
arguments corresponding to the optional parameter op1 and the keyword
parameter k exist. Otherwise the value is nil.

6-2 Local Functions

The special form `flet`

> (flet (($\langle\langle$function name$_1\rangle\rangle$ $\langle\langle$lambda list$_1\rangle\rangle$
> $\langle\langle$expression$\rangle\rangle$ . . . $\langle\langle$expression$\rangle\rangle$)
>   . . .
>   ($\langle\langle$function name$_m\rangle\rangle$ $\langle\langle$lambda list$_m\rangle\rangle$
> $\langle\langle$expression$\rangle\rangle$ . . . $\langle\langle$expression$\rangle\rangle$))
> $\langle\langle$expression$_1\rangle\rangle$
>   . . .
> $\langle\langle$expression$_n\rangle\rangle$)

defines a function which is used locally only inside the body $\langle\langle$expression$_1\rangle\rangle$ . . . $\langle\langle$expression$_n\rangle\rangle$. The definition of this function has the same format as a definition using a `defun` expression. The function's name comes first and it is followed by a lambda list and a body made up of some expressions. Just as in `defun`, the lambda list can specify the different kinds of parameters which were explained in the previous section and the value of the last expression becomes the value of the function. However, while a function defined by `defun` can be used anywhere, a function defined by `flet` can be used only inside of the body of the `flet` expression. In other words, the scope of the function defined by `flet` is only the body of the `flet` expression. Functions whose scope are limited like the ones defined by `flet` are called **local functions**. Other functions are called **global functions**. A function defined using `defun` is always a global function.

```
>(defun foo (x) (1+ x))
foo

>(flet ((foo (x) (1- x)))
    (foo 10))
9

>(foo 10)
11
```

The special form `labels` has the general form of an `flet` expression where `flet` is replaced by `labels`. `labels` has almost the same functionality as `flet`. The only difference is that the scope of a local function defined by `labels` is not the body of the `labels` expression but the whole area of the `labels` expression. This means that the system can refer the local function itself or other local functions defined together inside of the body of the local function to be defined. Let's look at an example:

```
>(defun foo (x) (1+ x))
foo

>(flet ((foo (x) (1- x))
        (bar (x) (foo x)))
   (bar 10))
11

>(labels ((foo (x) (1- x))
          (bar (x) (foo x)))
   (bar 10))
9
```

The scope of the local function `foo` defined in the `flet` is only the body of the `flet`, `(bar 10)`. The body of the local function `bar` is outside of the scope of the local function `foo`. This means that the function called by `bar` is not the local function `foo`, but the global function `foo` defined by the `defun` expression. When both `bar` and `foo` are defined using `labels`, the body of the local function `bar` belongs to the scope of the local function `foo` and thus `bar` calls the local function `foo`. The result will be the same if `bar` is defined first.

labels can be used to define local functions recursively using a set of functions each of which can call any of the others. `flet`, on the other hand, will call the global function with the same name as a local function when that name appears inside of the definition of a local function. The f in `flet` comes from the first letter of `function`. Old versions of Lisp used a form called `label` to define recursive functions. "labels" is the plural of "label."

Local functions cannot be referred to outside of a `flet` or a `labels` expression.

```
>(defun bar (x) (foo x))
foo
```

foo in the above definition is a global function. Even in

```
(labels ((foo (x) (1- x)))
   (bar 10))
```

where the call to `bar` is inside of the scope of a local function `foo`, `bar` calls the global function `foo`.

If the scope of local functions with the same name overlap, they are treated in the same way as variables and blocks.

```
(flet ((foo (x) (1+ x)))
  (flet ((foo (x) (1- x)))
    (foo 5)))
```

`(foo 5)` calls the `foo` defined by the inner `flet`.

By defining functions locally using `flet` and `labels`, you can avoid defining functions with the same name by mistake. If you define a function `foo` as a local function, you do not have to worry about this function destroying a function with the same name that has already been defined. Another important feature of defining a local function is that the scope of a local variable or a block will not be influenced by the definition of local functions. For example,

```
(let ((x 0))
  (flet ((flip ()
           (setq x (if (= x 0) 1 0))))
    ...))
```

Since the body of the local function `flip` is within the scope of the local variable x, the x which is referred in the body of `flip` is the local variable. Each time `flip` is called, the value of the local variable x will change from 0 to 1 or 1 to 0. This is true for the variable x no matter where `flip` is called in the `flet` expression.

```
(let ((x 0))
  (flet ((flip ()
           (setq x (if (= x 0) 1 0))))
    ...
    (let ((x '(z z z))) (flip))
    ...))
```

Even if x is called within the scope of another local variable, the x in the body of `flip` is the local variable bound by the outer `let` expression. This is because the scope of the x bound by the inner `let` expression is only the body of the `let` expression and the body of `flip` is not within that scope. The scope of blocks and tags can not be influenced by `flet` and `labels`.

```
(tagbody
   ...
  (flet ((foo () (go there))) ...)
   ...
  there
   ...)
```

When a local function **foo** is called, the system jumps to **there**.

```
(block lego
   ...
  (flet ((foo ()
            (return-from lego)))
    ...)
  ...)
```

In this form a call to **foo** always terminates the **lego** block.

6-3 Functions for Function Calls

When you want to call functions, you use a form starting with the function name or a lambda expression. Such forms can only be used when the name of the function and the arguments to the function are already known. If you want to call a function which is determined by calculation, you need to use functions which perform function calls. Two such functions are **apply** and **funcall**. Both **apply** and **funcall** specify a function to be called as their first argument. The arguments to this function are specified by the rest of the arguments to **apply** or **funcall**. The value of the called function becomes the value of the **apply** or the **funcall**.

funcall passes its arguments (except the first) to the function specified by its first arguments.

```
(funcall '+ 2 3 4)
```

calls a function **+** with 2, 3, and 4 as arguments. Since **funcall** is a function, the arguments to **funcall** are evaluated. The first argument to **funcall** is the value of '**+**, namely, a symbol **+**. Since **funcall** is a function, if the first argument to the **funcall** is a symbol, it is interpreted as a variable (in the usual way) and the value of this variable becomes the first argument to `funcall`. In

```
(funcall f 2 3 4)
```

`f` is a variable. If the value of `f` is `+`, the above expression does addition. If the value is `-`, it does subtraction.

```
>(let ((f '+))
   (funcall f 2 3 4))
9

>(let ((f '*))
   (funcall f 2 3 4))
24
```

The following function calculates the sum of the value of a function of one argument for all the integers from 0 to $n - 1$. (We are assuming here that the function for `square` has already been defined.)

```
>(defun sum-up (f n &aux (sum 0))
   (dotimes (i n sum)
     (setq sum (+ (funcall f i) sum)))))
sum-up
>(sum-up 'square 10)        ; the sum of the squares of 0 to 9
285
>(sum-up '1+ 10)            ; the sum of 1 to 10
55
```

The system function called `identity` takes one argument and simply returns it as a value. Using this on `sum-up`, we can get the total of 0 to $n - 1$.

```
>(sum-up 'identity 10000)
49995000
```

`funcall` can be used only when the number of arguments that a function will accept is known in advance and fixed. If the number is not known, `apply` should be used. The last argument to `apply` is a list. When n arguments are given to `apply`, the value of the second argument to the $n - 1$th argument and each element of the list (which is the nth and last argument to `apply`) become the arguments to the function to be called. In each of the next examples, `apply` gets 1 2 3 4 as an argument to a function to be called.

```
(apply f '(1 2 3 4))

(apply f 1 2 '(3 4))

(apply f 1 2 3 4 nil)
```

We can rewrite the above sum-up and fix it so that you can specify arguments to a function which can take more than two arguments.

```
>(defun sum-up* (f n &rest x
                        &aux (sum 0))
   (dotimes (i n sum)
     (setq sum (+ (apply f i x) sum)))))
sum-up*
```

```
>(sum-up* '* 5 2)       ; the sum of two times each number
20                      ; from 0 to 4

>(sum-up* '1+ 10)       ; the sum of the numbers from 1 to 10
55

>(sum-up* '+ 10 1)      ; the sum of the numbers from 1 to 10
55
```

The following can be given to funcall and apply as the first argument.

1. symbols which name a function
2. lambda expressions
3. definitions of a function
4. lexical closures

The above things are collectively called **functional data**. (Lambda expressions are not provided in the language definition of Common Lisp. However, many Common Lisp systems treat lambda expressions as functional data and this book also treats them as such.) We will talk about lexical closures in the next section. When a lambda expression is given to the system, it calls the function defined by the lambda expression. For example, for the row of numbers whose general term is

$$2n - 1 \quad (n = 0, 1, 2, \ldots)$$

the grand total of some number of terms can be obtained by using the lambda expression which uses $2n - 1$ in sum-up

```
(lambda (n) (1- (* n 2)))
```

Namely,

```
>(sum-up '(lambda (n) (1- (* n 2))) 10)
80

>(sum-up '(lambda (n) (1- (* n 2)))
         10000)
99980000
```

When a function is defined using **defun**, **flet**, and **labels**, the system remembers how the function was defined as well as the function name. It remembers the name of a function and its definition as a pair. When it evaluates

```
(cons 1 2)
```

it takes the function definition which is the other half of a pair for **cons** and executes the function call according to the definition. The data that is used as a function definition is different for different Common Lisp systems and may even be different for different functions. However, all of the systems agree on the one point: the definition of a function can be treated as data just like lists and numbers are data. Function definitions can be assigned to a variable and can be given to a function as an argument. To get the function definition, the special form **function** should be used.

```
(function ⟨⟨symbol⟩⟩ )
```

returns the definition of the function which has the same name as ⟨⟨symbol⟩⟩. For example, when the system evaluates

```
(function cons)
```

the definition of the function **cons** is returned. Just like (**quote** ⟨⟨data⟩⟩) can be written as '⟨⟨data⟩⟩, (**function** ⟨⟨symbol⟩⟩) can be written as #'⟨⟨symbol⟩⟩. The above **function** expression can be rewritten as

```
#'cons
```

If you type a function definition as the first argument to **apply** or **funcall**, the function which is defined by this function definition will be called.

```
(funcall #'cons 1 2)
```

```
(apply #'cons '(1 2))
```

Both of the above expressions have the same value as

```
(cons 1 2)
```

When called with a function definition as its first argument, funcall (or apply) may work in a different way from when it is called with a function name. The expression

```
(function ⟨⟨symbol⟩⟩ )
```

returns exactly the same function definition that is used when evaluating a function call expression when the above function expression is replaced by a function call using the same ⟨⟨symbol⟩⟩

```
( ⟨⟨symbol⟩⟩ ... )
```

Consider the example

```
(flet ((foo (x) ... ))
   (function foo))
```

(function foo) returns the definition of the local function foo. This will be clear if you replace (function foo) by (foo ...).

```
(flet ((foo (x) ... ))
   (foo ... ))
```

When you type

```
(flet ((foo (x) ... ))
   (funcall #'foo ... ))
```

the local function foo is called. On the other hand, when the function argument to funcall or apply is a symbol, the global function is called and a local function will never be called.

```
>(defun foo (x) (1+ x))
foo

>(flet ((foo (x) (1- x)))
    (funcall #'foo 10))
9
```

```
>(flet ((foo (x) (1- x)))
   (funcall 'foo 10))
11
```

When a symbol is given as a function name, `funcall` and `apply` use the function definition which exists at the time of function call. On the other hand, when a function definition is given, the actual definition given is used regardless of any existing definitions. Consider the following examples:

```
>(defun foo (x) (1+ x))
foo

>(setq fdef #'foo
       fname 'foo)
foo

>(funcall fdef 10)
11

>(funcall fname 10)
11

>(defun foo (x) (1- x))
foo

>(funcall fdef 10)
11

>(funcall fname 10)
9
```

First, the function definition of `foo` and the symbol `foo` are assigned to the two variables, `fdef` and `fname`, respectively. If you use `funcall` immediately, the result will be the same whether the function definition is given or the symbol is given. However, after `foo` is redefined, the new `foo` will be called if the symbol is given and the old definition of `foo` will be used if `fdef` is used.

For multiple-valued functions, the special form for function call is:

```
(multiple-value-call ⟨⟨function⟩⟩
            ⟨⟨expression₁⟩⟩ . . . ⟨⟨expressionₙ⟩⟩ )
```

This form calls the function specified by ⟨⟨function⟩⟩ with all the values of each ⟨⟨expression⟩⟩ as its arguments. The expression ⟨⟨function⟩⟩ is always evaluated and its value has to be some kind of functional data. During a call to `funcall`

(funcall ⟨⟨function⟩⟩ ⟨⟨expression$_1$⟩⟩ ... ⟨⟨expression$_n$⟩⟩)

only one value of each ⟨⟨expression⟩⟩ is used as an argument while `multiple-value-call` uses all the values of each ⟨⟨expression⟩⟩ as arguments.

```
>(funcall #'+ (floor 5 3) (floor 19 5))
4          ; (+ 1 3)

>(multiple-value-call #'+
   (floor 5 3) (floor 19 5))
10          ; (+ 1 2 3 4)
```

6-4 Lexical Closures

The value of the `quote` expression

```
'(a b c)
```

is simply the list of three elements, a, b, and c. When the system evaluates this expression, it does not ask whether the expression is calling the function a or not. Even when this expression is given as an argument to `eval`

```
(eval '(a b c))
```

the system simply gives the list (a b c) to `eval`. It is `eval` which treats (a b c) as a form. On the other hand, when `eval` is given an argument it never knows what expression was evaluated to get it nor does it know what local variables or local functions belonged to the scope of the expression that was evaluated to get its argument. When it is given (a b c) as an argument, `eval` simply thinks a is a global function and b and c are global variables. Therefore, the above call to `eval` is the same as

```
>(a b c)
```

When `funcall` and `apply` are called, the same thing happens. When you type

```
(funcall 'a)
```

the symbol a becomes the argument of the `funcall`. The purpose of `funcall` is to call the function which has the same name as the symbol and `funcall` does not know whether its own call is in the scope of some local variable and it simply calls the global function a. In

```
(funcall '(lambda (x) (* x x)) 3)
```

the same thing happens. The system simply evaluates

```
'(lambda (x) (* x x))
```

to the three element list containing `lambda`, (x), and (* x x) and gives this list to `funcall` as its first argument. The system does not know these constitute a lambda expression. `funcall` is the one who interprets them as "this must be the lambda expression since it starts with a `lambda`," binds x to 3, and starts to evaluate (* x x). In this case `funcall` successfully calculates the square of 3. However, for the lambda expression

```
(lambda (x) (* x y))
```

where the body contains a free variable, even if `funcall` is called

```
(let ((y 4))
  (funcall '(lambda (x) (* x y)) 3))
```

from within the scope of a local variable y, it does not know that the y in (* x y) is a local variable and that its value is 4. Thus it calculates three times the value of the global variable y. If instead of the `funcall` expression the system sees

```
(let ((y 4))
  ((lambda (x) (* x y)) 3))
```

it notices (lambda (x) (* x y)) is a lambda expression. During the evaluation of a list form the system determines whether it is a special form, a macro form, or a function call form. When the list form is a function call form, the system evaluates the arguments and calls the specified function. If the function is specified by name, it calls the function with that name. When the list form is a lambda expression, the system calls the function which the lambda expression defines. Thus, without recognizing a lambda expression, the system could not evaluate the form

```
((lambda (x) (* x y)) 3)
```

When the system evaluates this form (as opposed to a `funcall` expression) it knows that this form exists within the scope of a variable y. In the above example this would be the local variable y and that the value of this local variable is 4. Using this information the system can compute the value of (* x y).

```
>(let ((y 4))
    ((lambda (x) (* x y)) 3))
12
```

When the special form `function` is given a symbol

(function ⟨⟨symbol⟩⟩)

the system interprets the symbol as a function name, since the system knows that a `function` expression always specifies a function. If the specified function name is in the scope of a local function with the same name, it will take the definition of that local function as the value of the `function` expression. For the same reason, if a lambda expression is given to a `function` expression instead of a symbol

(function ⟨⟨lambda expression⟩⟩)

the system interprets that ⟨⟨lambda expression⟩⟩ not simply as a list but as a lambda expression which defines a function. A `function` expression will take either a symbol or a lambda expression as an argument but does not take a list form. When a `function` expression uses a symbol, the system uses the same function definition as when the function expression is replaced by the function call form

(⟨⟨symbol⟩⟩ ...)

When a `lambda` expression is given, the system interprets this as a function call expression starting with a lambda expression

(⟨⟨lambda expression⟩⟩ ...)

The system then creates a data object called a **closure** by adding all the information necessary to call the function defined by the lambda expression and takes this closure as the value of the `function` expression. When `funcall` and `apply` receive a closure, they execute the body of the lambda expression using all the information in the closure as if the closure was called in the place where it was created. For example,

```
>(let ((y 4))
   (funcall #'(lambda (x) (* x y)) 3))
```

A closure is created by the function expression "#' ⟨⟨lambda expression⟩⟩" which is an abbreviation of "(function ⟨⟨lambda expression⟩⟩)" and is given to funcall. With the help of such information, funcall finds out that a closure is created in the scope of a local variable y and that the present value of the local variable y is 4. So, funcall calls the function defined by the lambda expression as if it was called as

```
>(let ((y 4))
   ((lambda (x) (* x y)) 3))
```

The funcall executes the body assuming that in the body of the lambda expression, y is a local variable with 4 as its value. That is why we get

```
>(let ((y 4))
   (funcall #'(lambda (x) (* x y)) 3))
12
```

regardless what value the global variable y has.

A closure should be considered a function. In the above example, the closure can be thought of as a function which multiplies its argument by 4. The same thing happens when a closure is sent to sum-up. In this case funcall is called indirectly from sum-up.

```
>(defun sum-up (f n &aux (sum 0))
   (dotimes (i n sum)
     (setq sum (+ (funcall f i) sum))))
sum-up
>(dolist (y '(2 3 4))
   (print (sum-up #'(lambda (x) (* x y))
                  10)))
90       ; sum of the integers from 0 to 9 each multiplied by two
135      ; sum of the integers from 0 to 9 each multiplied by three
180      ; sum of the integers from 0 to 9 each multiplied by four
nil

>
```

This **dolist** executes the body three times with the value of the local variable y set to 2, 3, and 4, respectively and three closures are created and sent to **sum-up**. The first closure is a function which multiplies its argument by two, the next closure is a function which multiplies its argument by three, and the last closure multiplies its argument by four.

Just like a list or a number, a closure is a data object. That is why a closure can be used as an argument to **funcall** and can be given to other functions like **sum-up** as well as **funcall** and **apply**. A closure also can be assigned to a variable and it can be bound to a variable.

```
>(setq f (let ((y 4))
            #'(lambda (x) (* x y))))
   . . .


>(funcall f 3)
12


>(let* ((y 4)
        (f #'(lambda (x) (* x y))))
    (funcall f 3))
12
```

In place of "..." the system actually prints the closure that is assigned to the variable f. We used "..." here because the method of expressing a closure is completely different in each Common Lisp system. Some systems have a special type of data structure for construction of a closure. Others represent a closure using a list. The important thing in the above **let*** expression is that the **function** expression belongs to the scope of the local variable y which is bound by the **let*** expression. Therefore, the y in the body of the lambda expression, (* x y), refers to this local variable.

Beside keeping information about local variables, information on the following things can be found in closures:

blocks
tags
local functions
local macros

We will talk about local macros in Chapter 7. The following example will demonstrate that such information is saved in closures.

```
(block lego
  (flet ((foo (x) (1+ x)))
    (tagbody
      (bar #'(lambda (x)
               (cond
                 ((numberp x) (foo x))
                 ((symbolp x)
                  (return-from lego 0))
                 (t (go there)))))
        . . .
      there
        . . .  )))
```

The closure created here calls the local function **foo** if its argument is a number. It finishes the **lego** block if its argument is a symbol, and it jumps to the **there** tag if its argument is anything else. The closure will contain information about the local function **foo**, the block **lego**, and the tag **there**.

Let's look at the local variables more carefully. The thing actually kept in a closure as information about a local variable is not the value of that variable but its **binding**. The binding of a variable means the correspondence between the variable and the box for keeping the value of this variable, i.e., the box which exists for that variable at that time. When the system calls the following function:

```
(defun square (x) (* x x))
```

the system binds the local variable x to the argument to **square**. When the system binds x it makes a new box for x. The correspondence between x and this new box is the binding of the variable x which is in effect during this function call. The next time the system calls **square**, it creates another new box for the local variable x. This means that each time **square** is called, the binding of x will be different.

```
>(defun foo (x)
   (funcall
     #'(lambda (x) (* x y))
     3))
foo
```

When the system calls the above function, the closure given to **funcall** remembers the binding of the local variable y at the time the closure is created. **funcall**, after getting this closure, identifies the box for y from

the closure information and uses the content of this box when it evaluates
(* x y). The same thing happens for a new definition for foo.

```
>(defun foo (y)
   (funcall
     #'(lambda (x) (setq y (* x y)))
     3)
   y)
foo
```

The two occurrences of y in the body of the lambda expression
(setq y (* x y)) are the parameter y of foo. In this case, the binding of y kept in closure is used not only for calculating (* x y) but also
for the assignment. In other words, funcall identifies the box for y from
the closure information and puts the value of (* x y) in that box. As
a result, after the funcall is executed, the value of the parameter y is
multiplied by three.

```
>(foo 4)
12

>(foo 5)
15
```

If we change the definition of foo to

```
>(defun foo (y)
   #'(lambda (x) (setq y (* x y))))
foo
```

it returns a closure as its value. This closure keeps the binding of y which
was established at the time foo was called. So,

```
>(setq f (foo 4))
...

>(funcall f 3)
12
```

The content of the box that was created for the parameter y of foo when
(foo 4) was called is multiplied by three. Thus the current content of this
box is updated to 12. When the system evaluates the funcall expression
again, the content of this box is again multiplied by three, i.e., $12 \times 3 = 36$.

```
>(funcall f 3)
36

>(funcall f 3)
108
```

The box created for y when (foo 4) is called will not be thrown away after foo is called, but will be kept somewhere in the system so that its content can be examined or changed. After the above example, when the system evaluates (foo 4) again, it will have a closure as its value and the binding of y in that closure is different from the previous one.

```
>(setq g (foo 4))
. . .

>(funcall g 3)
12

>(funcall f 3)
324

>(funcall g 3)
36
```

More than two closures can jointly own the same variable binding. In the following example, the closures which are assigned to the global variables incr and decr jointly own the binding of the local variable x which was bound by let expression. In this case the content of a box for x can be changed by both closures.

```
>(multiple-value-setq (incr decr)
    (let ((x 0))
      (values
        #'(lambda () (setq x (1+ x)))
        #'(lambda () (setq x (1- x))))))
. . .

>(funcall incr)
1

>(dotimes (n 10) (funcall incr))
nil
```

```
>(funcall decr)
10
```

Sometimes when the system gives a symbol as a function name to a `funcall` expression, something like a closure is created. For example,

```
>(defun foo (x)
    (flet ((bar () (setq x (1+ x))))
       #'bar))
foo

>(setq f (foo 0))
  ...
```

The "definition" of the local function `bar` will be assigned to `f`. Since the `x` in the body of `bar`, `(setq x (1+ x))`, is the parameter of `foo`, the information about the binding of `x` remains as part of this definition. Every time this definition is given to `funcall`, the content of the box, which was created for `x` when `(foo 0)` was evaluated, is increased by 1 .

```
>(funcall f)
1

>(funcall f)
2
```

Closure literally means to close. In

```
(funcall '(lambda (x) (* x y)) 3)
```

the variable `y` is assumed to be "open" from the outside of this lambda expression. In many Lisp systems other than Common Lisp, the variable referred to by this `y` depends on the place where the `funcall` is executed, i.e, `y` is literally open. In these Lisps `y` simply takes the value which it has at the time the `funcall` is executed. In Common Lisp, since this `y` always represents the global variable, we can scarcely imagine that `y` is open. But, following the Lisp tradition, we use the term "closure" also with Common Lisp.

7   Macros

In the previous chapters, we described how some system macros worked. In this chapter, we will talk about the concept of the macro. We also discuss how to define macros yourself and introduce some functions that are useful for defining macros. We will also introduce some additional system macros (including `setf`) which are essential parts of Common Lisp.

7-1 Macros

Forms which are lists that start with symbols that represent the macro names are called macro forms. In the previous chapters, we said that a macro form is used as an abbreviated form of another form. When the system evaluates a macro form, it changes the macro form into another form using the **macro-expansion function** attached to the macro name and then evaluates the result. This process is called **macro expansion**. A macro form is written as a list and a macro-expansion function is defined as a general list processing function. In other words, macro expansion is a kind of list processing. For example, consider the macro form `incf`

```
(incf x)
```

which increases the value of the variable x by 1. To do this (incf x) could be macro-expanded to

```
(setq x (1+ x))
```

The results of the evaluation of the system macros such as `incf`, `cond`, `do`, and so on, including side effects, are the same on any Common Lisp system. How each macro form is macro-expanded may be different on different systems. For example, in KCL, (`incf x`) is actually expanded into the above assignment expression, but on some systems it may be done differently.

Let's look at another macro expansion. In KCL, the `cond` expression

```
(cond ((> x 0) 1)
      ((= x 0) 0)
      ((> x 0) -1))
```

is expanded to

```
(if (> x 0) 1
    (if (= x 0) 0
        (if (< x 0) -1 nil)))
```

The macro expansion is done automatically at the time of evaluation and a user usually cannot see how the macro is expanded. If you would like to see the actual expansion, you can use a system function `macroexpand`. By typing

```
(macroexpand ⟪expression⟫ )
```

the macro expansion continues as long as the value of ⟪expression⟫ is a macro form. When it stops, the expression which resulted from the expansion of ⟪expression⟫ is returned as the value. Since `macroexpand` is a function, the value as the result of the evaluation of ⟪expression⟫ will be given to `macroexpand` as an argument. For example, in KCL,

```
>(macroexpand '(incf x))
(setq x (1+ x))
t
```

Therefore,

```
>(eval (macroexpand '(incf x)))
```

increases the value of x by 1 in the same way as the following:

```
>(eval '(incf x))
```

The system function `macro-function` will get you the macro-expansion function that is associated with a macro name. A symbol is used for specifying a macro name. For example, if you type

```
>(macro-function 'incf)
```

the macro-expansion function of `incf` is returned as its value. The macro-expansion function can be called using `funcall` or `apply`. A macro-expansion function always takes a macro form as an argument. In the previous example of `incf`, in order to macro-expansion `(incf x)`, the list `(incf x)` should be given as an argument to the macro-expansion function for `incf`.

```
>(funcall (macro-function 'incf)
          '(incf x) nil)
(setq x (1+ x))
```

(The second argument to the macro-expansion function is seldom used. `nil` is enough in most cases.) Since `macro-function` returns `nil` for symbols which are not macro names, `macro-function` can be used as a predicate for deciding whether a symbol is being used as a macro name or not.

```
>(macro-function 'if)
nil
```

Sometimes when the system evaluates a system macro, it does not actually do a macro-expansion. Macro expression can take a long time because it may do a complicated calculation. Many Common Lisp systems implement frequently-used system macros as special forms. These will be directly executed without macro expanding. These system-macros, however, are indistinguishable from ordinary macros from the point of view of `macro-function` and `macroexpand`. The system function called `special-form-p` is used to confirm whether a symbol is the name of the special form.

```
>(special-form-p 'if)
t

>(special-form-p 'car)
nil
```

This function enables you to determine which system macros are implemented as special forms. In KCL, `incf` and `cond` are implemented as special forms. So,

```
>(special-form-p 'incf)
t

>(special-form-p 'cond)
t
```

7-2 `setf`

In this section we look at the system macro called `setf`. This is a typical system macro in Common Lisp. `setf` can be thought of as an extension of `setq`, although `setq` is a special form, not a macro. `setf` has, as a background notion, the idea of a **generalized variable** which is an extended notion of a variable. In order to make the value of a variable x 1, you can type

```
>(setq x 1)
```

After you type

```
>(setq cell (cons nil nil))
```

in order to make the `car` part of the cons cell in the variable `cell` to become 2 you would type

```
>(rplaca cell 2)
```

A variable, as well as the `car` part or the `cdr` part of a cons cell, contains one data object. Moreover, the data kept there can be replaced by another data object by some method. For example, the `car` part can be replaced using `rplaca` and the `cdr` part can be replaced by using `rplacd`. Elements of an array (see Chapter 10), properties of a symbol (see Chapter 8), and the fields of a structure (see Chapter 10) all have the same property. The place where a data object can be kept is called a generalized variable. Naturally, ordinary variables are generalized variables. A list starting with `car`, for example, (`car cell`), represents a place called the `car` part of the cons cell which is the value of the variable `cell`, therefore, it is considered to be a generalized variable.

Generalized variables are used in combination with some system functions. The most typical example is `setf`. `setf` is used as

    (setf ⟨⟨place⟩⟩ ⟨⟨expression⟩⟩)

The value of ⟨⟨expression⟩⟩ is put in ⟨⟨place⟩⟩.

For example, if you type

    (setf (car cell) 2)

the `car` part of cons cell, which is a value of `cell`, changes to 2. When ordinary variables are used in `setf`, it works the same as `setq`.

The expansion of `setf` is not the same in different versions of Common Lisp. For the above example, the following expansion is possible.

    (progn (rplaca cell 2) 2)

In this case the reason for putting everything in parentheses after the `progn` and making it return 2 as a value is that the value of `setf`, just like `setq`, is the value of ⟨⟨expression⟩⟩. Also, like `setq`, `setf` can take any number of pairs of places and expressions. If more than one such pair is given, the value of the last expression becomes the value of the `setf`. For example,

    >(setf x 1 (car cell) 2)
    2

The expressions in the `setf` expression are evaluated one by one from left to right. Now, suppose you type

    >(setf (car (foo)) (bar))

then the `car` part of cons cell which will be returned as the value of (foo) is replaced with the value of (bar). To do this, the following expansion is possible:

    >(progn (rplaca (foo) (bar)) (bar))

However, (bar) will be evaluated twice. Also, in

    >(progn (rplaca (foo) (bar)) (car (foo)))

the expression (foo) will be evaluated twice. If

```
>(let ((r (bar)))
   (rplaca (foo) r)
   r)
```

is used, since (bar) will be evaluated before (foo), the order will not match the order inside the setf expression. The correct expansion should be

```
>(let* ((c (foo)) (r (bar)))
   (rplaca c r)
   r)
```

or

```
>(let ((c (foo)))
   (rplaca c (bar))
   (car c))
```

Other system macros which change the value of a place like setf include psetf, incf, decf, push, and pop.

psetf, just like psetq, does all of the assignments at the same time, which makes it different from setf. The value of psetf, just like psetq, is nil.

The general form of incf is

(incf ⟨⟨place⟩⟩ ⟨⟨place⟩⟩)

The value of the data at ⟨⟨place⟩⟩ is increased by the amount of the value of ⟨⟨expression⟩⟩. For example,

```
>(incf x 1)
```

has the same effect as

```
>(setq x (1+ x))
```

The value of incf is the new value of ⟨⟨place⟩⟩. If the ⟨⟨expression⟩⟩ is omitted, 1 will be assumed as the default. This means that the above expression can be written as

```
>(incf x)
```

An example using lists

```
>(incf (car (foo)))
```

expands to

```
>(let* ((c (foo)) (r (1+ (car c))))
   (rplaca c r)
   r)
```

The system macro **decf** does the opposite of **incf**, i.e., it decreases the value of a place.

push is a macro which conses an element to a list. For example,

```
>(push 'a x)
```

has the same effect as

```
>(setq x (cons 'a x))
```

The general form of **push** is

```
(push ⟨⟨expression⟩⟩ ⟨⟨place⟩⟩ )
```

The value of the whole expression is the new value of ⟨⟨place⟩⟩.

pop is the opposite of **push**.

```
>(pop x)
```

has the same effect as

```
>(prog1 (car x) (setq x (cdr x)))
```

So, the value of

```
(pop ⟨⟨place⟩⟩ )
```

is the **car** of the initial value of ⟨⟨place⟩⟩ and as a side effect, the value of ⟨⟨place⟩⟩ becomes **cdr** of the initial value.

7-3 Macro Definitions

In this section we talk about how to define macros yourself. To define a macro means to define a macro expansion function and to associate it with a symbol which will become the name of that macro.

Let us define a macro called **when**. Of course **when** is actually a system macro which a user does not have to define. A **when** expression looks like

(when ⟨⟨condition⟩⟩ ⟨⟨expression₁⟩⟩...⟨⟨expressionₙ⟩⟩)

If we were to expand this using **if** and **progn** we might write

(if ⟨⟨condition⟩⟩ (progn ⟨⟨expression₁⟩⟩...⟨⟨expressionₙ⟩⟩))

The macro expansion function we need should take the whole macro form and return the macro expanded expression. In the above **when** expression, the ⟨⟨condition⟩⟩ and the body ⟨⟨expression₁⟩⟩...⟨⟨expressionₙ⟩⟩ represent **cdr** and **cddr** of the **when** expression, respectively. Using **lambda**, the macro expansion function for **when** can be written as

```
(lambda (form)
    (list 'if (cadr form)
          (cons 'progn (cddr form))))
```

The parameter **form** represents the whole macro form, **(cadr form)** is the condition, and **(cddr form)** is the body. We can rewrite this in a clearer way using **let**.

```
(lambda (form)
    (let ((condition (cadr form))
          (body (cddr form)))
      (list 'if condition
            (cons 'progn body))))
```

You can use **defmacro** to define a macro. A **defmacro** expression looks like

(defmacro ⟨⟨macro name⟩⟩ ⟨⟨lambda list⟩⟩
    ⟨⟨expression₁⟩⟩...⟨⟨expressionₙ⟩⟩)

The value of the last ⟨⟨expression$_n$⟩⟩ becomes the expanded form of a macro form. We can define the above mentioned when as

```
(defmacro when (condition &rest body)
   (list 'if condition
          (cons 'progn body)))
```

The above mentioned macro expansion function is defined to be the macro expansion function named when. Just as in a defun expression, the expression right after the when, i.e, ⟨⟨condition⟩⟩, is bound to the parameter called condition and the list made up of the rest of the expressions is bound to body. For example, when the system expands the when expression

```
(when (< x 0) (setq x (- x)))
```

the list (< x 0) is bound to condition and the list ((setq x (- x))) is bound to body.

A user can specify an optional parameter or a keyword parameter to the lambda list of defmacro expansion, just like in a defun expression or a lambda expression. In addition, the notion of the lambda list of a defmacro expression is extended so that a user can write a pattern for breaking up the macro form. For example, the when expression can be considered to have the form

```
(when ⟨⟨condition⟩⟩ . ⟨⟨body⟩⟩ )
```

Here, ⟨⟨body⟩⟩ is a list made up of several expressions. If the when is removed from the when expression, then you get

```
( ⟨⟨condition⟩⟩ . ⟨⟨body⟩⟩ )
```

In the lambda list of a defmacro, it is possible to specify the parameters using this pattern form of a lambda list. when can be rewritten as

```
(defmacro when (condition . body)
   (list 'if condition
           (cons 'progn body)))
```

As a second example, let's look at expanding dotimes to use do. To make

```
(dotimes ( ⟨⟨variable⟩⟩   ⟨⟨integer expression⟩⟩ )  .   ⟨⟨body⟩⟩ )
```

expand in the following way:

```
(do (( ⟨⟨variable⟩⟩ 0 (1+ ⟨⟨variable⟩⟩ ))
     (limit ⟨⟨integer expression⟩⟩ ))
    ((>= ⟨⟨variable⟩⟩ limit))
  . ⟨⟨body⟩⟩ )
```

dotimes can be defined as

```
(defmacro dotimes ((var form) . body)
  (let ((limit (gensym)))
    (list* 'do
       (list (list var '0 (list '1+ var))
             (list limit form))
       (list (list '>= var limit))
       body)))
```

The call to gensym produces a new symbol for limit each time the form
is expanded. Suppose when the system expands

```
(dotimes (x (progn (setq s 1) 100))
   (setq s (* s x)))
```

gensym returns the symbol #:g77. Then the following bindings occur

var	—	x
form	—	(progn (setq s 1)
body	—	((setq s (* s x)))
limit	—	#:g77

and the following expansion occurs

```
(do ((x 0 (1+ x))
     (#:g77 (progn (setq s 1) 100)))
    ((>= x #:g77))
  (setq s (* s x)))
```

You can specify the value of a dotimes expression by using ⟨⟨value⟩⟩.

```
(dotimes
   ( ⟨⟨variable⟩⟩ ⟨⟨integer expression⟩⟩ ⟨⟨value⟩⟩ )  .  ⟨⟨body⟩⟩ )
```

In such an expression, if ⟨⟨value⟩⟩ is omitted, the system uses nil as the ⟨⟨value⟩⟩. Considering this fact, dotimes can be defined using an optional parameter as

```
(defmacro dotimes ((var form
                          &optional
                             (result nil))
                       . body)
    (let ((limit (gensym)))
      (list* 'do
        (list (list var '0 (list '1+ var))
              (list limit form))
        (list (list '>= var limit) result)
        body)))
```

defmacro defines a global macro. Therefore, the scope of a macro defined using defmacro does not have a limit. On the other hand, the special form of macrolet

```
(macrolet (( ⟨⟨macro name₁⟩⟩ ⟨⟨lambda list₁⟩⟩
                     ⟨⟨expression⟩⟩...⟨⟨expression⟩⟩ )

                . . .

             ( ⟨⟨macro nameₘ⟩⟩ ⟨⟨lambda listₘ⟩⟩
                     ⟨⟨expression⟩⟩...⟨⟨expression⟩⟩ ))
  ⟨⟨expression₁⟩⟩
      . . .
  ⟨⟨expressionₙ⟩⟩ )
```

defines a local macro whose scope is its body ⟨⟨expression₁⟩⟩...⟨⟨expressionₙ⟩⟩. The definition of each local macro is the same as you would get using defmacro. When a local function is defined by flet and labels, the scope of the local variables is not limited by the definition expression of the local function. In case of macrolet, the scope is so limited. When you type

```
(macrolet ((foo (y) (list x y)))
      ...)
```

even if the macrolet expression exists within the scope of a local variable x, the scope of the macrolet is confined to the definition expression of the local macro foo, i.e.,

```
(foo (y) (list x y))
```

and the x here is a global variable. However, inside the body of macrolet, you can refer to local variables or blocks outside of the macrolet.

7-4 Backquote

We have used the following expression in the macro definition of `when`

```
(list 'if condition (cons 'progn body))
```

This expression creates the following expanded expression

```
(if ⟨⟨condition⟩⟩ (progn . ⟨⟨body⟩⟩ ))
```

which looks clearer and easier to understand than the first expression. Although

```
(if condition (progn . body))
```

cannot be evaluated, you should try to make the macro definition look as much like the expanded expression as possible.

To create a clearer expression, you can use the macro character " ` " called **backquote**. A **macro character** allows you to type an abbreviated version of the input. The reason that

```
(quote (a b c))
```

can be written as

```
'(a b c)
```

is that quote " ' " is a macro character.

Backquote is used in the following way:

```
`(if ,condition (progn .   ,body))
```

abbreviates

```
(list 'if condition (cons 'progn body))
```

You can put a list after a backquote just like after a quote. In the list, if you write a variable after a comma " , " the value of that variable will be put in the corresponding place in the list. More precisely, you will get an expression for placing the value of that variable in the proper place in the list. Not only variables but also any expression can come after a comma and the value of such an expression will be put in its corresponding places in the list. Consider

```
>'(a b)
(a b)
```

If the list after a backquote does not have comma, backquote and quote have the same effect. Anything other than a list can also come after back-quote, although it may not be so useful.

```
>'a
a
```

If we set

```
>(setq x '(c d))
```

then

```
>'(a b ,x e f)
(a b (c d) e f)
```

This is because at the time of input, `(a b ,x e f) is exchanged with

```
(list* 'a 'b x '(e f))
```

which then is evaluated to get (a b (c d) e f).

```
>(defun foo (x) '( a b ,x e f))
```

is equivalent to

```
>(defun foo (x) (list* 'a 'b x '(e f)))
```

and you will get

```
>(foo '(c d))
(a b (c d) e f)

>(foo 'cd)
(a b cd e f)
```

If you put an "@" right after a comma, you will get

```
>(setq x '(c d))
(c d)

>'(a b ,@x e f)
(a b c d e f)
```

Another way of expressing this is that '(a b ,@x e f) has the same value as

```
(list* 'a 'b (append x '(e f)))
```

The value of the expression which appears right after the ",@" will appear buried in the list using append. Since it is put in the list using append rather than nconc, the value of x is not changed and remains (c d). If you use a period "." instead of "@", the next expression after the "." will be embedded using nconc.

```
>(setq x '(c d))
(c d)

>'(a b ,.x e f)
(a b c d e f)

>x
(c d e f)
```

We can redefine **when** using backquote as

```
(defmacro when (condition . body)
  '(if ,condition (progn . ,body)))
```

or

```
(defmacro when (condition . body)
  '(if ,condition (progn ,@body)))
```

Backquote helps you abbreviate expressions which you input. The exact expression backquote abbreviates depends on which version of Common Lisp you are using. Some systems may use

```
'(if ,condition (progn ,@body))
```

as the abbreviation for

```
(list 'if condition (cons 'progn body))
```

Other systems may have other abbreviations for this expression. All the different systems, however, have the same value for the abbreviated expression when they are finished evaluating. To see which expression has been abbreviated by backquotes on your system, you should type

```
>''(if ,condition (progn ,@body))
(list 'if condition (list* 'progn body))
```

As a final example in this section let's redefine the macro **dotimes** using backquote:

```
(defmacro dotimes ((var form
                    &optional
                      (result nil))
                   . body)
  (let ((limit (gensym)))
    '(do ((,var 0 (1+ ,var))
          (,limit ,form))
         ((>= ,var ,limit) ,result)
       ,@body)))
```

8   List Processing

With the knowledge you acquired so far, it is possible to do all the essential list operations. You can make any list structure by combining five functions, `cons`, `car`, `cdr`, `rplaca`, and `rplacd`. If you use them combined with predicates such as `atom` and `endp`, you can extract any information about a list. In this chapter, we will talk about some functions which are useful for list processing, even though a user can do the same thing using the above-mentioned five functions. The functions we will introduce in this chapter come pre-defined. This removes the possibility of introducing an incorrect definition. They also work more efficiently than using the same functions defined by yourself since these functions have been optimized by the system designers. We also describe some techniques of more sophisticated list processing and their applications.

8-1   List Processing Functions

In this section, we will explain some additional system functions for list processing.

    `nth` takes a non-negative integer and a list and, if n is smaller than the length of the list, it returns the element which is $n + 1$th in the list. If n is larger than or equal to the length of a list, it returns `nil`.

```
>(nth 0 '(a b c d e))
a
```

```
>(nth 1 '(a b c d e))
b

>(nth 3 '(a b c d e))
d

>(nth 5 '(a b c d e))
nil
```

The first argument to nth specifies the $n + 1$th element. For example, 0 specifies the first element and 1 specifies the second element.

first returns the first element of a list.

```
>(first '(a b c))
a
```

first does exactly the same thing as car. If it gets nil, it returns nil just like car does.

```
>(first nil)
nil
```

The system has the following functions which return the 2nd to the 10th elements of a list:

second	third	fourth
fifth	sixth	seventh
eighth	ninth	tenth

rest works exactly in the same way as cdr.

```
>(rest '(a b c))
(b c)

>(rest '(a . b))
b

>(rest nil)
nil
```

nthcdr repeats cdr as many times as specified.

```
>(nthcdr 0 '(a b c d))
(a b c d)
```

```
>(nthcdr 2 '(a b c d))
(c d)

>(nthcdr 10 '(a b c d))
nil
```

last returns the last cons in a list (or a dotted-list)

```
>(last '(a b c))
(c)

>(last '(a b . c))
(b . c)
```

If the argument is **nil** or a dotted-pair, **last** returns the argument itself.

```
>(last '(a . b))
(a . b)

>(last nil)
nil
```

make-list makes a list from one required parameter and a keyword parameter called :initial-element. The required parameter specifies the length of the list and the keyword parameter specifies what data object should be used as the elements. If the keyword parameter is not given, **make-list** makes a list of **nil**s.

```
>(make-list 8 :initial-element 'man)
(man man man man man man man man)

>(make-list 3)
(nil nil nil)
```

reverse makes a new list in which elements of the original list it received are reversed.

```
>(reverse '(a b c d))
(d c b a)
```

Since **reverse** makes the new list using new cons cells, the initial list will not be destroyed.

```
>(setq x '(a b c d))
(a b c d)
>(reverse x)
(d c b a)
>x
(a b c d)
```

As opposed to **reverse**, **nreverse** destroys the initial list since it reverses the order of the elements by reusing the cons cells of the original list. Generally **nreverse** works faster than **reverse**.

```
>(nreverse x)
(d c b a)
```

After this, the value of x will have changed. This value will not always be the same as the value which is returned by **nreverse**. If you want to keep the value of **nreverse** in x, you should assign the value to x.

```
>(setq x (nreverse x))
(d c b a)
```

member checks whether some data object is an element of a list. It is defined as

```
(defun member (item list)
        &key (test #'eql s1)
             (test-not nil s2)
             (key #'identity))
   (when (and s1 s2)
       (error
        "Both :test & :test-not specified"))
   (if (not s2)
       (do ((x list (cdr x)))
           ((endp x) nil)
         (when (funcall test item
                  (funcall key (car x)))
           (return x)))
       (do ((x list (cdr x)))
           ((endp x) nil)
         (unless (funcall test-not item
                    (funcall key (car x)))
           (return x)))))
```

If you do not specify any keyword parameter, member checks whether item is an element of list or not. It compares each element of list from the beginning using eql with item and if it finds an element for which eql returns t, it returns a list made up of the elements right after that element. If it does not find such an element, it returns nil.

```
>(member 'c '(a b c d e))
(c d e)

>(member 'cc '(a b c d e))
nil

>(member c '(a b c c c))
(c c c)
```

If item is an element of list, member returns a list other than nil. That is why member can be used as predicate.

```
>(defun what-day (day)
    (cond ((member day
              '(mon tue wed thu fri))
            'week-day)
          ((member day '(sat sun))
           'week-end)
          (t 'i-dont-know)))
what-day

>(what-day 'tue)
week-day

>(what-day 'sun)
week-end

>(what-day 'every-day)
i-dont-know
```

The three keyword parameters of member are all function data. :test specifies a function which is used for comparing with item.

```
>(member '(c) '(a b (c) d e))
nil
```

If member compares item using equal instead of eql, it will type

```
>(member '(c) '(a b (c) d e)
         :test #'equal)
((c) d e)
```

Usually **member** compares each element in **list** with **item**. However, if you specify a **:key**, **member** compares **item** not to the element itself, but to the value which is returned by applying the function which follows **:key** to the element of **list**. For example, in

```
>(member 'c '((a . 1) (b . 2)
              (c . 3) (d . 4))
         :key #'car)
((c . 3) (d . 4))
```

the **car** of each element of **list** is compared with the symbol c. You may specify both **:test** and **:key**.

```
>(member '(c d) '((d) (c d) (b c d)
                  (a b c d))
         :key #'cdr
         :test #'equal)
((b c d) (a b c d))
```

If you specify **:test-not**, **member** uses the function of **:test-not** for the comparison, and returns the list of the rest of the elements which are right after the element whose value is **nil**.

```
>(member 'c '(c c a b c) :test-not #'eq)
(a b c)
```

You may specify **:test-not** and **:key** at the same time, but you cannot specify **:test** and **:test-not** at the same time. In the definition of **member** shown above, the **when** expression is used for checking this.

   member-if and **member-if-not** are system functions which are similar to **member**. **member-if** is defined as follows:

```
(defun member-if (test list
                  &key (key #'identity))
  (do ((x list (cdr x)))
      ((endp x) nil)
    (when (funcall test
            (funcall key (car x)))
      (return x))))
```

If you replace **when** by **unless**, you get the definition of **member-if-not**. The first argument of both functions is a function which specifies a condition. **member-if** looks for an element which satisfies such condition and **member-if-not** looks for an element which does not satisfy this condition. If they find such elements, they return a list of the rest of the elements that follow right after such an element. For example,

```
>(member-if #'numberp '(a (1) 2 b))
(2 b)

>(member-of-not #'numberp
                '(1 2 3 four 5 6))
(four 5 6)
```

remove, **remove-if**, and **remove-if-not** make a new list by removing some elements from a list. All of these system functions take two required parameters and some keyword parameters. When they are only given the required parameters, **remove** removes those elements which are **eql** to its first argument, **remove-if** removes those elements which satisfy the condition given by its first argument, and **remove-if-not** removes all the elements which do not satisfy the condition given by its first argument.

```
>(setq x '(1 2 3 4 5 2 7))
(1 2 3 4 5 2 7)

>(remove 2 x)
(1 3 4 5 7)

>(remove-if #'evenp x)
(1 3 5 7)

>(remove-if-not #'evenp x)
(2 4 2)
```

If you want to specify the number of elements which you want to remove, you can use a keyword parameter called :**count**.

```
>(remove 2 x :count 1)
(1 3 4 5 2 7)
```

Usually elements are removed from the front. If you want to remove elements from the back of the list, you can specify a value other than **nil** to the keyword called :**from-end**.

```
>(remove 2 x :count 1 :from-end t)
(1 2 3 4 5 7)
```

remove-if and remove-if-not work in the same way. However, remove takes the keyword parameters :test, :test-not, and :key, all of which work exactly like member. The functions remove-if and remove-if-not also take a keyword parameter called :key, which works just like member-if and member-if-not.

While these three functions do not destroy the list which is given to them as a second argument, the three system functions, delete, delete-if, and delete-if-not, use the list destructively to remove some elements.

8-2 Mapping Functions

Mapping function is the general term for functions which call some function repeatedly. mapcar, maplist, mapc, mapl, mapcan, and mapcon are the system mapping functions. These mapping functions specify which function to call repeatedly as their first argument and specify the arguments to be given at each call in a set of lists which appear as the rest of the arguments. Each mapping function treats the list made up of the second and remaining arguments differently and they also determine which value is returned as a result of calling the mapping functions

mapcar repeatedly calls the specified function using an element from each list as one of its arguments. It first calls the function on the first element of each list which appears as an argument, then it calls the same function using the second element of each list, and so on. It repeats this as long as the length of the lists that appear as the arguments have the same length. If the arguments have different lengths, mapcar repeats the function for as many times as the length of its shortest argument. The value of mapcar is a list made of elements which the function returns at each call.

```
>(mapcar 'cons '(a b c) '(1 2 3))
((a . 1) (b . 2) (c . 3))

>(mapcar 'cons '(a b c) '(1 2 3 4 5))
((a . 1) (b . 2) (c . 3))

>(mapcar #'(lambda (x) (* x x))
         '(7 2 3 8))
(49 4 9 64)
```

mapcar specifies the function which is repeatedly called in the same way as apply and funcall. mapcar can have as many lists as its arguments as long as the specified function can take.

maplist is similar to mapcar, however, it takes the cdr, not the car (that is, the elements), of each list, and uses it as the argument to the function. maplist first calls a function with each list as an argument. It then calls the same function with the cdr of each list as an argument. Then it calls the function again with the cddr of each list as an argument. It repeats this operation until one of the arguments becomes the empty list.

```
>(maplist 'cons '(a b c) '(1 2 3))
(((a b c) 1 2 3) ((b c) 2 3) ((c) 3))

>(maplist #'(lambda (x) (length x))
          '(7 2 3 8))
(4 3 2 1)
```

mapcar and maplist make a list of the values of the function at each call. However, if the function call is used just for a side effect, i.e., the value of the function is not important, using mapcar and maplist is a useless thing to do since they make a list which will not be used. In this case, it is more efficient to use mapc instead of mapcar and mapl instead of maplist. mapc and mapl work exactly like mapcar and maplist except that they ignore the value of the functions called. mapc and mapl return their second argument, i.e., the first list argument as a value.

```
>number-count
10

>(mapc #'(lambda (x)
           (when (numberp x)
               (incf number-count)))
       '(a 7 b c 2 3 d 8))
(a 7 b c 2 3 d 8)

>number-count
14
```

In the above example, mapc calls the function eight times which increases the value of a variable number-count by 1 when the argument is a number. Since the argument is a number 4 times out of 8, the value of number-count is increased by 4 as the result of this execution of mapc.

mapcan and mapcon call the specified function in the same way as mapcar and maplist. However, they assume the value of the function is a list and they return the list made of all the elements of the resulting lists, while `mapcar` and `maplist` make a list using the values of the function. In the following example, the function `cdr` is called three times. The first argument is (a b), the next one is (c), and the last one is (1 2 3). The values are (b), an empty list, and (2 3). The list made of all the elements of these lists, (b 2 3), is the value of `mapcan`.

```
>(mapcan 'cdr '((a b) (c) (1 2 3)))
(b 2 3)
```

You already know that `append` and `nconc` are the system functions which take some lists and return the lists made of all the elements of each list as the value. `append` makes a new list and `nconc` connects the two lists directly. `mapcan` and `mapcon` connect the values of the functions in the same way as `nconc`. You should be careful when you use it, since, if the function is called on part of an already-existing list, an unexpected side effect might happen. Let's look at the next example:

```
>(setq x '((a b) (c) (1 2 3)))
((a b) (c) (1 2 3))

>(mapcan 'cdr x)
(b 2 3)

>x
((a b 2 3) (c) (1 2 3))
```

The first element (a b) of the list contained in the variable x is the argument to the first call to `cdr`. This returns the value (b) which is part of the first sublist of x. `mapcan` then takes the `cdr` of (c), which is the empty list. When it connects this to (b) nothing changes. On the other hand, at the next step when `mapcan` connects the value (2 3), which is the value `cdr` applied to (1 2 3), it destructively changes (b) to (b 2 3). But this has the effect of changing the " front" of x. As a result, the value of x is changed after the call to `mapcan`.

8-3 Alists

An **alist** (association list) is a data structure which has been used very often in Lisp. An alist is a list of **pairs** and each pair is a cons cell. For example,

```
((usa . washington)
 (france . paris)
 (japan . kyoto))
```

is an alist made of three pairs: (usa . washington), (france . paris), and (japan . kyoto). The car part of a pair is called the key and the rest of the pair is called the data attached to a key. An alist is a data structure for keeping a key and its attached data.

A system function called assoc gets a pair with a specified key from an alist.

```
>(setq cc '((usa . washington)
            (france . paris)
            (japan . kyoto)))

>(assoc 'france cc)
(france . paris)

>(assoc 'japan cc)
(japan . kyoto)
```

If an alist does not have a pair with the specified key, assoc returns nil. If more than two pairs have the same key, assoc returns the first pair in the list.

```
>(assoc 'canada cc)
nil

>(setq cc1 (cons '(japan . tokyo) cc))
((japan . tokyo) (usa . washington)
 (france . paris) (japan . kyoto))

>(assoc 'japan cc1)
(japan . tokyo)
```

The advantage of using an alist for keeping information is that the system can add the information to an alist without destroying the old information. In the above example, although the data attached to the key called japan is tokyo in cc1, cc has kept the old information.

```
>(assoc 'japan cc1)
(japan . tokyo)
```

```
>(assoc 'japan cc)
(japan . kyoto)
```

Consider the following two system functions which are useful for adding information to an alist. `acons` receives three things: a key, some data, and an alist. It makes a pair of the key and the data, and then adds this pair to the alist. The "a" in `acons`, of course, comes from the word 'association.' Another function is called `pairlis` which makes an alist from a list of keys and a list of data. If an alist is also given to `pairlis`, it adds pairs to this alist.

```
>(acons 'japan 'tokyo cc)
((japan . tokyo) (usa . washington)
 (france . paris) (japan . kyoto))

>(pairlis '(usa france japan)
          '(washington paris kyoto))
((usa . washington) (france . paris)
 (japan . kyoto))

>(pairlis '(uk japan) '(london tokyo) cc)
((uk . london) (japan . tokyo)
 (usa . washington) (france . paris)
 (japan . kyoto))
```

8-4 Property Lists

Just like an alist, a **property list** (also called a plist) is a data structure for keeping a key and its associated data. However, while an alist is made up of pairs of keys and data, a property list is a list of alternating keys and data. Therefore, a property list has an even number of elements. Keys are the odd numbered elements and data are the even numbered elements.

```
(citizen japan age 33 pets (toto stretcher))
```

`citizen`, `age`, and `pets` are keys and `japan`, `33`, `(toto stretcher)` are the attached data in the property list.

Every symbol has a property list. The keys of this property list are thought of as a property of the symbol and the data is its value. In this way property lists are used to keep information about symbols. A user can give any properties to a symbol. For example, if you give the properties of kind, color, and size to the name of an animal, you can write a program which gives the description of the animal.

When a new symbol is made, the property list of the symbol is empty. Some symbols made by the system have properties, but such properties are only useful to the system, not generally for a user. Some old Lisps used to put the value of variables, the definition of functions, the name of the symbols, and so on, in these property lists. However, Common Lisp does not do this. In Common Lisp, even when you define a function or assign values to variables, the property list of a symbol does not change.

You can get the property list of a symbol using symbol-plist.

```
>(symbol-plist 'elephant)
(kind animal color gray size big)
```

You can add or change the property of a symbol by directly changing the value of symbol-plist using rplaca or rplacd. However, it is easier and safer to use the system functions and macros for manipulating the property lists of symbols which will be explained later in this section. As a result there will be less possibility of destroying a property which the system uses.

You can get the value of a symbol property using get.

```
>(get 'elephant 'color)
gray
```

If a symbol does not have the specified property, get returns nil. If the value of a property is a list or a logical value, you cannot tell whether a symbol does not have that property or it has the property but its value is nil. In either case get returns nil. In such cases, you should pre-specify a default value which get returns when a symbol does not have the property.

```
>(get 'elephant 'favorite-movies)
nil

>(get 'elephant
      'favorite-movies
      'not-found)
not-found
```

In order to add or change a symbol property, use a combination of setf and get.

```
(setf (get ⟨⟨symbol⟩⟩ ⟨⟨property⟩⟩ ) ⟨⟨value⟩⟩ )
```

⟨⟨symbol⟩⟩, ⟨⟨property⟩⟩, and ⟨⟨value⟩⟩ are all evaluated. If ⟨⟨symbol⟩⟩ has ⟨⟨property⟩⟩, the value of that property becomes ⟨⟨value⟩⟩, if not, a new property will be added with this value.

```
>(setf (get 'elephant 'favorite-movies)
       '(dumbo))
(dumbo)

>(get 'elephant 'favorite-movies)
(dumbo)
```

Generally, setf is a macro for putting a value in a place. get, just like car and cdr, is a function itself and can represent a place for a symbol property. Therefore, you can use macros such as push, pop, incf, decf, and so on, combined with get. When you use these macros combined with get, if a symbol does not have the specified property, get makes such property and then starts the actual operation. The value of the property would be the default value of get if there is one and it would be nil if there is none.

```
>(push 'peanuts (get 'elephant
                     'favorite-foods))
(peanuts)

>(push 'jelly-beans
       (get 'elephant 'favorite-foods))
(jelly-beans peanuts)

>(push 'india
       (get 'elephant 'home '(africa)))
(india africa)
```

You use remprop to remove an unuseful property. The value of remprop is nil if there is no such property. If there is such a property, the value would be anything other than nil. So, the value of remprop can be useful to find out whether a property exists or not.

```
>(get 'elephant 'favorite-foods)
(jelly-beans peanuts)

>(remprop 'elephant 'favorite-foods)
t
```

```
>(get 'elephant
      'favorite-foods
      'not-found)
not-found
```

Let's go on to some mechanisms for the general property lists. The function corresponding to **get** is **getf**. **getf** takes a property list where **get** takes a symbol.

```
>(getf '(a 1 b 2) 'b)
2
```

If you use **getf** combined with **setf**, you can add or change a property on a property list. In this case, there should be an expression for a place right after **getf** in order to change the property list in that place.

```
>(setq x '(a 1 b 2))
(a 1 b 2)

>(setf (getf x 'b) 20)
20

>x
(a 1 b 20)
```

You can specify the default value to **getf**, just as in **get**. The default value of **getf** works exactly the same way as the one in **get**.

The function corresponding to **remprop** is **remf**. It specifies the place while **remprop** specifies a symbol.

```
>(remf x 'a)
t

>x
(b 20)
```

The system function **get-properties** looks through a property list until it finds one of the properties. Its arguments are a property list and a list consisting of properties as elements.

```
>(get-properties '(a 1 b 2 c 3 d 4)
                 '(x c b))
b
2
(b 2 c 3 d 4)
```

get-properties returns three values. If one of the specified properties can be found in the property list, it returns, as its values, the property, the value of the property, and the rest of the property list after that property. If none of the specified properties is found in the property list, it returns nil for the property, nil for the value of the property, and nil for the property list after that property. Since the last value of get-properties would not be nil if the specified property is found, the last value will tell you whether there is a property or not. The last value also can be used to keep looking for the property. For example, in order to return a list of all the values of the properties which are in the property list we could define:

```
>(defun get-all-properties (plist properties)
   (multiple-value-bind (p v rest)
       (get-properties plist properties)
     (if (null rest)
         nil
         (cons v (get-all-properties
                   (cddr rest)
                   properties)))))
get-all-properties

>(get-all-properties '(a 1 b 2 c 3 d 4)
                     '(x c b))
(2 3)
```

9   Declarations

We have already talked about how to bind a local variable. In this chapter, we will explain how to bind a global variable and give some examples of its use. Since declarations are usually used for binding global variables, we will talk about general declarations as well.

9-1 Dynamic Binding

The system can bind global variables just like it can bind local variables. As we will explain later, let and let* can also bind global variables. We will first talk about a special form **progv** for binding global variables.

    (progv '(x) '(2) $\langle\!\langle$expression$_1\rangle\!\rangle$ ... $\langle\!\langle$expression$_n\rangle\!\rangle$)

executes the expressions in the body, $\langle\!\langle$expression$_1\rangle\!\rangle$ ... $\langle\!\langle$expression$_n\rangle\!\rangle$, one by one. Before execution, **progv** binds the global variable x to 2. It makes a new box for the global variable x and puts 2 there. If the global variable x already has a value, it means that the old box for this value will be stored somewhere during the execution of the **progv** and this box will be used again for the global variable x after the execution of the body. The new box which **progv** made for x will be thrown away after the execution of the body. In other words, the **progv** expression executes the body, $\langle\langle$expression$_1\rangle\rangle$ ... $\langle\langle$expression$_n\rangle\rangle$, with 2 temporarily as the value of the global variable x. Since the new box which **progv** prepares is used as the box for a global variable x during the execution of the body, the old box will not be changed even if the content of the box is changed when the value of x changes. Now, suppose we have defined a function for increasing a value of a global variable x by 1 as follows:

```
>(defun count () (setq x (1+ x)))
```

then

```
>(setq x 0)
0

>(count)
1

>x
1
```

When the above **progv** expression calls this function, the content of the box which **progv** has constructed is increased by 1, but the old value of x will not change.

```
>(progv '(x) '(2) (count) x)
3

>x
1
```

If there was not a value for x before the execution of this **progv** expression, x will not have the value after the execution of the **progv**. To check whether a global variable has a value or not, you can use the system predicate called **boundp** applied to a symbol which names the variable. If the variable has a value, **boundp** returns t and if not it returns **nil**.

```
>(boundp 'x)
t

>(boundp 'y)
nil
```

```
>(progv '(y) '((a b c)) (cdr y))
(b c)

>(boundp 'y)
nil
```

The general **progv** expression is

> (**progv** ⟨⟨variable list⟩⟩ ⟨⟨initial value list⟩⟩
> ⟨⟨expression₁⟩⟩ ... ⟨⟨expressionₙ⟩⟩)

The **progv** expression evaluates both ⟨⟨variable list⟩⟩ and ⟨⟨initial value list⟩⟩. The value of ⟨⟨variable list⟩⟩ should be a list of the names of the global variables each of which will be bound to an element of the list which is the value of ⟨⟨initial value list⟩⟩. If there is no element in the ⟨⟨initial value list⟩⟩ which corresponds to a variable in the ⟨⟨variable list⟩⟩, that variable will be bound to **nil**. If the list of initial values is too long, then the excess values will be thrown away. The value of the last ⟨⟨expressionₙ⟩⟩ becomes the value of the **progv**.

A **progv** expression does not affect the scope of a local variable. For example,

```
(let ((x 1))
  (progv '(x) '(2)
    (print x)))
```

Since the x of (print x) is a local variable which is bound by the **let** expression, the system prints 1. In this example, it is clear that **progv** binds x. However, since the global variables which are to be bound are determined by evaluating the ⟨⟨variable list⟩⟩ of the **progv**, it is possible that the **progv** expression in the scope of a local variable binds a global variable whose name happens to be the same as one of the local variables. It would not be reasonable if **progv**, which usually refers to a local variable, would refer to the global variable in such a case. To prevent this, a **progv** expression is made not to affect the scope of a local variable. If you want to have a **progv** expression refer to a global variable within the scope of a local variable, you should use the system functions **symbol-value** or **set**.

```
(let ((x 1))
  (progv '(x) '(2)
    (print (symbol-value 'x))))
```

The system will print 2, the present value of the global variable x.

The binding of local variables is called **static** (or lexical) binding and the binding of global variables is called **dynamic** binding. When you refer to a local variable, it is possible to see lexically, without executing the program, where the variable is bound. When you refer to a global variable, you need to run the program to find out where the variable is bound. For example, the x in

```
>(defun foo () (cons x x))
```

is a global variable. However, we cannot tell where x was bound by just looking at this definition.

```
>(defun f () (progv '(x) '(2) (foo)))
f

>(defun g () (progv '(x) '(3) (foo)))
g
```

If you type

```
>(f)
(2 . 2)
```

x is bound at f. If you type

```
>(g)
(3 . 3)
```

x is bound at g.

While a static binding can only be referenced within the scope of a local variable, a dynamic binding can be referenced anytime during the execution of the form in which the variable was bound. In other words, while the static binding has the lexical scope, the scope of a dynamic binding is indefinite. A static binding will stay as part of a closure even after the execution of the form in which the variable was bound. A dynamic binding will disappear from a closure after the execution of the form. In

```
>(setq fun (progv '(x) '(2)
              #'(lambda () x)))
```

the binding made by the **progv** will not remain in the closure assigned to **fun**. When the system calls this closure, it refers to the binding of the global variable at that time.

```
>(setq x '(a b c))
(a b c)

>(funcall fun)
(a b c)

>(progv '(x) '(100) (funcall fun))
100
```

The scope of a binding means the area in the program where the binding can be referenced. The limit of the time when a binding can be referenced is called its **extent**. A static binding can be referenced by calling a closure anytime as long as the closure continues to exist. So, a static binding has indefinite extent. On the other hand, a dynamic binding can be referenced only during the execution of the form which sets up that binding. A dynamic binding is said to have **dynamic extent**.

9-2 Special Variables

If you type the system function called `proclaim`

```
>(proclaim '(special x))
```

the variable x in this expression will acquire the special attribute called being a **special variable**. Being a special variable means that such a variable is bound using dynamic, not static binding, and that whenever this variable is mentioned it always refers to the global variable. (The use of the word "special" in special variable has nothing to do with special form.) For example,

```
>(let ((x 2)) (cons (symbol-value 'x) x))
```

If x is not a special variable, the `let` expression binds x as a local variable (a static binding) and `cons` returns the pair consisting of the value of the global variable x and the value of the local variable x as the value of `let` expression. If the global variable x has 1 as a value, the value of the `let` expression would be (1 . 2). If x is a special variable, the `let` expression binds the global variable x (causing a dynamic binding) and refers to the global variable x in the body of the `let` expression. So, the value of the `let` expression would be (2 . 2) no matter what value the global variable x had before. The same thing can be said when `let*`, `do`, `do*`, `multiple-value-bind`, etc. are used. When binding the parameters in calling the function `foo`

```
>(defun foo (x)
   (cons (symbol-value 'x) x))
```

if x is a special variable, the argument to `foo` will be bound to the global variable x.

```
>(foo 2)
(2 . 2)
```

When the system completes the execution of an expression which binds a special variable, the extent of this dynamic binding is also over and the value of the variable returns to the value before the binding. For example, if the value of x before `foo` is called is 1, the value of x would return to 1 when the execution of `foo` is over.

```
>x
1

>(foo 2)
(2 . 2)

>x
1
```

The fact that the binding of a special variable is always a dynamic binding means that a local variable whose name is the same as the name of a special variable could not exist. You can interpret

```
>(proclaim '(special x))
```

to mean that "the variable called x always refers to the global variable x."

Simple programs sometimes produce the same result either by using dynamic binding or static binding. For example, in the following program for factorial

```
(defun fact (x)
   (if (zerop x) 1 (* x (fact (1- x)))))
```

the value of **fact** will be the same whether or not **x** is a special variable, i.e., whether the binding to **x** is dynamic or static.

Dynamic binding is often used for passing an argument to a function without change. Let's look at an example.

```
>(defun queen (n)
    (queen1 n 0 0 nil nil nil))
queen

>(defun queen1 (n i j column left right)
   (cond ((= i n) column)
         ((= j n) nil)
         ((or (member j column)
              (member (+ i j) left)
              (member (- i j) right))
          (queen1 n i (1+ j)
                  column left right))
         ((queen1 n (1+ i) 0
                  (cons j column)
                  (cons (+ i j) left)
                  (cons (- i j) right)))
         ((queen1 n i (1+ j)
                  column left right)))))
queen1
```

This is a program to solve the famous "eight queens puzzle." We will not explain this program in detail here. We just say that if you type

```
>(queen 8)
```

you will solve this puzzle. 8 is bound to a parameter of **queen** and is then passed to the parameter **n** of the function **queen1** without change. When **queen1** calls itself recursively, **n** is again passed without change. We can rewrite the above program using a special variable **n** as follows:

```
>(proclaim '(special n))
nil

>(defun queen (n)
    (queen1 0 0 nil nil nil))
queen
```

```
>(defun queen1 (i j column left right)
   (cond ((= i n) column)
         ((= j n) nil)
         ((or (member j column)
              (member (+ i j) left)
              (member (- i j) right))
          (queen1 i (1+ j)
                  column left right))
         ((queen1 (1+ i) 0
                  (cons j column)
                  (cons (+ i j) left)
                  (cons (- i j) right)))
         ((queen1 i (1+ j)
                  column left right))))
queen1
```

In this program, since the binding of the parameter n of the function queen is dynamic, queen1 can refer to n as a global variable without it being passed explicitly to queen1 as an argument. n does not have to be transferred at each recursive call of queen1.

Although special variables and dynamic bindings are very useful when writing programs, their use sometimes makes it difficult to read the program because it is difficult to tell the status of variable bindings only by looking at the program. It is ideal to use special variables in programs which bind a variable once for each execution of the program like in the above queen program. In other programs, it would be better not to use special variables.

When you use special variables, you should call special variables by different names to make them distinct from ordinary variables. "*" is often used around the name of a special variable. In the above queen program, n could be named *n*. If you make it a rule to use "*" only for special variables, you can clearly see whether the binding is dynamic or static by looking at the program. Each special variable which is provided with the system has "*" around its name. *package* which contains the current package is a special variable. You will see many variables starting with "*print-" and ending with "*" in Chapter 11, they are all special variables. One important thing to remember is that once you make a special variable, such a variable cannot become an ordinary variable again. For this reason it is important to use distinctive names for special variables so that they can be kept separate from ordinary variables.

Let's try to express the dynamic binding using the static binding. Consider

```
(defun foo (*x*)
  (cons (symbol-value '*x*) *x*))
```

where *x* is a special variable. This definition can be rewritten as

```
(defun foo (x0)
  (let ((x1 *x*))
    (setq *x* x0)
    (prog1 (cons (symbol-value '*x*) *x*)
           (setq *x* x1))))
```

In this definition, we assume x0 and x1 are not special variables. First, this program keeps the old value of *x* in x1, assigns the argument of the function foo to *x*, calculates the cons, and finally puts the old value of *x* back using (setq *x* x1). In the above example, the value of *x* can not be made available nonlocally.

In the following example, the value of *x* can be passed out by a throw which is contained in h to the outside of f depending on what h does.

```
(defun f (*x*) (h))
```

In this case you need to replace the use of prog1 with unwind-protect.

```
(defun f (x0)
  (let ((x1 *x*))
    (setq *x* x0)
    (unwind-protect
      (h)
      (setq *x* x1))))
```

Otherwise, the value of *x* could be thrown out of f without retaining its old value. Unfortunately, the above change is not enough for restoring *x* because it is necessary to fix *x* so that it doesn't have a value if it did not have a value initially. In the above two examples, if *x* did not have a value initially, the program gets an error message. The correct program is the following which uses boundp:

```
(defun f (x0)
  (if (boundp '*x*)
      (let ((x1 *x*))
        (setq *x* x0)
        (unwind-protect
          (h)
          (setq *x* x1)))
      (progn
        (setq *x* x0)
        (unwind-protect
          (h)
          (makunbound '*x*)))))
```

makunbound is a system function which makes *x* into a variable without
a value.

Dynamic binding happens on exactly the same occasions as static binding. For example, in

```
(let ((*x* 1) (*y* *x*)) ... )
```

the system first evaluates 1 and *x* and binds them to *x* and *y*. So,
the system binds the old value of *x* to *y*. On the other hand, in

```
(let* ((*x* 1) (*y* *x*)) ... )
```

the system binds the new value of *x*, namely 1, to *y* since bindings
occur one by one. The old value of *x* will not be referred. In

```
(defun foo (*x* &optional (*y* *x*)) ... )
```

if the system does not get a second argument to foo, it binds the special
variable *y* to the value of *x*, that is, the first argument to foo. When
more than two forms which bind the same special variable exist, the binding
of the inner most form will be given priority.

```
>(let ((*x* 1))
   (cons *x* (let ((*x* 2)) *x*)))
(1 . 2)
```

9-3 Special Declaration

If you type

```
>(proclaim '(special *x*))
```

the symbol *x* becomes a special variable and after that, all bindings to *x* will be dynamic bindings and *x* will refer to the value of the global variable. In this sense, proclaim is the declaration of a global special variable. You can specify as many variables as you want after special.

```
>(proclaim '(special *x* *y* *z*))
```

Here *x*, *y*, and *z* are now the special variables. Since proclaim is a function and its argument will be evaluated, it has a quote sign. It is possible to type

```
>(proclaim
    (cons 'special (list '*x* '*y* '*z*)))
```

though we do not recommend this. If you want to make a dynamic binding only in part of a program, you can make a local special declaration using the special form called declare. Let's look at an example. Suppose x is not a special variable.

```
>(defun foo (x)
    (declare (special x))
    (h (1+ x)))
```

In this definition, x becomes a special variable, the binding to x becomes dynamic, and the value of the global variable x plus 1 will be passed to the function called h. Even if h uses a parameter whose name is x

```
>(defun h (x)
    (cons (symbol-value 'x) x))
```

the declare expression of foo will not affect h. h returns the cons of the value of the global variable x and the value of its argument.

```
>(foo 1)
(1 . 2)
```

The value of the global variable x is 1 and the argument to h is 2 when h is called.

You can put a declare expression anywhere as long as it is right before the body of the form that binds the variables. For example,

```
(defun f (x)
  (let ((x x0))
    (declare (special x))
    (h (1+ x))))
```

The let expression binds the global variable x and the system references the global variable x in the body of the let.

The special declaration using declare is only effective within the form of such a declaration. However, if, within this form, another form binds a variable with the same name, the special declaration becomes ineffective in that form. Let's look at an example. Suppose x is not a special variable.

```
(defun foo (x)                           ; 1
  (declare (special x))                  ; 2
  (let ((y (1+ x)))                      ; 3
    (let ((x (1+ y)))                    ; 4
      (+ x                               ; 5
        (let ()                          ; 6
          (declare (special x))          ; 7
          x)))))                         ; 8
```

If you type (foo 1), the system binds 1 to the global variable x in the first line because of the special declaration in the second line. It binds 2 to a local variable y in the third line and it binds 3 again to x in the fourth line. The special declaration will not affect this binding in the fourth line. Since the let expression in the fourth line does not have a special declaration, this let expression binds to a local variable x. The value of this local variable will be referred to in the fifth line. Since the let expression in the sixth line has a declaration, the x in the eighth line is the global variable. Therefore, its value would be 1. As a result, the value of (foo 1) is 4.

The above example is just a sample program for the purpose of explaining how declarations work in detail. You should not use declare so much in an actual program you write and you should not write a program in which a same variable name is used both for a local variable in some places and a global variable in other places in the the same program, because it just causes confusion. In the above example, if you call the local variable something other than x, the program would be much easier to read. Also, if possible, you should avoid using the local special declaration using `declare`. If a variable with the same name refers a special variable in some places and refers a local variable in other places, it would cause confusion in a big program. You should try to set aside some variables as special variables using the global special declaration.

Both `proclaim` and `declare` give the system some supplemental information in the form of a declaration. There are other kinds of extra information that can be described by declaration other than making a special declaration. For example, you can use a declaration for improving the efficiency of executing a program without affecting the result of the execution. By inserting a `declare` expression in the definition of factorial

```
(defun fact (x)
  (declare (integer x))
  (if (zerop x) 1 (* x (fact (1- x)))))
```

you give the system the information that the parameter is always an integer. `fact` still does what it is supposed to do without such information. This information may or may not help the program calculate faster. How the information affects the execution of the program depends on which version of Common Lisp you are using. In this book we will just explain in detail the general expression for `proclaim` and `declare`. The general expression of `declare` is

(declare ⟪declaration specifier$_1$⟫ . . . ⟪declaration specifier$_n$⟫)

Each declaration specifier is a list. The first element is the symbol specifying the kind of declaration. The rest of the elements are the information given to the system. In a special declaration, the first element is the symbol `special` and the rest of the elements are the symbols for variable names. A declaration specifier inside of a `declare` expression will not be evaluated. You can give as many declaration specifiers as you want to a `declare` expression.

```
(declare (special x) (special y z))
```

has the same effect as

```
(declare (special x y z))
```

While `declare` is a special form, `proclaim` is a function which takes only one declaration specifier.

You can put a `declare` expression in front of the body of a form which binds variables like `defun` or `let`. The following special forms and macros can accept `declare` expressions.

defmacro	flet
defun	labels
do*	let
do-all-symbols	let*
do-external-symbols	macrolet
do-symbols	multiple-value-bind
do	prog
dolist	prog*
dotimes	

These forms can take `declare` expressions before their body. For example, a general `defun` expression looks like

$(\text{defun } \langle\!\langle \text{function name}\rangle\!\rangle \ \langle\!\langle \text{lambda list}\rangle\!\rangle$
$\langle\!\langle \text{declaration}_1\rangle\!\rangle \ldots \langle\!\langle \text{declaration}_m\rangle\!\rangle$
$\langle\!\langle \text{expression}_1\rangle\!\rangle \ldots \langle\!\langle \text{expression}_n\rangle\!\rangle \ )$

`defun` and `defmacro` can take a character string in place of a $\langle\!\langle \text{declaration}\rangle\!\rangle$. In such case, the character string is called a **documentation string** and is a comment regarding the function or macro. For example,

```
>(defun foo (x)
   "Only for example."
   (declare (special x))
   (cons (symbol-value 'x) x))
foo
```

You can extract such comments using the system function called `documentation`. The first argument of `documentation` is a function name or a macro name and its second argument is the symbol `function`.

```
>(documentation 'foo 'function)
"Only for example."
```

The symbol `function` is required here because `documentation` can also be used to extract comments out of other things besides functions and macros.

Now let's look at the special form `the`. The form

```
(the ⟨⟨data type⟩⟩ ⟨⟨expression⟩⟩ )
```

returns the same value as just typing ⟨⟨expression⟩⟩, but this expression gives the system the additional information that the value is a data object whose type is ⟨⟨data type⟩⟩. In both

```
(setq x (* 2 (fact 10)))
```

and the expression

```
(setq x (* 2 (the integer (fact 10))))
```

the same value (twice the value of (fact 10)) will be assigned to a variable x. In the latter case, the system will also get the information that the value of (fact 10) is integer. This additional information might make it possible for the system to evaluate the latter expression in less time than to evaluate the former expression. Whether this is actually so or not depends on the system. Just like the effectiveness of a declaration other than special declaration would depend on the system, what ⟨⟨data type⟩⟩s of a the expression would improve the efficiency of the program's execution depends on the system.

9-4 Variables and Constants

A reference to a variable which is not a local variable is a reference to a global variable. However, in order to help in debugging and to make a program run reliably, it is frequently a good strategy to make a declaration for a reference to a global variable. Often global variables are referred to by mistake because the user types the wrong name for a local variable. Many Common Lisp systems including KCL give a user a warning when a global variable is referred to without having made a special declaration.

There are other methods of making a global declaration. One such method is to use defvar.

```
>(defvar *x*)
```

has almost the same effect as

```
>(proclaim '(special *x*))
```

defvar is a macro that expands into a proclaim statement. The reason we said 'almost' is that some systems do more when they encounter a defvar.

Because of this extra work, it is better to use `defvar` than to use `proclaim`. It is not an error to type `defvar` for a variable which is already a special variable.

After the variable name, `defvar` can take an expression for giving an initial value to a variable.

```
(defvar ⟪variable⟫ ⟪expression⟫ )
```

When the system evaluates the above expression, ⟪variable⟫ becomes a special variable and the value of ⟪expression⟫ becomes the initial value of ⟪variable⟫. For example,

```
>(defvar *x* (+ 1 2))
```

In this case the initial value of *x* would be 3. ⟪expression⟫ will be ignored if ⟪variable⟫ already has a value. In other words, ⟪expression⟫ is used only when the variable does not have a value; ⟪expression⟫ is not even evaluated if the variable has a value.

You can put a comment on the variable in a `defvar`.

```
(defvar ⟪variable⟫ ⟪expression⟫ ⟪character string⟫ )
```

In this case ⟪variable⟫ has the comment ⟪character string⟫. To extract the comment from the variable, you give the symbol `variable` to `documentation` as its second argument.

```
>(defvar *x* 3 "Only for example.")
*x*

>(documentation '*x* 'variable)
"Only for example."
```

A constant is a variable whose value never changes. To define a constant, you use the macro called `defconstant`.

```
>(defconstant one 1)
```

defines a constant called `one` whose value is 1. Generally, `defconstant` looks like

```
(defconstant ⟪variable⟫ ⟪expression⟫ )
```

In this form ⟨⟨expression⟩⟩ can not be omitted. Since the ⟨⟨expression⟩⟩ is evaluated, the above defconstant expression would be the same as

```
>(defconstant one (- 2 1))
```

If the system executes a defconstant twice over the same constant, it will not be an error as long as the two values of the constant are equal in the eql sense. This means that both of the above defconstant expressions can be executed. defconstant can take a comment after ⟨⟨expression⟩⟩. Since a constant is a kind of variable, you can use the symbol variable in the call to documentation to get the comment associated with the constant.

defparameter is something between defvar and defconstant. defparameter needs an ⟨⟨expression⟩⟩ just like defconstant and the values of ⟨⟨expression⟩⟩ need to be equal in the eql sense when defparameter is used twice with the same ⟨⟨variable⟩⟩. On the other hand, it is also possible to change its value in the program just like a defvar.

10   Data Types

In the previous chapters, we talked about lists and symbols. In this chapter, we will talk about numerical data and other Common Lisp data types.

10-1   Numbers

The numerical data types of Common Lisp are:

- integer
- ratio
- floating-point number
- complex number

An **integer** is an integer in the mathematical sense. A Common Lisp system can treat any integers without any restriction on their size. Usually, integers are input and output using base ten. Positive integers are written simply as unsigned numbers and negative integers are written using a minus sign "−".

A **ratio** is a fraction in the mathematical sense. A positive ratio is expressed as

$$\langle\!\langle\text{positive integer}\rangle\!\rangle / \langle\!\langle\text{positive integer}\rangle\!\rangle$$

A negative ratio has a minus symbol in front. The left side of the "/" is the numerator and the right side is the denominator. The function / returns a ratio when the integers have no common factors.

```
>(/ 14 4)
7/2

>(/ 1 -2)
-1/2
```

Integers and ratios are called **rational number**s. The functions for arithmetic

$$+, \quad -, \quad *, \quad /$$

calculate on rational numbers just like the usual arithmetic calculations.

```
>(+ 1/2 3/2 5)
7

>(- 1/2 1/3)
1/6

>(* 1/2 3/2 5)
15/4
```

A **floating point number** is the numerical data object for expressing a real number. For example, when you try to extract the square root of 2 using the system function sqrt,

```
>(sqrt 2)
1.414213
```

sqrt returns a floating point number. Since it is difficult to represent a real number precisely on a computer, an approximate value is used as in the above example. Consequently, the calculation of floating point numbers sometimes is not accurate. For example, if you square the above approximate value of the square root, you will not get 2.

```
>(* (sqrt 2) (sqrt 2))
1.999998
```

How a floating point number is represented depends on the computer hardware and each system has different methods for processing calculations on floating point numbers. On some systems you might get a more precise square root of 2 than on others.

A **complex number** is the same as a complex number in the mathematical sense. A complex number is made up of a real part and an imaginary part. The system inputs and outputs a complex number as

#c (⟪real part⟫ ⟪imaginary part⟫)

For example, the imaginary unit (the number which becomes −1 when squared) is expressed as

#c (0 1)

Then

```
>(* #c(0 1) #c(0 1))
-1
```

When you give a negative number to sqrt, you will get a complex number.

```
>(sqrt -9)
#c(0.0 3.0)
```

In chapter 2, we defined a function called quadratic-equation which could be used for solving a quadratic equation. This function returns a complex number when the specified quadratic equation has an imaginary root. For example,

```
>(quadratic-equation -2 3)
#c(1.0 1.414213)
#c(1.0 -1.414213)
```

The function numberp is used to determine whether a data structure is a number or not. Furthermore, the following predicates are used to determine what kind of numerical data a number is.

integerp	(integer or not)
rationalp	(rational number or not)
floatp	(floating point number or not)
complexp	(complex number or not)

There is no predicate for determining whether a number is a ratio or not. However,

```
(and (rationalp x) (not (integerp x)))
```

will tell you whether a number is a ratio.

Common Lisp has many functions for numerical computation. These are listed below:

(+ $\langle\langle$number$\rangle\rangle$ ... $\langle\langle$number$\rangle\rangle$)	sum
(* $\langle\langle$number$\rangle\rangle$ ... $\langle\langle$number$\rangle\rangle$)	product
(- $\langle\langle$number$\rangle\rangle$)	minus $\langle\langle$number$\rangle\rangle$
(- $\langle\langle$number$_1\rangle\rangle$ $\langle\langle$number$_2\rangle\rangle$ ... $\langle\langle$number$_n\rangle\rangle$)	$\langle\langle$number$_1\rangle\rangle$ minus $\langle\langle$number$_2\rangle\rangle$ ... minus $\langle\langle$number$_n\rangle\rangle$
(/ $\langle\langle$number$\rangle\rangle$)	reciprocal of $\langle\langle$number$\rangle\rangle$
(/ $\langle\langle$number$_1\rangle\rangle$ $\langle\langle$number$_2\rangle\rangle$ ... $\langle\langle$number$_n\rangle\rangle$)	$\langle\langle$number$_1\rangle\rangle$ divided by $\langle\langle$number$_2\rangle\rangle$ ... divided by $\langle\langle$number$_n\rangle\rangle$
(1+ $\langle\langle$number$\rangle\rangle$)	$\langle\langle$number$\rangle\rangle$ plus 1
(1- $\langle\langle$number$\rangle\rangle$)	$\langle\langle$number$\rangle\rangle$ minus 1
(gcd $\langle\langle$integer$\rangle\rangle$ ... $\langle\langle$integer$\rangle\rangle$)	the greatest common divisor
(lcm $\langle\langle$integer$\rangle\rangle$ ... $\langle\langle$integer$\rangle\rangle$)	the least common multiple
(max $\langle\langle$number$\rangle\rangle$ ... $\langle\langle$number$\rangle\rangle$)	the maximum
(min $\langle\langle$number$\rangle\rangle$ ... $\langle\langle$number$\rangle\rangle$)	the minimum
(expt $\langle\langle$number$_1\rangle\rangle$ $\langle\langle$number$_2\rangle\rangle$)	the $\langle\langle$number$_2\rangle\rangle^{\text{th}}$ power of $\langle\langle$number$_1\rangle\rangle$
(exp $\langle\langle$number$\rangle\rangle$)	$\langle\langle$number$\rangle\rangle^{\text{th}}$ power of e (base of the natural logarithms)
(log $\langle\langle$number$_1\rangle\rangle$ $\langle\langle$number$_2\rangle\rangle$)	log of $\langle\langle$number$_1\rangle\rangle$ with base $\langle\langle$number$_2\rangle\rangle$
(log $\langle\langle$number$\rangle\rangle$)	log of $\langle\langle$number$\rangle\rangle$ with base e
(sqrt $\langle\langle$number$\rangle\rangle$)	the square root
(isqrt $\langle\langle$non negative integer$\rangle\rangle$)	the biggest integers which is not bigger than the square root of $\langle\langle$non negative integer$\rangle\rangle$
(abs $\langle\langle$number$\rangle\rangle$)	absolute value
(sin $\langle\langle$number$\rangle\rangle$)	sine
(cos $\langle\langle$number$\rangle\rangle$)	cosine
(tan $\langle\langle$number$\rangle\rangle$)	tangent
(asin $\langle\langle$number$\rangle\rangle$)	arc sine
(acos $\langle\langle$number$\rangle\rangle$)	arc cosine
(atan $\langle\langle$number$\rangle\rangle$)	arc tangent

(floor ⟪number⟫)	the biggest integer not bigger than ⟪number⟫
(ceiling ⟪number⟫)	the smallest integer not smaller than ⟪number⟫
(truncate ⟪number⟫)	delete the digits after the decimal point
(round ⟪number⟫)	round to the nearest whole number

(floor ⟪number$_1$⟫ ⟪number$_2$⟫)
$\qquad$ = (floor (/ ⟪number$_1$⟫ ⟪number$_2$⟫))

(ceiling ⟪number$_1$⟫ ⟪number$_2$⟫)
$\qquad$ = (ceiling (/ ⟪number$_1$⟫ ⟪number$_2$⟫))

(truncate ⟪number$_1$⟫ ⟪number$_2$⟫)
$\qquad$ = (truncate (/ ⟪number$_1$⟫ ⟪number$_2$⟫))

(round ⟪number$_1$⟫ ⟪number$_2$⟫)
$\qquad$ = (round (/ ⟪number$_1$⟫ ⟪number$_2$⟫))

Although in the above list only the first value of floor, ceiling, truncate, and round is mentioned, they actually return two values. If there is only one argument, the difference between the argument and the first value becomes the second value.

```
>(floor 5.2)
5
0.2
```

If there are two arguments, the difference between the first argument and the product of the second argument and the first value becomes the second value.

```
>(floor 11 3)
3
2

>(floor 1/2 1/3)
1
1/6
```

```
>(truncate 3.5 1.2)
2
1.1
```

The second value of **floor** and **truncate** can also be computed by using the functions **mod** and **rem**.

```
>(mod 11 3)
2

>(mod 1/2 1/3)
1/6

>(rem 3.5 1.2)
1.1
```

To get a random number, use the function **random**.

(random $\langle\!\langle$positive integer$\rangle\!\rangle$)

returns a random integer between 0 and $\langle\!\langle$positive integer$\rangle\!\rangle$ − 1.

10-2 Arrays and Vectors

An **array** is a collection of data. Like a list, an array itself is a data object. Unlike a list, you can refer the elements of an array using its **index** without going through each element one by one. On the other hand, it is not as easy to change the size of an array as it is to change the size of a list. An array occupies one area of continuous memory in a computer and its elements are not connected using a cell like lists are. Elements of the array are stored in this continuous area and a specific element can be accessed simply by giving its index. The number of indexes necessary to refer to an element of an array is called the **rank** of the array. For example, the one-dimensional (one-rank, precisely speaking) array of seven elements; **sun**, **mon**, **tue**, **wed**, **thu**, **fri**, and **sat**, has the following structure:

The index of an array always starts from 0. The index for **sun**, the first
element of the above array, is 0 and the index for **mon** is 1.

The elements of an array can be accessed using **aref**. Suppose the
variable called **days** has the above array as its value.

```
>(aref days 0)
sun

>(aref days 1)
mon

>(aref days 6)
sat
```

If the rank of an array is n, **aref** is called with n indexes.

$$(\text{\textbf{aref}} \; \langle\!\langle\text{array}\rangle\!\rangle \; \langle\!\langle\text{index}_1\rangle\!\rangle \ldots \langle\!\langle\text{index}_n\rangle\!\rangle \;)$$

Since in the previous example, the array is one dimensional, there is only
one index.

We can represent the following matrix of two columns and three rows
using an array.

$$\begin{bmatrix} 1 & 2 & 3 \\ 4 & 5 & 6 \end{bmatrix}$$

Since this requires an index for both the column and the row, you need to
use a two-dimensional array. Suppose a variable called `matrix` contains this
array. The first index represents the column and the next index represents
the row. The array `matrix` should return

```
>(aref matrix 0 0)
1

>(aref matrix 0 1)
2

>(aref matrix 0 2)
3

>(areaf matrix 1 0)
4

>(aref matrix 1 1)
5

>(aref matrix 1 2)
6
```

The function called `make-array` is used to make a new array. `make-array`
takes one required parameter and some keyword parameters. The first
argument is a list of numbers each of which is 1 more than the maximum
index for its corresponding dimension. This first argument is called the
dimension list of the array. The dimension list of the example `days` is
(7) and the dimension list of the example `matrix` is (2 3). The length of
this list is the rank of the array. For example,

```
>(setq days (make-array '(7)))
```

makes a new array whose dimension list is (7) and assigns this array to
`days`. Since (7) is a one dimensional array, 7 can be used instead of (7).
So, you could have typed

```
>(setq days (make-array 7))
```

Next,

```
>(setq matrix (make-array '(2 3)))
```

constructs an array whose dimension list is (2 3) and assigns it to matrix.

The initial value of each element in an array made by make-array is not usually determined. If you want to specify an initial value, you should use the keyword parameter :initial-element. By typing

```
>(setq days (make-array 7
                :initial-element 'sun))
```

all the elements of the array are initialized to sun, therefore every day is sunday.

To change the value of an element of an array, you can use a combination of setf and aref. For example, by typing

```
>(setf (aref days 1) 'mon)
```

the element of days whose index is 1 becomes mon. For matrix,

```
>(setf (aref matrix 1 2) 6)
```

As an example, let us define a function called matrix-times which returns the product of two matrices a and b each of which is represented using a two-dimensional array whose dimensions are (n n) where n is a non-negative integer.

```
(defun matrix-times (n a b
          &aux (c (make-array (list n n))))
   (dotimes (i n c)
      (dotimes (j n)
         (let ((s 0))
            (dotimes (k n)
               (incf s (* (aref a i k)
                          (aref b k j))))
            (setf (aref c i j) s)))))
```

A one-dimensional array is sometimes called a **vector**. The array days is a vector. A vector can be input by typing

```
#( ⟨⟨element₁⟩⟩ . . . ⟨⟨elementₙ⟩⟩ )
```

When the system reads this expression, it makes a new vector where $\langle\langle element_1 \rangle\rangle \ldots \langle\langle element_n \rangle\rangle$ are the elements of the vector whose indexes are $0 \ldots (n-1)$, respectively. The same expression is used when this vector is printed. For example, to create a vector called **days**

```
>(setq days #(sun mon tue wed thu fri sat))
#(sun mon tue wed thu fri sat)
```

An array of other than one-dimension is input as

$\#\langle\langle dimension \rangle\rangle$ **a** $\langle\langle content\ of\ the\ array \rangle\rangle$

The small **a** can be a capital **A**. The same expression is used when printing an array. For example, to create the previously-mentioned **matrix**

```
>(setq matrix #2a((1 2 3) (4 5 6)))
#2A((1 2 3) (4 5 6))
```

To get the product of the matrices

$$\begin{bmatrix} 1 & 1 \\ 0 & 1 \end{bmatrix} \times \begin{bmatrix} 1 & 2 \\ 3 & 4 \end{bmatrix} = \begin{bmatrix} 4 & 6 \\ 3 & 4 \end{bmatrix}$$

using **matrix-times**, you could type

```
>(matrix-times 2 #2a((1 1) (0 1))
                 #2a((1 2) (3 4)))
#2A((4 6) (3 4))
```

To find the rank and the dimension list of an array, you use **array-rank** and **array-dimensions**

```
>(array-rank days)
1

>(array-dimensions days)
(7)

>(array-rank matrix)
2

>(array-dimensions matrix)
(2 3)
```

In order to check whether a data object is an array or not, you use the system predicate **arrayp**. This will return **t** if its argument is an array and **nil** if not. To check whether a data object is a vector or not, you use **vectorp**. Since a vector is a kind of an array, if the value of **vectorp** is **t**, the value of **arrayp** will be **t**.

Some arrays limit the kinds of data that can be used as their elements. An array made of only integers is one of them. In such a case, you specify the type of data that can be used as elements by adding a keyword parameter called :**element-type** to **make-array**. Specifications using this keyword parameter do not always work and when it does not work, the system makes an array which contains general elements. Which specifications will work depends on each system.

Vectors can be considered to be a sequence of data just like a list. Sometimes vectors and lists are grouped together and called **sequences**. Some of the functions to be used for list processing can take a vector as the argument. These include the following functions:

```
length      reverse       nreverse
remove      remove-if     remove-if-not
delete      delete-if     delete-if-not
```

For example,

```
>(length #(a b c d))
4

>(reverse #(a b c d))
#(d c b a)

>(remove 2 #(1 2 3 2 5))
#(1 3 5)
```

Let us look at three new functions which can be used for both lists and vectors: **copy-seq**, **subseq**, and **concatenate**. **copy-seq** takes a sequence and makes a new sequence which contains the same elements. In other words, it makes a copy of the initial sequence.

```
>(setq x '(1 2 3) y #(a b c))
#(a b c)

>(setq x1 (copy-seq x))
(1 2 3)

>(setq y1 (copy-seq y))
#(a b c)
```

After this, x and x1 and y and y1 are equal in the equal sense but not
equal in the eq sense.

concatenate takes some sequences and makes a new sequence that
lists all the elements of its arguments one by one. The first argument of
concatenate can specify whether to make a list or a vector.

```
>(concatenate 'list '(1 2 3) #(a b c))
(1 2 3 a b c)

>(concatenate 'vector '(1 2 3) #(a b c))
#(1 2 3 a b c)
```

As you can see, concatenate can be used to exchange a list and a vector.
It is easy to add or delete elements from a list, but it is not efficient to refer
elements in the list since you need to refer them through cells. It is easy to
refer elements in a vector, but it is not easy to add or delete elements of the
vector. You can increase the efficiency of your programs by representing
data as a list when you add or delete elements and by changing them using
concatenate to a vector when you need to refer to the elements.

subseq makes a new sequence from a part of the initial sequence. The
first argument to subseq is the original sequence. The second argument
specifies the first index of the elements to be extracted and the third argument specifies the last index.

```
>(subseq '(a b c d e f) 2 4)
(c d)

>(subseq #(a b c d e f) 0 3)
#(a b c)
```

The third argument is optional and the default value is the length of the
sequence, i.e., you can extract all of the elements that appear after the
index specified by the second argument.

10-3 Characters and Strings

A **character** is the character data used by the computer. A Character
data object is written as

#\⟨⟨character⟩⟩

For example, lower case "a" is written as

    #\a

and upper case "A" is written as

    #\A

If you type

    >(setq x #\a)
    #\a

the system will assign the character object a to x. A character object evaluates to the character itself, so it does not require a quotation mark.

The collection of available characters, i.e., the character set, is different for each system and we cannot say which characters exactly can be used. We will use ASCII (American Standard Code for Information Interchange) characters in this book.

Special characters such as empty space or line feed are expressed as

    #\⟨⟨special character⟩⟩

Every Common Lisp system initially defines the following as ⟨⟨special characters⟩⟩:

Space	empty space
Tab	tab
Backspace	backspace
Rubout	rubout
Return	carriage return
Linefeed	linefeed
Page	new page
Newline	new line

Some systems define additional special characters. Depending on the system the Newline character representing the printing of a new line could actually be the same character as either Return or Linefeed.

A predicate called characterp will check if a data object is a character or not. eql is more appropriate to compare characters than eq just like when comparing numbers. The function called char= with n arguments returns t when all n characters are equal. In this case all the arguments need to be characters. The following are the predicates for the character data.

(alpha-char-p ⟨⟨character⟩⟩)   alphabetic or not
(upper-case-p ⟨⟨character⟩⟩)   upper case or not
(lower-case-p ⟨⟨character⟩⟩)   lower case or not
(digit-char-p ⟨⟨character⟩⟩)   digit or not
(alphanumericp ⟨⟨character⟩⟩)   alphabetic or digit

(char/= ⟨⟨character$_1$⟩⟩ ... ⟨⟨character$_n$⟩⟩)
            all characters are not equal
(char< ⟨⟨character$_1$⟩⟩ ... ⟨⟨character$_n$⟩⟩)
            whether or not ⟨⟨character$_1$⟩⟩ $<$ ... $<$ ⟨⟨character$_n$⟩⟩
(char> ⟨⟨character$_1$⟩⟩ ... ⟨⟨character$_n$⟩⟩)
            whether or not ⟨⟨character$_1$⟩⟩ $>$ ... $>$ ⟨⟨character$_n$⟩⟩
(char<= ⟨⟨character$_1$⟩⟩ ... ⟨⟨character$_n$⟩⟩)
            whether or not ⟨⟨character$_1$⟩⟩ $\leq$ ... $\leq$ ⟨⟨character$_n$⟩⟩
(char>= ⟨⟨character$_1$⟩⟩ ... ⟨⟨character$_n$⟩⟩)
            whether or not ⟨⟨character$_1$⟩⟩ $\geq$ ... $\geq$ ⟨⟨character$_n$⟩⟩

Almost all Common Lisp systems including KCL decide if one character is
"bigger" than another based on the details of the implementation of the
character codes for the system. This makes it possible that the order of
characters might be different in different versions of Common Lisp. However, at least the following order is true on every system.

$$\#\backslash A < \#\backslash B < ... < \#\backslash Y < \#\backslash Z$$
$$\#\backslash a < \#\backslash b < ... < \#\backslash y < \#\backslash z$$
$$\#\backslash 0 < \#\backslash 1 < ... < \#\backslash 8 < \#\backslash 9$$

The functions called **char-code** and **code-char** change character data to
number code and number code to character data, respectively. For example, on a system using ASCII,

```
>(char-code #\a)
97

>(code-char 97)
#\a
```

The exchange between upper case and lower case is done using **char-upcase** and **char-downcase**. **char-upcase** changes lower case letters to
upper case and keeps upper case as upper case. **char-downcase** changes
uppercase letters to lower case and keeps lower case as lower case.

A **string** is a one-dimensional array whose elements are limited to character data. That is, it is a vector of characters. Precisely speaking, the elements of a string should be data objects of a type called **string-char**. Ordinary character data objects are of type **string-char**. Some systems can handle character data objects other than **string-char** and some systems cannot. Here, to make it simple, we assume a string is a vector of character data.

Since a string is a vector, it can be made using **make-array**. For example,

```
>(setq x (make-array 10
            :element-type 'string-char
            :initial-element #\a))
"aaaaaaaaaa"
```

makes a string out of ten instances of #\a and assigns this string to x. You can also create this string using **make-string**, but this can only be used for making strings.

```
>(setq x (make-string 10
            :initial-element #\a))
"aaaaaaaaaa"
```

Another way to type a string is to directly specify the elements.

```
>(setq x "aaaaaaaaaa")
"aaaaaaaaaa"
```

Since a string is a vector, a string can be referenced or changed using **aref** as well as **char** which can only be used for strings.

```
>(char x 3)
#\a

>(setf (char x 3) #\A)
#\A

>x
"aaaAaaaaaa"
```

You can input or output a string by putting double quotes "" around the string. If double quote is a character that needs to appear in the string, you should type "\"" and if "\" needs to appear, you should type "\\".

```
>(aref "a\"b" 1)
#\"

>(aref "a\\b" 1)
#\\
```

The system compares each character of a string when **equal** is called.

```
>(eql "abc" "abc")
nil

>(equal "abc" "abc")
t
```

You can use **string=** instead of **equal**. **string=** takes two arguments both of which should be strings. The following are other predicates for comparing strings

(**string/=** $\langle\!\langle string_1 \rangle\!\rangle \langle\!\langle string_2 \rangle\!\rangle$)	$\langle\!\langle string_1 \rangle\!\rangle \neq \langle\!\langle string_2 \rangle\!\rangle$
(**string<** $\langle\!\langle string_1 \rangle\!\rangle \langle\!\langle string_2 \rangle\!\rangle$)	$\langle\!\langle string_1 \rangle\!\rangle < \langle\!\langle string_2 \rangle\!\rangle$
(**string>** $\langle\!\langle string_1 \rangle\!\rangle \langle\!\langle string_2 \rangle\!\rangle$)	$\langle\!\langle string_1 \rangle\!\rangle > \langle\!\langle string_2 \rangle\!\rangle$
(**string<=** $\langle\!\langle string_1 \rangle\!\rangle \langle\!\langle string_2 \rangle\!\rangle$)	$\langle\!\langle string_1 \rangle\!\rangle \leq \langle\!\langle string_2 \rangle\!\rangle$
(**string>=** $\langle\!\langle string_1 \rangle\!\rangle \langle\!\langle string_2 \rangle\!\rangle$)	$\langle\!\langle string_1 \rangle\!\rangle \geq \langle\!\langle string_2 \rangle\!\rangle$

The fact that one string is bigger or smaller than another string is decided by **lexicographic order**. The system compares characters one by one from left to right in the two strings. If the system finds two unequal characters, it decides which string is smaller by comparing which character is smaller in the **char<** sense. If there are no unequal characters, the system decides that the shorter string is smaller. For example,

$$\text{"ab"} < \text{"abc"} < \text{"abd"} < \text{"ac"} < \text{"b"}$$

The above five predicates return **nil** if the condition of the predicate is not true. If the condition is true, they return the value which indicates where the difference occurs in the two strings, instead of **t**.

```
>(string/= "abc" "abc")
nil

>(string/= "abc" "abd")
2
```

The predicate called **stringp** is used to check whether a data object is a string or not. If it is a string, **stringp** returns **t**. It not, it returns **nil**.

Since a string is a kind of array and a kind of vector, if the value of `stringp` is t on a data object, the value of `arrayp` and `vectorp` will also be t.

There are several functions for exchanging upper case and lower case of characters in a string. `string-upcase` changes lower case to upper case and `string-downcase` changes upper case to lower case.

```
>(string-upcase "This is a pen.")
"THIS IS A PEN."

>(string-downcase "This is a pen.")
"this is a pen."
```

These two functions do not change the existing string, but rather they make new strings. `nstring-upcase` and `nstring-downcase` change the string directly.

Since a string is a kind of vector, the functions used for the sequences, which we talked about in the previous section, can be used for strings.

```
>(length "abcd")
4

>(reverse "abcd")
"dcba"

>(remove #\Space "This is a pen.")
"Thisisapen."

>(subseq "abcdef" 2 4)
"cd"

>(subseq "abcdef" 2)
"cdef"
```

If you want the result of `concatenate` to be a string, you can use `string` as the first argument to `concatenate`. In this case, the elements should all be character data.

```
>(concatenate 'list "ab" '(1 2) #(x y))
(#\a #\b 1 2 x y)

>(concatenate 'string "abc" "def")
"abcdef"
```

```
>(concatenate 'string "ab" '(#\c #\d) #(#\e #\f))
"abcdef"
```

You should notice that a and b in the following expression

```
>(concatenate 'string '(a b))
```

are symbols, not character data, and you will get an error message.

10-4 Structures

A **structure**, like an array, is a collection of data. The difference between a structure and an array is how you refer to its contents. In the case of a structure the system refers to an element using the name of that part of the structure, while in the case of an array it uses the index (an integer) to access an element of an array. In order to use a structure, you need to declare the structure and give names to each part of the structure. Each part of a structure is called a **field**. To define structures with different fields, it is necessary for each structure to have a structure name for specifying what kind of structure it is. You can declare a structure using the macro called **defstruct** which specifies the structure name and the names of its fields.

```
(defstruct ⟨⟨structure name⟩⟩
   ⟨⟨field₁⟩⟩
      . . .
   ⟨⟨fieldₙ⟩⟩ )
```

Suppose we define a structure called **student** which is made of four fields, **department**, **grade**, **name**, and **sex**. To do this, we use the following defstruct expression.

```
>(defstruct student
    department
    grade
    name
    sex)
student
```

After this **defstruct** command, the following things happen. First, the system defines four **access functions**:

```
student-department
student-grade
student-name
student-sex
```

in order to access the four fields of the structure called **student**. Each access function takes a structure of this type as an argument and returns the value of the field corresponding to this accessor. Then, the system defines the function called

```
make-student
```

in order to create a new data object of the type of structure called **student**. This function takes the following keyword parameters:

```
:department
:grade
:name
:sex
```

which correspond to each field. For example, by typing

```
>(setq x (make-student
    :department 'computer-science
    :grade 3
    :name 'hagiya
    :sex 'male))
```

the system will initialize each field using the specified value and make a new data object which is a structure of the type called **student**. Therefore, after this operation, you can type

```
>(student-department x)
computer-science

>(student-name x)
hagiya
```

make-student is called the **constructor** for the **student** structure. The value of each field can be changed by using a combination of **setf** and the access function. For example,

```
>(setf (student-department x)
       'literature)
```

The field called **department** of x will become the symbol **literature**.

To check whether a data object is a structure of a particular type or not, use the system function called **typep** with the data to be checked and the structure name as the argument. If the data object is a structure of the specified type, **typep** will return **t**, if not, it will return **nil**.

```
>(typep x 'student)
t

>(typep 100 'student)
nil
```

As you can see from the above example, a constructor takes the name of the structure type and adds "**make-**" in front of it as in

    make-⟨⟨structure name⟩⟩

and each access function will be called

    ⟨⟨structure name⟩⟩-⟨⟨field⟩⟩

The value of a field where its initial value is not specified is **nil**. If you want to give the field a default value other than **nil**, change ⟨⟨field⟩⟩ in **defstruct** to

    (⟨⟨field⟩⟩   ⟨⟨expression⟩⟩)

For example, after you type

```
(defstruct student
  department
  (grade 100)
  name
  male)
```

if you do not specify the parameter called :**grade** to the constructor, 100 will be used as the default value. ⟨⟨expression⟩⟩ is evaluated every time the constructor is called. So,

```
>(defvar *student-id* 0)
*student-id*
```

```
>(defstruct student
   department
   (grade '100)
   name
   sex
   (id (incf *student-id*)))
student
```

The value of the global variable *student-id* is incremented by 1 each time a new structure of type **student** is made.

A structure is input in the following way:

#s(〈〈structure name〉〉
            〈〈field〉〉   〈〈value〉〉
                  . . .
            〈〈field〉〉   〈〈value〉〉)

where "s" can be "S".

Instead of calling the constructor

```
>(setq x (make-student
              :department 'computer-science
              :grade 3
              :name 'hagiya
              :sex 'male))
```

you can also input the data directly

```
>(setq x #s(student
              department computer-science
              grade 3
              name hagiya
              sex male))
```

A structure will be output in the same format as it is input.

11   Input and Output

Since input and output are very important in the programming languages, some people say that a person who understands input and output will understand the language. Input and output are important because they are the only way of connecting a program to the outside world. On the other hand, because of the connection with the outside world, input and output are influenced most by the outside world and they take a complicated and non-standard form compared to other aspects of the programming language.

Common Lisp pays much attention to input and output and allows for detailed specifications of input and output. We cannot explain all of the details here, but we will explain the most essential part in making everyday programs in this chapter.

11-1   Streams

Terminals and files for keeping programs or data can be input and output. The data type called a **stream** connects these files or a terminal to the system. A stream is a channel for input and output. For example, if a stream is connected to a terminal and if you output to that stream, then characters and data are shown on the screen of that terminal. If you input from that stream, characters and data input from the keyboard are given to the program. If a stream is connected to a file and input and output are made to and from this stream, then it becomes input and output to and from the file. While the terminal and files which are connected to a stream exist outside of the program, a stream is a data object of Common Lisp and can be treated just like other data objects. In other words, a stream is a data object defined inside of Common Lisp which can input and output other data. It is also possible to write a program independent of hardware and the operating system by defining most of the input and output operation as input and output to a stream. In such a case, when you actually want to use the stream you need to connect it to a terminal or a file using the method explained below.

Unlike symbols or lists, you cannot type an expression directly to the system that is a stream data object. A stream is printed as

```
#<...>
```

A concrete example is

```
#<input stream from "foo.lsp">
```

which cannot be input by simply typing.

Every Common Lisp system comes with some predefined streams. Two of these are **standard output** and **standard input**. If you omit the arguments which name a stream in an output function, the system will use the standard output as the stream. If you omit the arguments which name a stream in an input function, the system will use the standard input for the stream. Standard output is usually a stream which is connected to a terminal, however, it is stored as the value of a variable called *standard-output*, so, if you change the value of *standard-output* to another stream, you can change where standard output goes.

The value of the variable *standard-input* is set to the standard input which usually is the stream from your terminal. If you want to input to or output from your terminal, you can use a stream called **terminal I/O**. Terminal I/O is the value of a variable called *terminal-io*. Even if the standard output or the standard input is changed, you can still do inputting and outputting to the terminal using *terminal-io*. Terminal I/O is a stream which can do both input and output.

Streams are broadly divided into

- streams for files (input, output, and I/O)
- streams for devices (input, output, and I/O)
- streams to a string (output)
- streams from a string (input)
- two-way streams (I/O)

- echo streams (I/O)
- concatenate streams (input)
- broadcast streams (output)

Each stream can do either only input, only output, or both input and output.

11-2 Outputting Data

The most basic function for outputting data is **write**. The output functions such as **print**, **princ**, and **print1** which are often used can all be replaced by **write**. **write** takes the data to be output as a required parameter and also takes eleven keyword-parameters in order to control the method of output. The eleven keyword-parameters are:

:stream	(the stream to use for output)
:escape	(can be re-input or not)
:radix	(can output number base or not)
:base	(number base for output)
:circle	(consider circular list or not)
:pretty	(do pretty-printing or not)
:level	(limit of the depth)
:length	(limit of the length)
:case	(upper case or lower case)
:gensym	(output #: or not)
:array	(can output an array or not)

The value of **write** is the data for output which is passed as its first argument. Let's look at these keyword-parameters more closely.

The keyword :**stream** specifies the stream to use for output. If you do not specify :**stream** or specify **nil**, the system takes the standard output (the value of *standard-output*) as the default. If you specify **t** as the :**stream**, the system takes the terminal I/O (the value of *terminal-io*). You should specify a stream for :**stream** if you do not specify **nil** or **t**.

:**escape** specifies whether the output is to be printed in a form which can be re-input or not. This specification influences the way a symbol or a string is output. If you specify anything other than **nil** for :**escape**, the system prints objects in a way that it can be re-input. For example, a symbol whose print name is **"123"** is output as

The string made of #\1, #\2, and #\3 is output as

    "123"

If you specify nil for :escape, both |123| and "123" will be output as

    123

If you were to re-input this, you would get the number 123. When :escape
is nil, the system will not output the package name of a symbol even when
necessary. :escape has the same effect with respect to lists of symbols or
strings.

In this book, we have always output things as if :escape is not nil
unless it is explicitly specified as nil.

If you do not specify :escape in write, the system uses the value of the
variable *print-escape* as the default value of :escape. Each parameter
of write will take the value of the variable which appears below in the
definition as its default. write is defined as

```
(defun write (x &key
                   (stream nil)
                   (escape *print-escape*)
                   (radix *print-radix*)
                   (base *print-base*)
                   (circle *print-circle*)
                   (pretty *print-pretty*)
                   (level *print-level*)
                   (length *print-length*)
                   (case *print-case*)
                   (gensym *print-gensym*)
                   (array *print-array*))
  (cond ((null stream)
         (setq stream *standard-output*))
        ((eq stream t)
         (setq stream *terminal-io*)))
  ...)
```

You can use the function called princ instead of using nil as the :escape
parameter. princ is defined as

```
(defun princ (x &optional (stream nil))
   (write x :stream stream :escape nil))
```

You can also use prin1 instead of using t. prin1 is defined as

```
(defun prin1 (x &optional (stream nil))
  (write x :stream stream :escape t))
```

A function called print can also be used. print is defined as

```
(defun print (x &optional (stream nil))
  (terpri stream)
  (write x :stream stream :escape t))
```

terpri is a function which outputs a line break. terpri takes a stream as the argument. If it does not have the argument or it has nil as an argument, it outputs to the standard output. If the argument is t, it outputs to the terminal I/O. While terpri always outputs a line break, the function called fresh-line outputs a line break only when the current line of the specified stream is not an empty line. If the line of the stream is an empty line, fresh-line does not do anything.

: base specifies the number base of the output, i.e., in what base integers and ratios are printed. : base should be more than 2 and less than 36. : radix specifies whether to show the number base in the output or not. When the number base is output, i.e., when radix is not nil, the output looks like

#⟨⟨number base⟩⟩r⟨⟨number⟩⟩

(The number base itself is always output using the decimal system.) For example, the number 123 will look like the following when :radix is not nil and :base is 3.

#3r11120

When :radix is nil and :base is 3, the output will be

11120

The notation for the binary scale, the octal scale, the hexadecimal scale are expressed as #b, #o, and #x instead of #2r, #8r, #16r. Suppose :radix is not nil. 123 will be expressed as the following when :base is 2, 8, and 16, respectively.

```
#b1111011
#o173
#x7B
```

When :radix is not nil and :base is 10, the output would not be #10r123 but would simply print

        123.

The "." at the end indicates the decimal system. 123. is an integer, not a floating-point number, since a floating-point number would be printed with one or more decimal places after the ".". :radix and :base do not effect the output of floating-point numbers which are always output using the decimal system.

:circle specifies whether to consider **circular list**s when printing. For example,

        >(setq x '(a b c))
        (a b c)

        >(nconc x x)

makes the following circular list.

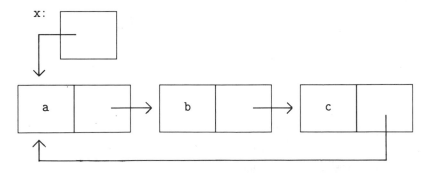

If :circle is nil, the system will not recognize the circularity in this list and (nconc x x) will print

        (a b c a b c a b c a b c ...

infinitely. If we print the left most cell of (nconc x x) as "???", then (nconc x x) can be rewritten as

        (a b c . ???)

Since ??? represents the whole list, we will get

```
???=(a b c . ???)
```

When :circle is not nil, the system will use a label which looks like #n# (where n is non-negative integer) instead of ???.

```
#0=(a b c . #0#)
```

#0# is the reference to a label and #0= (not #0#) is the definition.

Let's look at another example. If *print-circle* is not nil, the system recognizes a circular list and outputs

```
>(setq x '(a))
(a)

>(rplacd x x)
#0=(a . #0#)

>(setq y '(b))
(b)

>(rplacd y y)
#0=(b . #0#)

>(setq x (list x y))
(#0=(a . #0#) #1=(b . #1#))

>(nconc x x)
#0=(#1=(a . #1#) #2=(b . #2#) . #0#)
```

As you can see, the label is relative to each output. If circle is not nil and the same cell appears in the list more than once, the system will make a label for the cell even if there is no circular list. For example,

```
>(setq x '(a b c))
(a b c)

>(list x x x)
(#0=(a b c) #0# #0#)
```

:pretty specifies whether to use **pretty-print**, i.e., to use empty space or carriage return in places which make a list easy to look at. If :pretty is not nil, the system uses pretty printing. Instead of specifying :pretty not to be nil, you can use the function called pprint, which is defined as

```
(defun pprint (x &optional (stream nil))
   (terpri stream)
   (write x :stream stream
             :escape t
             :pretty t)
   (values))
```

:level and :length are used to specify the depth and the length of the output of a list. When :level or :length are nil, there is no limit for the depth or the length. To prevent a circular list from being printed infinitely, you can specify level or length rather than setting :circle to something other than nil. For example, if *print-length* is 5

```
>(setq x '(a b c))
(a b c)

>(nconc x x)
(a b c a b ...)
```

As you can see, the list whose length is longer than 5 is printed as "...". The list whose depth is deeper than what is specified is printed as "#". The list

```
(a (b c) (d (e f) (g (h i) j) k) l)
```

will be expressed as the following if :level is 2 and :length is nil,

```
(a (b c) (d # # k) l)
```

If :level is nil and :length is 3,

```
(a (b c) (d (e f) (g (h i) j) ...) ...)
```

If :level is 2 and :length is 3

```
(a (b c) (d # # ...) ...)
```

:case specifies whether to output symbols in upper case. As we said in Chapter 4, when you input symbols, the system automatically changes lower case letters to upper case letters. When the system prints symbols, you can specify whether the system should output in upper case or in lower case. The value of :case should be either :upcase, :downcase, or :capitalize. :upcase means to use upper case letters in the print name, :downcase means use lower case letters, and :capitalize means to use the upper case only for the first character. For example, the symbol this-is-a-symbol whose print name is "THIS-IS-A-SYMBOL" is output with :upcase, :downcase, and :capitalize as

```
THIS-IS-A-SYMBOL
this-is-a-symbol
This-Is-A-Symbol
```

:gensym specifies whether to output symbols without a home-package (for example, symbols created by a function gensym) as

#: ⟪symbol name⟫

or simply

⟪symbol name⟫

If :gensym is not nil, it will be printed as

#: ⟪symbol name⟫

:array specifies whether to output the content of an array. If :array is not nil, the system will output the contents. If :array is nil, the system will print only the information that the system tried to output an array. This could look like

```
#<an array>
```

for an array and the same for a vector. A string will not be affected by the value of :array. Even if the value of :array is nil, the system will print the character array "abc" as

```
"abc"
```

Sometimes output by write or some other functions are kept in a buffer in the system without being written on the file or on the terminal. If you type

(finish-output ⟪stream⟫)

you will force the system to write the content of this buffer to the file or on the terminal. If you omit the argument to `finish-output` or if you specify `nil`, the system assumes the standard output. If you specify `t`, it assumes the terminal I/O.

We described the variables which give the default value the keyword parameter of `write`. Changing the value of one of these variables makes a difference in how the system displays data objects. If you want the system to output integers using the octal system, you can set the value of `*print-base*` to 8.

```
>*print-base*
10

>(expt 10 3)
1000

>(setq *print-base* 8)
10

>(expt 10 3)
1750
```

The value of this assignment expression is, of course, 8. The system prints "10" in octal system on the terminal rather than 8. By the time the printing is to be done, the system already knows that the value of `*print-base*` is 8.

11-3 Inputting Data

To input data you use the function called `read`. `read` takes several optional parameters and the first optional parameter is the stream for inputting. If you omit this parameter or specify `nil`, the system uses the standard input. If you specify `t`, it uses the terminal I/O. So, if you type

```
(read)
```

the system reads one data object from the standard input and returns this as the value of `read`. We will describe the other parameters later. When the system reads a form, it uses this version of `read` without arguments. This means that if you change the standard input, you can input a form from a file.

The input of data is controlled by the value of some variables, one of which is *read-base*. *read-base* is used for specifying the number base of integers and ratios when they are input. For example, if the value of *read-base* is 8

    123

will be read as 83 (in the decimal system). When you specify a number base which is bigger than 10, you should be careful. You can input numbers in the following form which is the same as for output.

    #⟨⟨number base⟩⟩r⟨⟨number⟩⟩

The number base should be more than 2 and less than 36. You can use #b, #o, #x for #2r, #8r, and #16r (the r, b, o, and x can also be R, B, O, X). Therefore, no matter what the value of *read-base* is, you will get

    >#xabc
    2748

(assuming *print-base* is 10). You can also use ABC instead of abc. If you put "." at the end of an integer, the data is always input in decimal system. For example,

    >(setq *read-base* 8)
    8

    >100.
    100

As you can see, setting *read-base* does not affect the output.

A variable called *readtable* which controls the input will be explained in Section 7 in this chapter.

Finding the end of a stream sometimes causes problems. The stream which is connected to your terminal usually does not have an end, but a stream from a file ends with an end-of-file. When you try to input beyond an end-of-stream, you will get an error message. If you want to find the end-of-stream without getting an error message, you should type

    (read ⟨⟨stream⟩⟩ nil ⟨⟨final value⟩⟩)

instead of

    (read ⟨⟨stream⟩⟩)

When you try to input beyond the end-of-stream, the system returns the value of ⟨⟨final value⟩⟩ as the value of **read** without giving an error message. (the second argument to **read** specifies whether to print the error message and its default value is **t**.) If you specify a value which will never be read as ⟨⟨final value⟩⟩, you can find the end-of-stream. One thing that is often used is

```
(setq eos (cons nil nil))
(read stream nil eos)
```

which uses a cons as its ⟨⟨final value⟩⟩. Since ⟨⟨read⟩⟩ will always use a new cell each time a list is input, a cons which is the same as **eos** will never be read. The following program lets the system read data and evaluate it until the end-of-stream is encountered.

```
(do* ((eos (cons nil nil))
      (x (read stream nil eos)
         (read stream nil eos)))
     ((eq x eos))
  (eval x))
```

Another problem in inputting is to find out how much of a stream has been read while inputting. For example, suppose the content of a stream looks like

```
_ _abc_de(fgh_ijkl)_mn_ _o
```

Here we are using "_" to show empty space. Suppose no input has been done on this stream. At this point, the pointer for displaying the next character sits at the beginning of the stream. We use "↑" to show this pointer and place it under the content of the stream.

```
_ _abc_de(fgh_ijkl)_mn_ _o
↑
```

When the system does a **read** to this stream once, the pointer skips two empty spaces and stops at **a**.

```
_ _abc_de(fgh_ _ijkl)_mn_ _o
  ↑
```

The system reads the symbol **abc** and returns it as the value of **read**. In order to acknowledge the end of the symbol **abc**, the pointer has to read the next empty space. So, actually when abc is read using read, the pointer sits here

```
_ _abc _de(fgh _ijkl) _mn _ _o
      ↑
```

In other words, the empty space after c is skipped without being read. When you type read for the second time, the "(" which is next to the e will not be skipped and pointer will sit at the "(".

```
_ _abc _de(fgh _ijkl) _mn _ _o
          ↑
```

If you type read for the third time, the system reads the list (fgh ijkl). Since the system notices the end of the list by reading the ")", the pointer sits here

```
_ _abc _de(fgh _ijkl) _mn _ _o
              ↑
```

Next, read reads mn and the pointer skips one empty space and sits here

```
_ _abc _de(fgh _ijkl) _mn _ _o
                        ↑
```

When the symbol is terminated by a tab or a line feed instead of empty space, the same thing happens.

The above description may sound too detailed for some readers, but it is important to remember this when inputting characters. If you do not want the system to skip empty space next to a symbol or a number, you should use a function called read-preserving-whitespace which works exactly in the same way as read except not skipping the empty space next to a symbol or a number.

11-4 Input and Output of Characters

In order to output characters, you can call write by setting :escape to nil or by using princ. However, there is a function called write-char made specially for outputting characters. The first argument of write-char should be a character data object and the second argument is a stream.

The second argument can be omitted. If you specify **nil** for the second argument or omit the argument, the system assumes the standard output. If you specify **t**, it assumes the terminal I/O.

To input characters, use the function called **read-char**. The arguments to **read-char** are the same as the ones for **read**. The way to find the end of a stream is also the same as in **read**. **read-char** reads one character from a stream and returns it as a character data object. The pointer in the stream proceeds only one character at a time.

When the system is reading characters from a stream, you can undo the fact that the system reads the last character using the function **unread-char**. For example, suppose the pointer sits in the following stream

```
_ _abc_de(fgh_ijkl)_mn_ _o
       ↑
```

When you call the function **read-char**, the system returns the character #\d and the pointer moves forward one place

```
_ _abc_de(fgh_ijkl)_mn_ _o
      ↑
```

If you type

```
(unread-char #\d stream)
```

the system cancels the fact that it read #\d and the pointer is moved back to

```
_ _abc_de(fgh_ijkl)_mn_ _o
       ↑
```

If you call **read** now, the system returns

```
de
```

You cannot call **unread-char** more than once in a row. If you type

```
(unread-char #\Space stream)
```

following **unread-char** in the above example, the pointer will not move. Another function called **peek-char** is a combination of **read-char** and **unread-char**. This function is used to input characters without moving the pointer. **peek-char** can take an argument called **peek-type** in front of

its argument. peek-type is optional and can be omitted. The default value
of peek-type is nil. In this case the system returns the next character in
the stream without moving the pointer. When peek-type is not nil, the
system moves the pointer forward over empty space, tab, or line feed, to
the first character it finds and returns this character. If there is no empty
space, tab, or line feed, the system returns the next character without
moving the pointer. An expression with peek-type nil, for example,

```
(peek-char nil stream)
```

does exactly the same thing as

```
(let ((char (read-char stream)))
  (unread-char char stream)
  char)
```

11-5 The File System

In this section we talk about the way to connect files to streams. Interaction
with the file system is not standardized in programming languages. Each
operating system has a different file system, especially the structure of file
names. Common Lisp has a data type called **pathname** for dealing with
files independent of the operating system, but we will not use pathnames
since the functions and macros explained in this section do not require
pathnames and can use character strings to express file names.

To get a stream for a file from the file name you use the function called
open. open takes the file name as the argument. When you type

```
>(setq stream (open "foo.lsp"))
```

the system assigns the input stream connecting to the file foo.lsp to the
variable called stream. If the specified file does not exist, you will get an
error message. The pointer of the stream is set at the beginning of the file.
If you call read or read-char for this stream, characters will be input from
the beginning of the file. open takes some keyword parameters in addition
to the file name. If you do not specify any more information the system
returns an input stream as in the above example. If you want to use an
output stream, you should set the value of the keyword parameter called
:direction to the keyword :output (the default value of :direction is
:input). For example, if you type

```
(setq another-stream
  (open "bar.lsp" :direction :output))
```

you will get an output stream for the file called `bar.lsp`. If the file `bar.lsp` does not exist, the system makes a new file called `bar.lsp`. If such a file exists, the initial content of the file will be lost. If you do not want the initial contents of the file with the same name to disappear, you can type

```
(setq another-stream
   (open "bar.lsp" :direction :output
                   :if-exists :append))
```

In this case output will be added to the end of the existing file.

When you finish inputting or outputting to a file, you close the file using the function `close` on the stream connected to this file. For example,

```
(close another-stream)
```

Many people forget to type `close`. Also when a program ends because of an error, it may be impossible to call `close`. To prevent this, it is better to use a macro called `with-open-file` when you want to use a file.

```
(with-open-file ( 《variable》 《file name》
                              《option》...《option》 )
       《expression》...《expression》 )
```

is equivalent to

```
(let (( 《variable》 (open 《file name》
                          《option》...《option》 )))
      (unwind-protect
         (progn 《expression》...《expression》 )
         (close 《variable》 )))
```

The system first opens the file with 《file name》 and binds the stream for this file to 《variable》. The system, then, evaluates each 《expression》 and closes the stream automatically. It evaluates each of 《file name》 and 《option》 ... 《option》. For example,

```
(with-open-file (stream "bar.lsp"
                         :direction :output)
      (dotimes (i 100)
         (print (fact i) stream)))
```

The system prints the factorial of 0 to 99 in the file bar.1sp. Since the system expands with-open-file to an expression including unwind-protect, the stream will be closed even if it jumps non-locally out of the with-open-file. The expression

```
(with-open-file (stream "foo.lsp")
  (do* ((eos (cons nil nil))
        (x (read stream nil eos)
           (read stream nil eos)))
       ((eq x eos))
    (eval x)))
```

causes the system to evaluate the expressions inside of foo.1sp one by one.

The following three system functions operate on files. probe-file is used to check whether a file exists or not.

```
(probe-file "bar.lsp")
```

If a file named bar.1sp exists, probe-file will return something other than nil. If not, it returns nil. delete-file is used to erase an already-existing file.

```
(delete-file "bar.lsp")
```

will erase the file called bar.1sp. If bar.1sp does not exist, the system may return an error message. For this reason it is better to check the existence of a file before trying to erase it.

```
(when (probe-file "bar.lsp")
  (delete-file "bar.lsp"))
```

rename-file is used to change the name of a file.

```
(rename-file "foo.lsp" "bar.lsp")
```

will change the name of foo.1sp to bar.1sp. The system may return an error message if a file called foo.1sp does not exist or a file called bar.1sp already exists. It is better to check the existence of the file using probe-file before using rename-file.

11-6 Input and Output to Strings

There are string-output-streams and string-input-streams. `with-input-from-string` is similar to `with-open-file`.

```
(with-input-from-string ( ⟨⟨variable⟩⟩ ⟨⟨string⟩⟩ )
    ⟨⟨expression₁⟩⟩ ... ⟨⟨expressionₙ⟩⟩ )
```

When the system is evaluating $\langle\langle expression_1 \rangle\rangle$ ... $\langle\langle expression_n \rangle\rangle$ it binds the string-input-stream constructed from ⟨⟨string⟩⟩ to ⟨⟨variable⟩⟩. You can think of a string-input-stream as an input-stream from a file whose content is the same as the string. ⟨⟨string⟩⟩ is evaluated. For example, in

```
(with-input-from-string
        (stream "(a b) (c d)")
    (setq x (read stream))
    (setq y (read stream)))
```

the system assigns (a b) to x and (c d) to y.

`with-output-to-string` is a macro for outputting to a string. `with-output-to-string` is also similar to `with-open-file`. During the evaluation of

```
(with-output-to-string ( ⟨⟨variable⟩⟩ )
    ⟨⟨expression₁⟩⟩ ... ⟨⟨expressionₙ⟩⟩ )
```

the system will make a string-output-stream, bind it to ⟨⟨variable⟩⟩, and then evaluate $\langle\langle expression_1 \rangle\rangle$ ... $\langle\langle expression_n \rangle\rangle$. It will put all the outputs into one string and return this string as the value of the `with-output-to-string` expression.

```
(with-output-to-string (stream)
    (dotimes (i 10) (prin1 i stream)
        (princ " " stream)))
```

The string returns

```
"0 1 2 3 4 5 6 7 8 9 "
```

`write-to-string` is a function which is a simplified version of `with-output-to-string`. This function takes more than one argument and returns the output of the first argument as a string. We can define `write-to-string` using `with-output-to-string` as follows:

```
(defun write-to-string (x &rest args)
  (with-output-to-string (stream)
    (apply #'write x :stream stream
           args)))
```

For example,

```
>(write-to-string (cons 'a 'b))
"(a . b)"
```

11-7 Read Macros

When **read** inputs data it uses a unified mechanism called read macros. Read macros are different from the macros explained in Chapter 7 and are the mechanism which associates the characters called **macro characters** to the input function which corresponds to such characters. For example, "(" is a macro character and associated with it is the input function for reading a list. A macro character influences the input in a simple way. When the system sees a macro character it calls the input function corresponding to that macro character. In other words, it leaves most of the analysis of the construction of Lisp objects to the input function corresponding to some macro character. A data structure called a **readtable** remembers a macro character and its corresponding input function. A readtable is a type of Lisp data and can be used in a program. If you change the readtable you can change the construction of Lisp objects easily.

The readtable which is used during input from a stream is stored in the variable `*readtable*`. Although the value of `*readtable*` can be overwritten with another readtable, here we will only talk about how to change the readtable stored in `*readtable*`.

The following characters are already registered in the readtable as the macro characters.

> "   #   '   (   )
>   ,   ;   '

The function corresponding to each of these macro characters can be obtained by using `get-macro-character`.

```
(get-macro-character 《character》 )
```

For example, if you type

```
>(get-macro-character #\')
```

the system returns the function corresponding to "'". This function changes
input from

'⟨⟨data⟩⟩

to

(quote ⟨⟨data⟩⟩)

The value of `get-macro-character` is a function data object. The function
`set-macro-character` is used to define a macro character. Its general
form is

(set-macro-character ⟨⟨character⟩⟩ ⟨⟨function⟩⟩)

For example,

```
>(set-macro-character #\!
   (get-macro-character #\'))
```

turns "!" into a macro character and the function that corresponds to "'"
will now correspond to "!". This means that you will get

```
>'!(a b)
(quote (a b))

>!(a b)
(a b)
```

The following expression is called when the macro character appears in the
input stream (with function corresponding to the macro character).

(funcall ⟨⟨function⟩⟩ ⟨⟨input stream⟩⟩ ⟨⟨macro character⟩⟩)

`read` puts the result of this `funcall` into the input. For example, suppose
we try to define "!" as a macro character which works the same as "'".
You need to arrange that after the system sees a "!", it should read one

data object, ⟨⟨data⟩⟩, from the input stream and return (quote ⟨⟨data⟩⟩).
This task can be done using the following function:

```
(lambda (stream char)
  (list 'quote (read stream)))
```

Therefore you should type

```
(set-macro-character #\!
  #'(lambda (stream char)
      (list 'quote (read stream)))))
```

You could use a lambda expression instead of the closure. Also the following
is acceptable:

```
(defun foo (stream char)
  (list 'quote (read stream)))

(set-macro-character #\! #'foo)
```

If the function does not return a value, read is considered to have received
no input. Using this fact, you can define the macro character ";" for
putting comments into the input stream. The definition of ";" looks like

```
(defun semicolon-reader (stream char)
  (do ((char (read-char stream)
             (read-char stream)))
      ((char= char #\Newline))
    (values)))

(set-macro-character #\;
  #'semicolon-reader)
```

11-8 The Sharp Sign Macro

In Common Lisp there are many expressions starting with a sharp sign
"#". For example,

```
#\a
```

means a character a.

```
#o123
```

is an integer in the octal system. Data which usually cannot be read is
printed in the following format:

```
#<...>
```

Packages and streams are such data.

An expression starting with a "#" is called a **sharp sign macro** and is
processed by the input function which corresponds to the macro character
"#". The general form of a sharp sign macro is

#⟪non negative integer⟫ ⟪character⟫ . . .

⟪non negative integer⟫ is always interpreted in the decimal system but
can be omitted. ⟪character⟫ signals the start of the processing for each
sharp sign macro. As you can see, a sharp sign macro becomes effective
by combining "#" and ⟪character⟫. Such a macro is called a **dispatching
macro** and "#" is called the dispatching character. A user can define a
dispatching macro, however, we will just summarize the sharp sign macro
here.

#\⟪character⟫   #\⟪special character name⟫
        input characters

#:⟪symbol name⟫
        make a new symbol with symbol name and return the symbol with-
        out registering it in any package.

#.⟪expression⟫
        the system evaluates the expressions following this when they are
        input and pretends the value was read.

#⟪number base⟫ r   #⟪number base⟫ R
#b   #B
#o   #O
#x   #X
        input an integer or a ratio in the appropriate number base

#| ··· |#
        comment. "···" can be anything

#n=   #n#
        n is non negative integer. Was output when :circle is other than
        nil and can be used as input.

#(...)
    input of a vector

#a   #A
    input an array other than a vector

#s   #S
    input a structure

11-9 Formatted Output

To do **formatted output**, that is, output which follows an appropriate
format, requires a function called `format`. The general call to `format` looks
like

   (format ⟨⟨stream⟩⟩ ⟨⟨format string⟩⟩ ⟨⟨argument₁⟩⟩ ... ⟨⟨argumentₙ⟩⟩)

⟨⟨stream⟩⟩ specifies the place to send the output. If this argument is `t` the
output will be printed on standard output. When it is `nil` the result of the
format output becomes a string and is returned as in `write-to-string`.
⟨⟨stream⟩⟩ should be a stream if it is not `t` or `nil`. ⟨⟨format string⟩⟩ is a
string which controls the formatted output. The system formats the output
of ⟨⟨argument₁⟩⟩ ... ⟨⟨argumentₙ⟩⟩ depending on the content of this string.
We will call these arguments "the arguments for the formatted output."

   You control the formatted output with the formatted string by inserting
format directives which start with "~" into the string. Characters other
than format directives are output on the output stream without being
changed. For example,

```
>(format nil "This is a format-string.")
"This is a format-string."
```

The format directives inside of a format string will consume the arguments
of the formatted output one by one. When a format directive consumes
one argument, the next format directive cannot consume this argument; it
has to use the next argument. We will explain the simple format directives.

~s   ~S

~a   ~A

The above format directives do `write` their argument on the output stream
and consume their argument. ~s or ~S does the output with `:escape` set to
non-`nil`. ~a or ~A does the output with `:escape` set to `nil`. For example,

```
>(format nil "~s loves ~s." 'john 'mary)
"john loves mary."
```

~⟨⟨number base⟩⟩ r	~⟨⟨number base⟩⟩ R
~b	~B
~o	~O
~d	~D
~x	~X

The above format directives output an argument using the specified number base and consume an argument. The argument must be an integer. ~d and ~D use the decimal system. For example,

```
>(format nil "~d is ~o in octal."
            123 123)
"123 is 173 in octal."
```

The following

```
~%
```

does a line feed to the output stream.

12   Programming

In this chapter, we will discuss some functions that are useful when writing a program.

12-1   A Program File

A form can be directed to the system by directly typing it from the terminal, but you can also input it from the file which contains the form by using the function called `load`. When you type

    (load 《file name》)

the system evaluates each of the forms in the specified file, although it will not display the value of each form. If you want to have the system display each of the values, you should type

    (load 《file name》 :print t)

Each time the system evaluates a form, it prints the value on the standard output stream. For example, suppose the content of a file called `foo.lsp` is as follows:

```
(defun square (x) (* x x))
(defun squaresquare (x &aux (y (* x x)))
      (* y y))
```

If you type

```
>(load "foo.lsp")
Loading foo.lsp
Finished loading foo.lsp
t

>
```

the definition of the functions **square** and **squaresquare** has been made.
If you want the system to display the value of each **defun** expression, i.e.,
the name of the function to be defined, you should type

```
>(load "foo.lsp" :print t)
Loading foo.lsp
square
squaresquare
Finished loading foo.lsp
t
```

A file which is used for keeping forms is called a **program file** or a **source
file**. It is the usual custom to use a program file when making a program.
The user creates this file using an editor and he loads the file into the system
when the program is ready. He tests the program by actually calling some
defined functions. If he finds some mistakes in a program, he corrects the
content of the program file using the editor again. KCL has a function
called **ed**. If you type

```
>(ed "foo.lsp")
```

you will call the editor on the file called **foo.lsp**. Which editor you get
will depend on the system. Some systems may have an editor especially
made for editing Lisp programs and some systems may have an ordinary
editor. After you correct the program file, you can load the program again
and repeat the test.

The results which you get by inputting a file using **load** and which you
get by typing the contents of the file directly at the terminal are basically
the same. Any forms which can be input from the terminal can be input
from the file. This means that you make a program for loading a collection

of files and put it in a file, i.e., you can load a collection of files by having multiple load instructions in just one file. For example, if you keep the forms

```
(load "file1.lsp")
(load "file2.lsp")
(load "file3.lsp")
```

in a file called fload.lsp, the loading of three files will be done just by loading the file fload.lsp.

```
>(load "fload.lsp")
Loading fload.lsp
Loading file1.lsp
Finished loading file1.lsp
Loading file2.lsp
Finished loading file2.lsp
Loading file3.lsp
Finished loading file3.lsp
Finished loading fload.lsp
t

>
```

If you do not want to see messages such as "Loading ..." or "Finished ...," you can set the system special variable *load-verbose* to nil.

```
>(setq *load-verbose* nil)
nil

>(load "fload.lsp")
t
```

You can also get rid of the messages by setting the keyword parameter :verbose to nil when you use load.

12-2 The Compiler

The **compiler** in Lisp is a program for altering a program to make it run faster. This changing is called **compiling**. A system macro called time will show you the time spent for evaluating a form.

```
>(defun fib (x)
    (cond ((= x 0) 1)
          ((= x 1) 1)
          (t (+ (fib (1- x))
                (fib (- x 2)))))))
fib
>(time (fib 20))
real time : 35.000 secs
run time  : 28.233 secs
10946

>
```

The above example prints the time spent when 20 is given as an argument
to the function fib which calculates the Fibonacci numbers. The output
of the actual time is different on each system. KCL shows both the real
time, which is the total time for the evaluation, and the run time, which is
the actual time that the computer was in use. In the above example, the
computer was in use for 28.233 seconds. The last line 10946 is the value
of (fib 20). We compile fib using the system function called compile.

```
>(compile 'fib)
fib
>(time (fib 20))
real time : 2.000 secs
run time  : 1.561 secs
10946
```

As you can see, after the compiling, the actual time is reduced to less than
one tenth.

You can compile the content of an entire program file by typing

```
>(compile-file "foo.lsp"
    :output-file "foo.out")
```

After evaluating this form, the content of the source file foo.lsp has been
compiled and the result is output in a file called foo.out. The content of
the source file is unchanged. If you type

```
>(load "foo.out")
```

the system loads the compiled program. It should take less time to execute
this program than to load and execute foo.lsp. The file which is used for

keeping the result of the compiling is called an **object file**. In the above
example, `foo.out` is an object file.

When using the function `compile-file` you should use the keyword parameter `:output-file` as in the example to specify the name of an object
file. If you omit this specification, the system specifies the object file according to the name of the source file in a predetermined way that depends
on which system you are using. For example, the object file generated
from a "$\cdots$.lsp" file will be called "$\cdots$.fasl" by changing the "lsp" part
of the file name to "fasl". Depending on which system you are using,
`compile-file` can also take parameters other than `:output-file` as keyword parameters.

The compiler reads each form in a source file and changes all the "top
level" forms. During this process, the compiler evaluates the top-level forms
which it reads, for example, `defmacro` expressions. All macro forms of the
program are expanded during compiling, since it is more time efficient to
do it then rather than to expand each macro during the execution of the
compiled program. However, in order to be able to expand all the macros
during compiling, the macros which are used in the program have to be
defined. That is why the compiler evaluates the `defmacro` expressions
in the source file to prepare to expand macros whenever needed. Some
systems evaluate some top-level forms other than `defmacro` expressions
during compiling and some systems (like KCL) evaluate all top-level forms.
If you want a top-level $\langle\langle$form$\rangle\rangle$ to be evaluated during compiling and the
compiler does not normally evaluate this form, you can embed the $\langle\langle$form$\rangle\rangle$
in the special form called `eval-when`.

```
(eval-when (compile load eval) ⟨⟨form⟩⟩ )
```

When the compiler reads this top-level form, it evaluates $\langle\langle$form$\rangle\rangle$ and then
compiles $\langle\langle$form$\rangle\rangle$ as usual. When used in an `eval-when` form

```
(compile load eval)
```

is used to specify when an evaluation is to take place and these symbols
mean the following:

compile	at the time of compiling
load	at the time of loading the object file
eval	at the time of loading the source file

This specification should always be a list and each element has to be one
of the above symbols in any order. $\langle\langle$form$\rangle\rangle$ will be evaluated as specified
in the specification.

If ⟨⟨form⟩⟩ does not exist in an `eval-when`, the compiler can decide whether or not to evaluate ⟨⟨form⟩⟩ during compiling. If ⟨⟨form⟩⟩ exists in an `eval-when` and you did not specify `compile` as the specification at the evaluation, this ⟨⟨form⟩⟩ will not be evaluated during compiling.

When you load a source file, ⟨⟨form⟩⟩ will be evaluated if this ⟨⟨form⟩⟩ does not exist in `eval-when`. If ⟨⟨form⟩⟩ exists inside of `eval-when` and you did not specify `eval`, this ⟨⟨form⟩⟩ will not be evaluated during loading.

The fact that ⟨⟨form⟩⟩ is evaluated during loading of the object file means that the compiled version of ⟨⟨form⟩⟩ has the same effect as the evaluation of the initial ⟨⟨form⟩⟩. If ⟨⟨form⟩⟩ is a `defun` expression, the system will define a function. If ⟨⟨form⟩⟩ is a special declaration using `proclaim`, the declaration will become effective. If ⟨⟨form⟩⟩ is an assignment expression like

```
(setq x 1)
```

the value of the variable x will become 1. The compiler does all the work necessary to make this assignment. In other words, orders like "define this function," "change this variable to a special variable," or "assign this value to this variable" are kept in the object file and the function `load` simply follows such orders. If ⟨⟨form⟩⟩ is not embedded in an `eval-when`, the compiler does the preparation for the assignment automatically. But if a ⟨⟨form⟩⟩ is in an `eval-when` and `load` does not appear in the specification list, the compiler does not do this preparation. For example, if you compile the file of

```
(defun f1 () ... )
(eval-when (eval)
   (defun f2 () ... ))
```

and load its object file, the system will define f1 but will not define f2. If you have already defined f2 before loading, the definition will be still effective. Since this `eval-when` does not specify `compile`, the `defun` expression for defining f2 will not be evaluated at compiling. Therefore, the compiler will ignore this `defun` expression.

We now look at the special form `compiler-let` which is related to the compiler.

```
(compiler-let (( ⟨⟨variable₁⟩⟩ ⟨⟨initial value₁⟩⟩ )
                     . . .
                ( ⟨⟨variableₘ⟩⟩ ⟨⟨initial valueₘ⟩⟩ ))
     ⟨⟨expression₁⟩⟩ . . . ⟨⟨expressionₙ⟩⟩ )
```

This special form is usually treated in the same way as

$$(\texttt{progv} \ \text{'(} \ \langle\langle\text{variable}_1\rangle\rangle\ldots\langle\langle\text{variable}_m\rangle\rangle \ )$$
$$(\texttt{list} \ \langle\langle\text{initial value}_1\rangle\rangle\ldots\langle\langle\text{initial value}_m\rangle\rangle \ )$$
$$\langle\langle\text{expression}_1\rangle\rangle\ldots\langle\langle\text{expression}_n\rangle\rangle \ )$$

However, when you compile `compiler-let`, the system binds $\langle\langle\text{variable}_1\rangle\rangle$ ... $\langle\langle\text{variable}_m\rangle\rangle$ during compiling but it will not bind them when it executes the compiled code. `compiler-let` is usually used when a user wants to control an evaluation during compiling, especially macro expansion, using the value of a global variable.

12-3 Module Structure

When a program is big, it may be necessary to divide it into several parts. Parts of a program are called **modules**. The modules of a program can be kept in several files and one module might be kept in several files or in one file.

When you divide a program into modules, you should give a name to each module using

(provide ⟨⟨module name⟩⟩)

at the beginning of the file. `provide` is a function and $\langle\langle\text{module name}\rangle\rangle$ is either a symbol or a string. For example,

(provide 'westcoast)

declares that the module in this file is to have the name `westcoast`. When the system reads a file and executes a `provide`, it `cons` the module name onto the value of the variable `*modules*`. In other words, a variable `*module*` keeps the list of the names of all the modules and `provide` simply adds a module name to this list.

A function called `require` is used in conjunction with `provide`. `require` specifies another module on which the executed module depends. For example, suppose the following expression

(require 'eastcoast)

exists in the module called `westcoast` and the system executes (`require` `'eastcoast`) in the middle of reading the module called `westcoast`. If the system has already read a module called `eastcoast` (i.e., the symbol `eastcoast` is in `*modules*`), the system will not do anything. If the system has not read the module called `eastcoast`, it reads the file `eastcoast` before it reads the rest of the file `westcoast`. If the module to be read is made up of several files or you do not want to use the standard name for the file containing the module to be read, you can add the name of the file or the list of the file names after the module of `require`. For example,

```
(require 'eastcoast "boston.lsp")
```

You should put `in-package` right after `provide` and specify the current package of the module. We recommend the use of a package name which is the same as the module name.

It is desirable to place functions such as `export`, `import`, `use-package`, etc, which influence the reading of the symbols, at the beginning of a file. It is also better to place `provide` and `require` at the beginning of a file, preferably, in the following order:

1. `provide`
2. `in-package`
3. `shadow`
4. `export`
5. `require`
6. `use-package`
7. `import`
8. the content of the module such as function definitions and variable declarations

12-4 Features

The value of a system special variable called `*features*` is a list of symbols and each symbol records a **feature** of the system. KCL running on a SUN workstation has the seven features.

```
>*features*
(sun mc68k ieee-floating-point unix bsd
 common kcl)
```

Let us briefly explain what they are. These features are the name of the computer where the system is running, CPU of the computer, the format of the floating-point numbers, the operating system, the version of the operating system, common which means that the system is a Common Lisp system, and kcl which is the name of the Common Lisp. KCL running on the workstation called E15 has the following features:

```
>*features*
(e15 mc68k ieee-floating-point unix
 system-v common kcl)
```

In addition to what we explained in Chapter 11, the sharp sign macro can be used as follows:

#+⟨⟨feature specification⟩⟩ ⟨⟨form⟩⟩

When the value of *features* "satisfies" ⟨⟨feature specification⟩⟩, the system reads the next ⟨⟨form⟩⟩ in a usual way. If the value does not "satisfy" the ⟨⟨feature specification⟩⟩, the system will not read the ⟨⟨form⟩⟩. A ⟨⟨feature specification⟩⟩ is a symbol or a list. If it is a symbol and the same symbol exists in the list of *features* then it satisfies the ⟨⟨feature specification⟩⟩. Suppose the system reads

```
(setq machine-name
      #+sun "SUN Workstation"
      #+e15 "E15 Workstation")
```

If you are using KCL on a SUN workstation, the above satisfies the feature sun, but does not satisfy the feature e15. So, the system reads

```
"SUN Workstation"
```

in a usually way, but the system does not read

```
"E15 Workstation"
```

Thus, the system reads

```
(setq machine-name "SUN Workstation")
```

On the other hand, the system reads

```
(setq machine-name "E15 Workstation")
```

for KCL on E15. If the ⟪feature specification⟫ is a list, it should start with one of the following:

and   or   not

The following list

$$(\text{and } \langle\!\langle \text{feature specification}_1 \rangle\!\rangle \ldots \langle\!\langle \text{feature specification}_n \rangle\!\rangle \ )$$

will be satisfied when all the specifications are satisfied.

$$(\text{or } \langle\!\langle \text{feature specification}_1 \rangle\!\rangle \ldots \langle\!\langle \text{feature specification}_n \rangle\!\rangle \ )$$

will be satisfied when one of ⟪feature specification$_1$⟫ ... ⟪feature specification$_n$⟫ is satisfied. And

$$(\text{not } \langle\!\langle \text{feature specification} \rangle\!\rangle \ )$$

is satisfied only when ⟪feature specification⟫ is not satisfied. For example, when the system reads

```
(setq operating-system
    #+(and unix bsd) "Unix 4.2bsd"
    #+(and unix system-v) "Unix System V"
    #+(and unix (not (or bsd system-v)))
      "Some Unix"
    #+(not unix) "Some Operating System")
```

KCL on a SUN will read

```
(setq operating-system "Unix 4.2bsd")
```

and KCL on the E15 will read

```
(setq operating-systems "Unix System V")
```

A system whose features include unix but do not include bsd and system-v will read

```
(setq operating-system "Some Unix")
```

A system whose features do not include unix will read

```
(setq operating-system
      "Some Operating System")
```

Another sharp sign macro relating to features looks like

#-⟨⟨feature specification⟩⟩ ⟨⟨form⟩⟩

which is the same as

#+(not ⟨⟨feature specification⟩⟩) ⟨⟨form⟩⟩

Since *features* is a variable, the user can change its value. When the system processes "#+" and "#-", it uses the values which are available in *features* at that time. When a user changes the value of *features*, the new value should also be a list of symbols. In general, a user should not delete features which the system comes with initially since the system itself might be assuming the existence of such features. It is best to change the value of *features* by adding new features to the old ones.

12-5 Miscellaneous Information

It is useful to remember that both **describe** and **inspect** are functions of one argument. They can take any data as arguments. The system will show the information relevant to such data. For example, if you type

```
>(describe 'cons)
```

the system will output the information that **cons** is an external symbol of the **lisp** package and the function **cons** is already defined, etc.

While **describe** has the system display all the information on the data, **inspect** gives a user information interactively. The details of what information you can expect to get will be different on each system.

The system function **apropos** is also very useful. If you type

```
>(apropos ⟨⟨string⟩⟩ )
```

the system will show all the symbols whose print name has ⟨⟨string⟩⟩ as a part of the name. The system also displays the function definition for each symbol or the value of the global variable, etc., at the same time. This function is useful when you forget the name of a function or a variable. If you type just ⟨⟨string⟩⟩ after **apropos**, the system will look through all the packages. If you want to limit the package for the search, you can type

```
>(apropos ⟨⟨string⟩⟩ ⟨⟨package⟩⟩ )
```

KCL will display the following information for you.

```
>(apropos "PRINT" (find-package 'lisp))
*print-base*     has value: 10
print Function
*print-case*     has value: :downcase
print Function
*print-array*    has value: t
*print-level*    has value: nil
*print-radix*    has value: nil
*print-gensym*   has value: t
*print-length*   has value: nil
*print-escape*   has value: t
*print-circle*   has value: nil
*print-pretty*   has value: t

>
```

Appendix 1
Sample Lisp Programs

In this appendix, we will show you some actual sample Lisp programs to make the knowledge of Common Lisp that you acquired in this book more useful. Since Common Lisp is designed with the wide application areas in mind, it is difficult to choose a program which represents an application area. The traditional sample programs written in Lisp are "the tower of hanoi," or the "eight queens puzzle," and other puzzles or classic methods for artificial intelligence such as "mini-max," "alpha-beta," or a program for analyzing the natural language sentences. However, the application areas of Lisp are not limited to artificial intelligence and especially Common Lisp can be used for general purpose programming and as a language in an introductory course for programming. As a matter of fact, we wrote this book from such a point of view. Here, we will show you a text processing program as an introductory lesson for programming in Lisp.

A1-1 A Text Editor

In this section, we will write a very simple text editor using Common Lisp. There are several kinds of text editors. The editor we will make in this section is a screen editor on a character display. Recently a high powered editor using a bit map display has been becoming popular, however, a screen editor using characters is the basis of such a high powered editor and remains useful as a software technique.

Since each character display is different, we need to pick one particular character display. However, we can make a display editor which can be used on many different character displays if we restrict ourselves to using only some basic functions. In order to do this, it is important to make a distinction between functions which only exist on some special displays and functions which generally exist on displays of all kinds. One more thing to remember is that since an editor requires input and output from the terminal, the editor depends on not only the kinds of character display you are using but also the operating system in which Lisp is executed.

Here we will assume the following things about the character display: it has a cursor and the system puts the character at the cursor when it is output to the display and then moves the cursor one character space to the right; the cursor can be moved to any row or to any column on the screen; the character display can erase the whole screen; it can erase the part of a line which is between the cursor and the right end. Let us also suppose that the operating system allows you to input a character from the keyboard without buffering it.

The definition of the editor is as follows. The text which the editor edits is shown on the screen and any corrections to the text should appear on the screen as soon as they are made. When the text does not fit on the screen, only part of it will be shown on the screen. The text is separated by line feed characters (#\Newline). One line of the text appears as one line on the screen, however, if the line of the text does not fit on one line of the screen, the text is displayed in multiple lines on the screen. This is called wrapping. Tab stop is set at every eight characters and the tab character (#\Tab) means the empty space till the next tab stop. For example, the text

```
This is   sample text.#\Newline
This line is longer than a display
  line.#\Newline
Here is a tab.#\TabOK?#\Newline
Now the end of the text.
```

will look like the following on the screen of 24 × 4

```
This is _sample text.
This line is longer than
 a display line.
Here is a tab.  OK?
```

When no writing is being done, the cursor on the display (in the above
sample, the "_" in front of sample is the cursor) shows the current point
on the screen. Many of the editor commands are executed at this current
point. For example, the input of #\Rubout erases the character before the
current point. Generally, each character input from the keyboard starts
up a specific command. However, characters other than control characters
mean to insert the character itself in front of the current point. For example, if you type the key a, the character a will be inserted in front of
the current point and the cursor will move one character to the right. The
above sample will change to

```
This is a_sample text.
This line is longer than
 a display line.
Here is a tab.  OK?
```

#\Space, #\Tab, and #\Newline also insert themselves in front of the cur-
rent pointer. Several control characters are commands that move the current point. For example, control-F (push the F key while holding down
the control key) moves the current pointer one character forward, i.e., to
the right. If the cursor was at the end of a line, this command will move
the cursor to the beginning of the next line. If the cursor would be off the
screen as a result of this move, the part of the text that appears on the
screen moves so that the current point always appears on the screen.

In KCL, control characters look like

   #\^《character》

For example, Control-F looks like

   #\^F

The following is the list of the commands that can be used with this
editor. We will simply say line for a line of text and display line for a line
on the screen.

#\^F	move the current pointer forward one character
#\^B	move the current pointer backward one character
#\^N	move the current pointer one display line down
#\^P	move the current pointer one display line up
#\^A	move the current pointer to the start of the display line
#\^E	move the current pointer to the end of the display line

#\^Rubout	delete the character in front of the current pointer
#\^D	delete the character at the current pointer
#\^K	delete the right part of the line from the current pointer
#\^[	evaluate the content of the text exiting the editor
#\^C	get out of the editor
#\Page	place the display line with the cursor to the center of the display
#\Newline	insert a #\Newline
#\Return	insert a #\Return
#\Tab	insert a #\Tab
#\Space	insert a #\Space
other characters	insert the character itself

The editor will simply ignore control characters other than ones listed above. The closing parenthesis #\) not only inserts a ")" but also moves the character cursor to the corresponding "(" for one second to show the correctness of the parentheses. The above mentioned commands are based on the editor called EMACS.

Now, we will talk about the data structures which the editor uses. The text being edited is stored in a so-called holed buffer which has a hole between the text before the current pointer and the text after the current pointer. This buffer is a one dimensional array of the characters, i.e., a character string. The two parts of the text represent the beginning of this array and the end of the array. For example, the above example will look like

```
This is a...........................
..........(the hole)...............
...................................
........ sample text.#\Newline
This line is longer than a display
 line.#\Newline
Here is a tab.#\TabOK?#\Newline
Now the end of the text.
```

In the editor program, this array is stored in the variable called *buf*. The size of this array is in the variable *bufsize*. The variable *hstart* (hole start) has the index for the beginning of the hole and the variable *hend* (hole end) has the index for the end of the hole (more precisely, the character next to the hole).

The variable *ncol* has the number of the columns on the display and the variable *nrow* has the number of the rows on the display. The

variables *ccol* and *crow* show the position of the cursor when no
editing is being done. The top and the left most part on the display is row
0 column 0. *crow* sometimes becomes negative or bigger than *nrow*
during processing.

In order to control the display lines, a structure called line is used.
Suppose you put the whole text on an imaginary display in which the
length of the line is the same as the display and the number of lines is
limitless. For each line, one line structure applies. A line structure has the
following fields:

start	index of *buf* which is the front of the display line
nchar	the number of the characters in the display line
next	one display line under
last	one display line above
nlp	t if it ends with #\Newline.
	nil if not

A line which goes over more than one display line will have nil for nlp
except the last display line.

When nlp is t, #\Newline is not included in nchar.

The display line with the current pointer is divided into two parts which
straddle the hole. start contains the index which is the front of the first
half part of the display line.

The first display line in this imaginary display will be put in a variable
tl (top line). The field last of *tl* is nil. Suppose the part of this
imaginary display starting with *tl* is displayed on the actual display.
The top display line on this display is a variable *wtl* (window top line).
The display line with the current point is the variable *cl* (current line
or cursor line).

Let's prepare some functions (or macros) for displaying. Such functions
depend on which character display you are using

(begin-screen)	initialize the display
(end-screen)	processing at the end
(throw-cursor col row)	throw the cursor to col column
	row row
(clear-screen)	erase the whole display
(clear-line)	erase the rest of the lines
	after the cursor
(flush-screen)	output the buffer on the screen
(write-char-screen char)	output char on the screen
(terpri-screen)	terpri the screen

We also need to prepare the following functions or macros for keyboard input.

    (begin-keyboard)   initialize the keyboard
    (end-keyboard)   ending the processing
    (keyin)   input from the keyboard without buffering

A function print-line is defined using functions for the screen.

    (print-line col row start nchar)

prints nchar characters from start in *buf* at col column and row row. Tab stops are, of course, considered in the evaluation of this function.

refresh is a function for refreshing the screen. It draws each display line starting at *wtl*, with special processing for *cl*. It also puts the cursor at column *ccol* and row *crow*.

center is a function for moving *cl* to the center of the screen and calls the function refresh.

The top level of the editor is a function called edit and this function appears at the very end of the program. edit initializes the screen and the keyboard and enters into the main loop using do. In the main loop, the process of reading one character from keyboard using keyin and executing the command corresponding to this character is repeated. Such commands usually are expressed by one function, for example, #\^F calls forward.

The command for moving the current point calls a function move.

    (move index)

If index is smaller than *hstart*, the system moves the current point so that *hstart* becomes index. If index is bigger than *hend, it moves the current point so that *hend* becomes index. If the cursor is no longer on the screen, it calls center.

A function insert-char is called for inserting characters. insert-char calls the function putchar which inserts a character next to *hstart* and recomputes *ccol*, *crow*, and *cl*. insert-char, after calling putchar, calls rescan and partial-refresh.

rescan is a function for reconstructing the display lines after an insertion or deletion of characters. rescan takes two arguments cl-end and cl-nlp. cl-end should be t if the last index (which should be bigger than the *hend*) of the display line with the current point ends with #\Newline and it returns nil if not. cl-nlp should be t if the the display line with the current pointer ends with #\Newline and it returns nil if not. You can get cl-end by typing

    (cl-end)

However, since the line with the current pointer is out of order because of the insertion and deletion, you have to specially call it. You can also get cl-nlp by typing

```
(line-nlp *cl*)
```

rescan returns two values. The first value is the change in the number of display lines and the second value is the number of the display lines that have been changed. These values are used by partial-refresh.

partial-refresh is a function that rewrites part of the screen.

```
(partial-refresh
  col row line index ninc nmod)
```

rewrites nmod lines under line. First, it writes out the content of the index specified by index on the line shown by line from col column row row of the screen. It then writes the content of the next line from 0 column row+1 row to the right. ninc shows the increase or the decrease of the number of the display lines. If ninc is not 0, partial-refresh rewrites not only the nmod line but all the lines after line in the screen.

rubout or del deletes characters. rubout calls del which calls rescan and partial-refresh just like insert-char.

kill deletes from the current pointer to the end of the line with the current pointer and then calls rescan and partial-refresh. It sometimes deletes several display lines.

right-paren moves the current pointer to "(" corresponding to the left parentheses and makes the current pointer sleep for one second.

Finally, we will explain the top level edit. edit takes one optional parameter, which has to be a symbol. If there is no argument or the optional parameter is nil, it starts the editing where it left off last time. If the optional parameter is t, it starts editing from scratch. If the optional parameter is neither t nor nil, it edits the function definition for such a symbol. If edit is stopped by typing a #\^[, it evaluates the corrected function definition and it redefines the function. The value of edit is nil if it is terminated with a #\^C. The value of edit is the value of the evaluation of the content of the text if it ends with #\^[.

```
;;;; Editor in Common Lisp

(in-package 'editor)
(shadow 'last)
(export 'edit 'lisp)
```

```
;;;      Machine-dependent Part
#+unix
(eval-when (compile eval)

  (defmacro begin-screen () nil)

  (defmacro end-screen () nil)

  (defmacro throw-cursor (col row)
    `(progn (princ #\^[)
            (princ #\[)
            (princ (1+ ,row))
            (princ #\;)
            (princ (1+ ,col))
            (princ #\H)))

  (defmacro clear-screen ()
    `(progn (princ #\Page)
            (finish-output)))

  (defmacro clear-line ()
    `(progn (princ #\^[)
            (princ #\[)
            (princ #\K)))

  (defmacro flush-screen ()
    `(finish-output))

  (defmacro write-char-screen (char)
    `(princ ,char))

  (defmacro terpri-screen ()
    `(progn (write-char #\Return)
            (write-char #\Linefeed)))

  (defmacro begin-keyboard ()
    `(progn (read-char)
            (system "stty raw -echo")))

  (defmacro end-keyboard ()
    `(system "stty -raw echo"))

  (defmacro keyin ()
    `(read-char)))
```

```
#+aosvs
(eval-when (compile eval)

  (defmacro begin-screen () nil)

  (defmacro end-screen () nil)

  (defmacro throw-cursor (col row)
     '(progn (princ (code-char #o220))
             (princ (code-char
                        (+ ,col #o200)))
             (princ (code-char
                        (+ ,row #o200)))))

  (defmacro clear-screen ()
     '(progn (princ #\Page)
             (finish-output)))

  (defmacro clear-line ()
     '(princ #\^K))

  (defmacro flush-screen ()
     '(finish-output))

  (defmacro write-char-screen (char)
     '(princ ,char))

  (defmacro terpri-screen ()
     '(terpri))

  (defmacro begin-keyboard () nil)

  (defmacro end-keyboard () nil))

;;;    Machine-independent Part
(defstruct line
  start
  nchar
  next
  last
  nlp)

(defvar *ncol* 79)
(defvar *nrow* 24)
```

```lisp
(defvar *bufsize* 2048)
(defvar *buf*
  (make-array *bufsize*
    :element-type 'string-char))
(defvar *tl*
  (make-line :start 0 :nchar 0))
(defvar *wtl* *tl*)
(defvar *ccol* 0)
(defvar *ccol1* 0)
(defvar *crow* 0)
(defvar *cl* *tl*)
(defvar *hstart* 0)
(defvar *hend* *bufsize*)

(eval-when (compile eval)

  (defmacro cl-end ()
    '(+ (line-start *cl*)
        (line-nchar *cl*)
        (- *hend* *hstart*)))

  (defmacro next-col (col char)
    '(if (char= ,char #\Tab)
         (+ (* (floor ,col 8) 8) 8)
         (1+ ,col))))

(defun print-line (col row start nchar)
  (when (<= nchar 0)
    (return-from print-line))
  (do ((col col)
       (index start (1+ index))
       (char #\Space)
       (i 0 (1+ i)))
      ((>= i nchar))
    (setq char (aref *buf* index))
    (cond ((char= char #\Tab)
             (setq col
                (+ (* (floor col 8) 8) 8))
             (when (< col *ncol*)
               (throw-cursor col row)))
          (t (write-char-screen char)
             (incf col)))))
```

```
(defun refresh ()
  (clear-screen)
  (do* ((1 *wtl* (line-next 1))
        (row 0 (1+ row)))
       ((or (>= row *nrow*) (null 1)))
    (throw-cursor 0 row)
    (if (eq 1 *cl*)
        (let* ((s (line-start 1))
               (n (- *hstart* s)))
          (print-line 0 *crow* s n)
          (print-line *ccol* *crow*
             *hend* (- (line-nchar 1) n)))
        (print-line 0 row (line-start 1)
           (line-nchar 1))))
  (throw-cursor *ccol* *crow*)
  (flush-screen))

(defun center ()
  (let ((k (- *crow* (floor *nrow* 2))))
    (cond ((> k 0)
           (dotimes (i k)
             (setq *wtl*
                   (line-next *wtl*)))
           (decf *crow* k))
          ((< k 0)
           (setq k (- k))
           (dotimes (i k)
             (when (null
                       (line-last *wtl*))
               (setq k i)
               (return))
             (setq *wtl*
                (line-last *wtl*)))
           (incf *crow* k))))
  (refresh))

(defun get-index (line to-col)
  (do ((col 0 next-col)
       (next-col)
       (i (line-start line) (1+ i))
       (n 0 (1+ n))
       (nchar (line-nchar line)))
```

```
     ((or (>= n nchar)
          (> (setq next-col
                (next-col col
                   (areaf *buf* i)))
              to-col))
  i)))

(defun move (index)
  (cond
    ((< index *hstart*)
     (do ((i (1- *hstart*) (1- i))
          (j (1- *hend*) (1- j)))
         ((< i index)
          (setq *hstart* (1+ i)
                *hend* (1+ j)))
       (setf (aref *buf* j)
          (aref *buf* i)))
     (do ((k (- *hend* *hstart*)))
         ((>= index
              (line-start *cl*)))
       (incf (line-start *cl*) k)
       (setq *cl* (line-last *cl*))
       (decf *crow*)))
    ((> index *hend*)
     (do ((i *hstart* (1+ i))
          (j *hend* (1+ j)))
         ((>= j index)
          (setq *hstart* i *hend* j))
       (setf (aref *buf* i)
          (aref *buf* j)))
     (do ((k (- *hend* *hstart*)))
         ((or (null (line-next *cl*))
              (< index
                 (line-start
                    (line-next *cl*)))))
       (setq *cl* (line-next *cl*))
       (incf *crow*)
       (decf (line-start *cl*) k))))
  (setq *ccol* 0)
  (do ((i (line-start *cl*) (1+ i)))
      ((>= i *hstart*))
    (setq *ccol*
       (next-col *ccol* (aref *buf* i)))))
```

```
   (cond ((or (< *crow* 0)
              (>= *crow* *nrow*))
          (center))
         (t (throw-cursor *ccol* *crow*)
            (flush-screen)))))

(defun forward ()
  (when (>= *hend* *bufsize*)
    (return-from forward))
  (move (1+ *hend*)))

(defun backward ()
  (when (<= *hstart* 0)
    (return-from backward))
  (move (1- *hstart*)))

(defun next ()
  (when (null (line-next *cl*))
    (return-from next))
  (move (get-index (line-next *cl*)
                   *ccol1*)))

(defun last ()
  (when (null (line-last *cl*))
    (return-from last))
  (move (get-index (line-last *cl*)
                   *ccol1*)))

(defun bol ()
  (do ((i (1- *hstart*) (1- i)))
      ((or (< i 0)
           (char= (aref *buf* i)
                  #\Newline))
       (move (1+ i)))))

(defun eol ()
  (do ((j *hend* (1+ j)))
      ((or (>= j *bufsize*)
           (char= (aref *buf* j)
                  #\Newline))
       (move j))))

(defun putchar (char)
  (when (>= *hstart* *hend*)
    (error "Buffer overflow."))
```

```
(setf (aref *buf* *hstart*) char)
(incf *hstart*)
(when (cond
         ((char= char #\Newline)
          (setf (line-nlp *cl*) t))
         ((progn
            (incf (line-nchar *cl*))
            (setq *ccol*
              (next-col *ccol* char))
            (>= *ccol* *ncol*))
          (setf (line-nlp *cl*) nil)
          t))
    (setq *cl*
      (setf (line-next *cl*)
         (make-line :start *hstart*
                    :nchar 0
                    :next (line-next *cl*)
                    :last *cl*)))
    (when (line-next *cl*)
      (setf (line-last (line-next *cl*))
         *cl*))
    (setq *ccol* 0)
    (incf *crow*)))

(defun rescan (col-end cl-nlp)
  (let* ((ccol *ccol*) (cl *cl*)
         (cl-next (line-next cl))
         (l cl)
         (l-nchar (- *hstart*
                     (line-start l)))
         (ninc 0) (nmod 1))
    (setf (line-nlp cl) nil)
    (do () ((or cl-nlp (null cl-next)))
      (setq cl cl-next
            cl-end (+ (line-start cl)
                      (line-nchar cl))
            cl-nlp (line-nlp cl)
            cl-next (line-next cl)))
    (do ((i *hend* (1+ i)))
        ((>= i cl-end))
      (setq ccol
         (next-col ccol (aref *buf* i)))
```

```
            (incf l-nchar)
            (when (>= ccol *ncol*)
               (setf (line-nchar l) l-nchar
                     (line-nlp l) nil)
               (cond
                  ((eq (line-next l) cl-next)
                   (setf (line-next l)
                     (make-line :start (1+ i)
                                :next cl-next
                                :last l))
                   (when cl-next
                     (setf (line-last cl-next)
                       (line-next l)))
                   (incf ninc))
                  (t (setf (line-start
                             (line-next l))
                       (1+ i)))))
               (setq l (line-next l) l-nchar 0)
               (setq ccol 0)
               (incf nmod)))
         (setf (line-nchar l) l-nchar
               (line-nlp l) cl-nlp)
         (unless (eq (line-next l) cl-next)
           (do ((l-next (line-next l)
                        (line-next l-next)))
               ((eq l-next cl-next))
             (decf ninc))
           (setf (line-next l) cl-next)
           (when cl-next
             (setf (line-laste cl-next) l)))
         (values ninc nmod)))

  (defun partial-refresh
      (col row line index ninc nmod)
    (when (or (< row 0)
              (>= row *nrow*)
              (< *crow* 0)
              (>= *crow* *nrow*))
        (center)
        (return-from partial-refresh))
      (if (= ninc 0)
          (setq nmod
            (min nmod (- *nrow* row)))
```

```
            (setq nmod (- *nrow* row)))
        (do* ((col col 0)
              (row row (1+ row))
              (n 0 (1+ n))
              (nchar (- (line-nchar line)
                        (- index
                           (line-start line)))))
             ((>= n nmod))
          (cond
            ((null line)
             (when (>= ninc 0) (return))
             (throw-cursor col row)
             (clear-line)
             (incf ninc))
            (t (throw-cursor col row)
               (clear-line)
               (cond ((eq line *cl*)
                      (print-line
                        col *crow* index
                        (- *hstart* index))
                      (print-line
                        *ccol* *crow* *hend*
                        (- nchar
                           (- *hstart*
                              index))))
                     (t (print-line
                          col row
                          index nchar)))
               (when (setq line
                           (line-next line))
                 (setq index
                   (line-start line))
                 (setq nchar
                   (line-nchar line)))))))
    (throw-cursor *ccol* *crow*)
    (flush-screen))

(defun insert-char (char)
  (let* ((ccol *ccol*)
         (crow *crow*) (cl *cl*)
         (cl-end (cl-end))
         (cl-nlp (line-nlp *cl*)))
```

```
      (setf (line-nchar *cl*)
        (- *hstart* (line-start *cl*)))
    (putchar char)
    (multiple-value-bind (ninc nmod)
        (rescan cl-end cl-nlp)
      (partial-refresh
        ccol crow cl (1- *hstart*)
        (+ (- *crow* crow) ninc)
        (+ (- *crow* crow) nmod)))))

(defun insert-string (string)
  (let* ((ccol *ccol*) (crow *crow*)
         (cl *cl*) (hstart *hstart*)
         (cl-end (cl-end))
         (cl-nlp (line-nlp *cl*)))
    (setf (line-nchar *cl*)
      (- *hstart* (line-start *cl*)))
    (dotimes (i (length string))
      (putchar (aref string i)))
    (multiple-value-bind (ninc nmod)
        (rescan cl-end cl-nlp)
      (partial-refresh
        ccol crow cl hstart
        (+ (- *crow* crow) ninc)
        (+ (- *crow* crow) nmod)))))

(defun rubout ()
  (when (= *hstart* 0)
    (return-from rubout))
  (move (1- *hstart*))
  (del))

(defun del ()
  (when (= *hend* *bufsize*)
    (return-from del))
  (let (cl-end cl-nlp)
    (cond
      ((char= (aref *buf* *hend*)
              #\Newline)
       (setq cl-end (1+ *hend*))
       (setq cl-nlp nil))
      (t (setq cl-end (cl-end))
         (setq cl-nlp
           (line-nlp *cl*))))
```

```
      (incf *hend*)
      (multiple-value-call
        #'partial-refresh
        *ccol* *crow* *cl* *hstart*
        (rescan cl-end cl-nlp))))

 (defun kill ()
   (when (and (< *hend* *bufsize*)
              (char=
                (aref *buf* *hend*)
                #\Newline))
     (return-from kill (del)))
   (do* ((ndec 0 (1+ ndec))
         (cl *cl* (line-next cl))
         (cl-end (cl-end)
                 (+ (line-start cl)
                    (line-nchar cl)))
         (cl-nlp (line-nlp cl)
                 (line-nlp cl)))
        ((or cl-nlp
             (null (line-next cl)))
         (unless (eq cl *cl*)
           (setf (line-next *cl*)
             (line-next cl))
           (when (line-next cl)
             (setf (line-last
                     (line-next cl))
               *cl*)))
         (setq *hend* cl-end)
         (multiple-value-bind (ninc nmod)
             (rescan cl-end cl-nlp)
           (partial-refresh
             *ccol* *crow* *cl* *hstart*
             (- ndec) nmod)))))

 (defun right-paren ()
   (insert-char #\))
   (do ((hend *hend*)
        (i (- *hstart* 2) (1- i))
        (level 1))
       ((< i 0)
        (write-char #\^G)
        (finish-output))
```

```
          (cond ((char= (aref *buf* i) #\()
                 (when (= (decf level) 0)
                   (move i)
                   (sleep 1)
                   (move hend)
                       (return)))
                ((char= (aref *buf* i) #\))
                      (incf level)))))


(defun edit (&optional symbol nil)
             &aux (form nil))
  (when symbol
    (setq *tl*
       (make-line :start 0 :nchar 0))
    (setq *wtl* *tl*
          *ccol* 0
          *crow* 0
          *cl* *tl*
          *hstart* 0
          *hend* *bufsize*))
  (unwind-protect
    (progn
      (begin-screen)
      (begin-keyboard)
      (refresh)
      ;; KCL only
      (when (and symbol
                 (not (eq symbol t)))
         (insert-string
           (write-to-string
             (cons 'defun
                   (cdr (symbol-function
                         symbol)))
             :escape t
             :pretty t)))
      (do ((char #\Space)
           ;; KCL only
           (*break-enable* nil))
          (nil)
        (case (setq char (keyin))
          (#\^F (forward))
          (#\^B (backword))
```

```
                    (#\^N (next))
                    (#\^P (last))
                    (#\^A (bol))
                    (#\^E (eol))
                    (#\Rubout (rubout))
                    (#\^D (del))
                    (#\^K (kill))
                    (#\^[ (move *bufsize*)
                         (setq form
                           (read-from-string
                             *buf* :end *hstart*))
                         (terpri-screen)
                         (flush-screen)
                         (return))
                    (#\^C (clear-screen)
                         (return))
                    (#\Page (center))
                    (#\Return
                      (insert-char #\Newline))
                    ((#\Space #\Tab #\Newline)
                      (insert-char char))
                    (#\) (right-paren))
                    (t (when (char> char #\Space)
                         (insert-char char))))
                  (when (and (char/= char #\^N)
                             (char/= char #\^P))
                    (setq *ccol1* *ccol*))))
             (end-screen)
             (end-keyboard))
         (if form (eval form) nil))
```

A1-2 Cross Reference

In this section, we will describe a program for making a cross reference for
Common Lisp programs.

The function called ~load starts the program. ~load, like load, reads
the program from the file and at the same time, adds the cross reference in
property lists of variable names and function names. The properties which
~load recorded for the functions are as follows:

`call`	the list of functions which this function calls
`called-by`	the list of functions which call this function
`refer`	the list of functions which this function refers to
`referred-by`	the list of functions which refers to this function
`bind`	the list of special variables which this function binds
`read`	the list of special variables that this function reads
`write`	the list of the special variables that this function writes

That a function `foo` refers to a function `bar` means that `bar` occurs as

    (function bar)

inside of `foo`. The properties which ~`load` records for the variable names
are as follows:

`bound-by`	the list of functions which bind this variable
`read-by`	the list of functions which use this variable
`written-by`	the list of functions which alter this variable

These properties are renewed by functions such as `call-fun`, `bind-var`,
etc.

The function

    ~eval

analyzes an expression. This function analyzes the content of an expression
and records the cross reference while pretending it evaluates the expression.
~`eval` uses the following three variables:

`*current-fun*`	the name of the function which it is analyzing
`*local-var-list*`	the list of local variables
`*local-fun-list*`	the list of local functions

`*local-var-list*` is a list of dotted pairs which looks like

    (⟪ variable name⟫ . lexical)

or

    (⟪ variable name⟫ . special)

The first dotted pair means that the binding of a local variable occurred
and the latter pair means that the binding of a special variable occurred.
`*local-fun-list*` is a list of local function names.

In a macro expression, since the result of the macro expansion is analyzed, the macro call is not recorded in the cross reference. Also, our program cannot use a local macro made by `macrolet`.

The analysis of a special form is done by associating a macro to each special form. Since this process is a little tricky, the program defines a macro called `defspecial`. For example, for the special form `if`, if you type

```
(defspecial if (cond then
                     &optional (else nil))
  (~eval cond)
  (~eval then)
  (~eval else))
```

this `defspecial` expression will expand to

```
(progn
  (setf (get 'if 'special-form) '~if)
  (defmacro ~if (cond then
                      &optional (else nil))
    (~eval cond)
    (~eval then)
    (~eval else)))
```

So, the special form `if` corresponds to the macro called `~if`. This `~if` is started by the expression

```
((get fun 'special-form)
 (funcall (get fun 'special-form) form))
```

in the `cond` expression inside of `~eval`. We used a macro here because we wanted to expand the special form using the lambda list of `defmacro`.

`*local-var-list*` is kept up to date using a macro called `enter-var`. `enter-var` is usually used along with the macro called `do-body`. For example, two macros were used for the special form `let*` in the following way:

```
(defspecial let* (var-list &rest body)
  (do-body nil
    (dolist (x var-list)
      (cond ((symbolp x) (enter-var x))
            (t (~eval (cadr x))
               (enter-var (car x)))))))
```

As a result, you will define the macro `~let*` as

```
(defmacro ~let* (var-list &rest body)
  (do-body nil
    (dolist (x var-list)
      (cond ((symbolp x) (enter-var x))
            (t (~eval (cadr x))
               (enter-var (car x)))))))
```

If you expand do-body and enter-var, you will further get

```
(defmacro ~let* (var-list &rest body)
  (multiple-value-bind (specials body)
      (find-specials body nil)
    (let ((*local-var-list*
           *local-var-kist*))
      (dolist (v specials)
        (bind-var v)
        (push (cons v 'special)
          *local-var-list*))
      (dolist (x var-list)
        (cond
          ((symbolp x)
           (cond
             ((member x specials)
              (bind-var x)
              (push
                (cons x 'special)
                *local-var-list*))
             (t (push
                  (cons x 'lexical)
                  *local-var-list*))))
          (t (~eval (cadr x))
             (let ((v (car x)))
               (cond
                 ((member v specials)
                  (bind-var v)
                  (push
                    (cons v 'special)
                    *local-var-list*))
                 (t (push
                      (cons v 'lexical)
                      *local-var-list*)
          ))))))
      (mapc #'~eval body))))
```

find-specials returns the special declaration from body. The first argument of do-body, that is, the second argument of find-specials, is t if the special form can take a documentation string and it returns nil if the special form cannot take a documentation string. An important thing to remember here is that the body of a special form must be the argument named body since do-body assumes this.

A function called ~lambda analyzes both a lambda expression and a defun expression. ~lambda looks for &optional and &key and calls enter-var.

In this program, there is one part which depends on the system. It is the function called special-var-p for checking whether a variable is a special variable or not. Since KCL can use the internal function called system:specialp of the system, this program defines special-var-p as

```
(defun special-var-p (x)
  (system:specialp x))
```

Although it takes longer to execute, special-var-p defined as

```
(defun special-var-p (x)
  (progv (list x) (list 1)
    (eval
      '(let ((,x 2))
        (= (symbol-value ',x) 2)))))
```

works in any Common Lisp system.

The following program is not complete. Some special forms do not have defspecial expressions. Also, this program will not analyze programs using macrolet. The rest of the program will be left to the reader to complete.

```
;;;   Cross-reference for Common Lisp
;;;

(defun special-var-p (x)
  (system:specialp x))      ; KCL only

(defvar *current-fun*)

(defun read-var (var)
  (pushnew var
    (get *current-fun* 'read))
  (pushnew *current-fun*
    (get var 'read-by)))
```

```
(defun write-var (var)
  (pushnew var
    (get *current-fun* 'write))
  (pushnew *current-fun*
    (*get var 'written-by)))

(defun bind-var (var)
  (pushnew var
    (get *current-fun* 'bind))
  (pushnew *current-fun*
    (get var 'bound-by)))

(defun call-fun (fun)
  (pushnew fun
    (get *current-fun* 'call))
  (pushnew *current-fun*
    (get fun 'called-by)))

(defun refer-fun (fun)
  (pushnew fun
    (get *current-fun* 'refer))
  (pushnew *current-fun*
    (get fun 'referred-by)))

(defvar *local-var-list* nil)
(defvar *local-fun-list* nil)

(defun ~load (file
              &aux (*package* *package*))
  (with-open-file (stream file)
    (do* ((eof (cons nil nil))
          (form (read stream nil eof)
                (read stream nil eof)))
         ((eq form eof))
      (eval form)
      (~top-level-eval form))))

(defun ~top-level-eval (form)
  (when (consp form)
    (case (car form)
      ((defvar defparameter defconstant))
      (defun
        (let ((*current-fun*
               (cadr form)))
```

```
                    (remprop *current-fun* 'call)
                    (remprop *current-fun* 'refer)
                    (remprop *current-fun* 'read)
                    (remprop *current-fun* 'write)
                    (remprop *current-fun* 'bind)
                    (let ((*local-var-list* nil)
                          (*local-fun-list* nil))
                       (~lambda (caddr form)
                                (cdddr form)))))
              (defmacro)
              (eval-when
                 (when (or (member 'eval
                                   (cadr form))
                           (member 'load
                                   (cadr form)))
                     (dolist (x (cddr form))
                       (~top-level-eval x))))
              (progn
                 (dolist (x (cdr form))
                   (~top-level-eval x)))
              (t (when (macro-function (car form))
                   (~top-level-eval
                     (macroexpand-1 form)))))))))

    (defun ~eval (form)
      (if (atom form)
          (if (symbolp form)
              (unless
                (and
                  (assoc form
                    *local-var-list*)
                  (eq
                    (cdr
                      (assoc form *local-var-list*))
                    'lexical))
                (read-var form)))
          (let ((fun (car form))
                (args (cdr form)))
            (cond
              ((consp fun)
               (mapc #'~eval args)
               (~lambda (cadr fun)
                        (cddr fun)))
```

```
              ((get fun 'special-form)
               (funcall
                 (macro-function
                    (get fun 'special-form))
                 form))
              ((member fun *local-fun-list*)
               (mapc #'~eval args))
              ((macro-function fun)
               (~eval (macroexpand-1 form)))
              (t (call-fun fun)
                 (mapc #'~eval args))))))

(defun find-specials
    (body has-doc-string)
  (do ((b body (cdr b)) (s nil) (form))
      ((endp b) (values s nil))
    (setq form (macroexpand (car b)))
    (cond ((and has-doc-string
                (stringp form)))
          ((or (atom form)
               (not (eq 'declare
                        (car form))))
           (return (values s b)))
          (t (dolist (d (cdr form))
               (when (eq (car d)
                         'special)
                 (dolist (v (cdr d))
                   (pushnew v s)))))))))

(defmacro enter-var (v)
   (if (atom v)
       '(cond
          ((member ,v specials))
          ((special-var-p ,v)
           (bind-var ,v)
           (push (cons ,v 'special)
             *local-var-list*))
          (t (push (cons ,v 'lexical)
               *local-var-list*)))
       '(let ((v ,v))
          (cond
             ((member v specials))
```

```
      ((special-var-p v)
       (bind-var v)
       (push (cons v 'special)
         *local-var-list*))
      (t (push (cons v 'lexical)
           *local-var-list*))))))

(defmacro do-body (has-doc-string
                      &rest body)
  '(multiple-value-bind (specials body)
       (find-specials body
          ,has-doc-string)
     (let ((*local-var-list*
            *local-var-list*))
       (dolist (v specials)
         (bind-var v)
         (push (cons v 'special)
           *local-var-list*))
       ,@body
       (mapc #'~eval body))))

(defun ~lambda (lambda-list body &aux v)
  (do-body t
    (tagbody
     REQUIRED
       (when (endp lambda-list) (go END))
       (case (setq v (pop lambda-list))
         (&optional (go OPTIONAL))
         (&rest (go REST))
         (&keyword (go KEYWORD))
         (&aux (go AUX)))
       (enter-var v)
       (go REQUIRED)
     OPTIONAL
       (when (endp lambda-list) (go END))
       (case (setq v (pop lambda-list))
         (&rest (go REST))
         (&keyword (go KEYWORD))
         (&aux (go AUX)))
       (cond
         ((symbolp v)(enter-var v))
         (t (enter-var (car v))
            (unless (endp (cdr v))
```

```
                 (~eval (cadr v))
                 (unless (endp (cddr v))
                   (enter-var (caddr v))))))))
       (go OPTIONAL)
     REST
       (enter-var (pop lambda-list))
       (when (endp lambda-list) (go END))
       (when (eq (pop lambda-list) '&aux)
         (go AUX)))
   KEYWORD
     (when (endp lambda-list) (go END))
     (case (setq v (pop lambda-list))
       (&allow-other-keys
         (cond ((endp lambda-list)
                (go END))
               (t (pop lambda-list)
                  (go AUX))))
       (&aux (go AUX)))
     (cond
       ((symbolp v) (enter-var v))
       (t (if (symbolp (car v))
              (enter-var (car v))
              (enter-var (cadar v)))
          (unless (endp (cdr v))
            (~eval (cadr v))
            (unless (endp (cddr v))
              (enter-var (caddr v))))))
       (go KEYWORD)
   AUX
     (when (endp lambda-list) (go END))
     (setq v (pop lambda-list))
     (cond ((symbolp v) (enter-var v))
           (t (enter-var (car v))
           (unless (endp (cdr v))
             (~eval (cadr v)))))
   END)))

(defmacro defspecial
    (symbol lambda-list . body)
  (let ((macro
           (intern
             (concatenate 'string "~"
               (symbol-name symbol)))))
```

```
         '(progn
           (setf (get ',symbol 'special-form)
              ',macro)
           (defmacro ,macro ,lambda-list
             ,@body))))

(defspecial quote (value))

(defspecial function (fun)
  (cond ((symbolp fun)
         (unless
             (member fun
               *local-fun-list*)
           (refer-fun fun)))
        (t (~lambda (cadr fun)
                    (cddr fun)))))

(defspecial setq (&rest r)
  (do ((r r (cddr r)))
      ((endp r))
    (unless
        (and (assoc (car r)
                *local-var-list*)
             (eq (cdr
                  (assoc (car r)
                    *local-var-list*))
                 'lexical))
      (write-var (car r)))
    (~eval (cadr r))))

(defspecial if (cond then
                &optional (else nil))
  (~eval cond)
  (~eval then)
  (~eval else))

(defspecial progn (&rest body)
  (mapc #'~eval body))

(defspecial block (&rest body)
  (mapc #'~eval body))
```

```
(defspecial return-from (block
                           &optional
                              (form nil))
  (~eval form))

(defspecial tagbody (&rest tagbody)
  (dolist (x tagbody)
    (unless (atom x) (~eval x))))

(defspecial go (tag))

(defspecial let (var-list &rest body)
  (do-body nil
    (dolist (v var-list)
      (when (consp v) (~eval (cadr v))))
    (dolist (v var-list)
      (enter-var
        (if (atom v) v (car v))))))

(defspecial let* (var-list &rest body)
  (do-body nil
    (dolist (v var-list)
      (cond ((atom v) (enter-var v))
            (t (~eval (cadr v))
               (enter-var (car v)))))))

(defspecial multiple-value-bind
    (var-list form &rest body)
  (do-body nil
    (~eval form)
    (dolist (v var-list) (enter-var v))))

(defspecial flet (fun-list &rest body)
  (let ((*local-fun-list*
          *local-fun-list*))
    (dolist (x fun-list)
      (~lambda (cadr x) (cddr x)))
    (dolist (x fun-list)
      (push (car x) *local-fun-list*))
    (do-body t)))
```

```
(defspecial labels (fun-list &rest body)
  (let ((*local-fun-list*
          *local-fun-list*))
    (dolist (x fun-list)
      (push (car x) *local-fun-list*))
    (dolist (x fun-list)
      (~lambda (cadr x) (cddr x)))
    (do-body t)))
```

Appendix 2
Debugging Lisp Programs

In this section, we will talk about debugging Lisp programs.

There are many different debugging tools in the Lisp system and it is hard to say which one is best. We will describe several debugging techniques and leave the reader to choose one he likes.

A2-1 Break Level

The basic activity of a Lisp system is to repeat the process of reading an expression, evaluating it, and displaying its result. This process is called a `read-eval-print` loop or, in short, the **top-level loop**. If an error occurs in the middle of the evaluation of an expression, control moves from where it is to another `read-eval-print` loop. This is called the **break-level loop**. In the break-level loop, unlike the top-level loop, variables are evaluated in the environment that was current when the error occurred. Let's look at an example in KCL:

```
>(defun fact (x)
   (if (zerop x) one (* (fact (1- x)))))
fact
```

```
>(fact 10)
```

After printing the following error message, the system moves to the break level.

```
Error: The variable ONE is unbound.
Error signaled by IF.

>>
```

In KCL the prompt sign at the break level is ">>". If we evaluate x here we will see

```
>>x
0
```

At the break level, unlike the top level, the system executes some special commands which are for examining errors and are called break-level-commands. In KCL you can execute break-level-commands by typing the keyword corresponding to each command.

One of the most used break-level-commands is the backtrace. This command prints all the function calls that have been made up until the time the error occurred. In KCL, you type :b to get a backtrace.

```
>>:b
Backtrace: funcall > fact > if > fact >
if > fact > if > fact > if > fact >
If > fact > if > fact > if > fact >
if > fact > if > fact > if > fact > IF

>>
```

The above printout shows that the system repeated the process in which fact was called from funcall and if was called from this fact and another fact was called by this if until the error occurred at the last if. The first funcall can be assumed to be at the top level. The IF in upper case tells you that the error occurs there and the break level is active in that form.

Since the break-level-commands are different in each Common Lisp system, we will not explain these further. One important thing to remember is that typing :q gets you back to the top level in KCL.

A2-2 Break and Error

If you cannot determine the error using the break level, the simplest thing
to do is to run the program once more. However, if you run the program
exactly like before, you will end up with the same result. You could insert
some debugging commands into the program and let the system print the
state of the variables several times. By inserting

```
#+debug (print x)
```

into your program you can use a feature to do this. If you put the symbol
debug in the *features* list, this form will print the value of the variable
x and you can delete **debug** from the *features* list after debugging.
   Rather than calling **print**, you can also call

```
(break)
```

When you call the function **break**, the system enters the break-level as if
an error had occurred at this call. For example,

```
>(defun foo (x)
    (break)
    (cons x x))
foo

>(foo 1)

Break.

>>
```

Here you can check the value of a variable or execute a break command:

```
>>x
1

>>:b
Backtrace: funcall >> FOO

>>
```

In KCL, if you type :r instead of :q you can get out of the break level and
continue the execution of the program.

```
>>:r
(1 . 1)

>
```

By inserting **break** at some critical places in your program, you can check
the state of the execution of the program while it is executing.

   The function **error** is like **break** except that you cannot restart the
program. This function allows a program to print an error. A program
usually calls **error** when it enters into an unusual state. **error** takes one
required parameter and some number of optional parameters. The required
parameter is a format string which will be used as the error message. The
rest of the parameters are the arguments to this format string. For example,

```
>(defun fact (x)
   (when (< x 0)
     (error "~S is negative." x))
     (if (zerop x) 1 (* x (fact 1- x)))))
fact

>(fact -1)

Error: -1 is negative.
Error signaled by WHEN.

>>
```

A2-3 trace and step

Debugging using the function **trace**, which was first explained in Section
3-1 on recursive function calls, may be the most typical debugging tool in
Lisp. If you type

```
>(trace foo)
```

you will start to trace the function **foo**. After this, whenever **foo** is called,
the system prints the arguments to **foo** and prints the value of **foo** when
foo returns. KCL will type

```
⟪depth⟫ > ( ⟪function name⟫ ⟪argument⟫ ... )
```

when a function is called and

$$\langle\!\langle \text{depth} \rangle\!\rangle \ < \ (\ \langle\!\langle \text{function name} \rangle\!\rangle \ \langle\!\langle \text{value} \rangle\!\rangle \ \dots \ )$$

when a function returns.

You can type any number of function names after `trace` or if you type

```
>(trace)
```

the system returns the list of the functions being traced.

To stop a trace you should use `untrace`.

```
>(untrace foo)
```

Or, if you type

```
>(untrace)
```

you can stop all the traces.

Both `trace` and `untrace` are macros.

Another macro `step` makes the system evaluate an expression in steps one sub-expression at a time or execute a program one command at a time. For example, the evaluation of

```
(+ (* 2 3) 1)
```

consists of

the evaluation of (* 2 3)
the evaluation of 1
the call for +

and the evaluation of (* 2 3) consists of

the evaluation of 2
the evaluation of 3
the call for +

If you type the following using the macro `step`

```
>(step (+ (* 2 3) 1))
```

the system will execute all the above steps one by one. In KCL, if you type

```
>(step (+ (* 2 3) 1))
```

you will get

```
Type ? and a newline for help.
  (+ (* 2 3) 1)
    (* 2 3)
       2
       3
     = 6
     1
   = 7
 7

>
```

In this example, the execution stops at (+ (* 2 3) 1) and at (* 2 3) and restarts the execution whenever you type a new line. You can also input some commands before restarting the computation.

The details printed by **step** differ depending on the system.

A2-4 Terminal Interrupt

A terminal interrupt is treated as an error. In KCL running under UNIX, the usual terminal interrupt character can cause an error. For example,

```
>(loop (cons nil nil))
^C
Correctable error: Console interrupt.
Signaled by CONS.

>>
```

If you type :q following the above, you will go back to the top level. If you type :r, you will restart the execution.

A terminal interrupt is useful to stop the infinite loop in the program.

A2-5 Sample Debugging

In this section we will show you an actual example of debugging in KCL a program which solves the eight queens puzzle. Bugs exist at (1) and (2). We add the call for **break** at (3) during the debugging. Let's assume the program is in a file called qp.lsp.

```
===========================================================
(defun queen (n)
   (queen1 n 0 0 nil nil nil))

(defun queen1 (n i j column left right)
  (cond ((equal i n)
         (terpri)
         (print-solution n column)
         nil)
        ((equal j n) nil)
        ((or (member j column)
            ;(member (+ i j) left)        ; (1)
            (member (- i j) right))
         (queen n i (1+ j)
               column left right))        ; (2)
        ((queen1 n (1+ i) 0
                (cons j column)
                (cons (+ i j) left)
                (cons (- i j) right)))
        ((queen1 n i (1+ j)
               column left right)))))

(defun print-solution (n x)
  ;(break)                                 ; (3)
  (do ((y x (cdr y)))
      ((null y))
    (terpri)
    (do ((i 0 (1+ i)))
        ((equal i (car y)))
      (princ ". "))
    (princ "Q ")
    (do ((i 0 (1+ i)))
        ((equal i (- n (car y) 1)))
      (princ ". "))))

===========================================================

>(load "qp.lsp")              ; load the file qp.lsp
Loading QP.LSP
Finished loading QP.LSP
t

>(queen 8)                    ; execution of 8-queen
```

```
Error: QUEEN requires only
       one argument,
       but six were          ; error message saying the number
       supplied.             ; of arguments for queen is
                             ; wrong
Error signalled by QUEEN.

>>:b                         ; back trace
Backtrace: funcall > queen > queen1 >
cond > queen1 > cond > QUEEN

>>(ed "qp.lsp")

;; go back to the editor and restart loading
;; after changing (2) of queen to queen1

Loading QP.LSP
Finished loading QP.LSP
t

>>:q                         ; back to the top level

Top level.

>(queen 8)                   ; execution of 8-queen again

 . . . . Q . . .
 . Q . . . . . .
 . . . Q . . . .
 . . . . . . Q .
 . . . . . . . Q
 . . . . . Q . .
 . . Q . . . . .
 Q . . . . . . .

 . . . Q . . . .
 . Q . . . . . .
 . . . . Q . . .
 . . . . . . Q .
 . . . . . . . Q
 . . . . . Q . .
 . . Q . . . . .
 Q . . . . . . .
```

```
.  Q  .  .  .  .  .  .
.  .  .  Q  .  .  .  .
.  .  .  .  Q  .  .  .
.  .  .  .  .  .  Q  .
.  .  .  .  .  .  .  Q
.  .  .  .  .  Q  .  .          ; something is wrong
.  .  Q  .  .  .  .  .
Q  .  .  .  .  .  .  .          ; terminal interrupt
```

```
Correctable error: Console interrupt.
Signalled by CONS.
```

```
>>:q                           ; go back to the top level
```

```
Top level.
```

```
>(ed 'qp.lsp)
```

;; in the editor, add (break) at (3)

```
Loading QP.LSP
Finished loading QP.LSP
t
```

```
>(queen 8)                     ; reexecution
```

```
Break.                         ; execution of break
```

```
>>:b                           ; back trace
Backtrace: funcall > queen >
queen1 > cond > queen1 > cond >
queen1 > cond > queen1 > cond >
queen1 > cond > queen1 > cond >
queen1 > cond > queen1 > cond >
queen1 > cond > queen1 > cond >
queen1 > cond > queen1 > cond >
queen1 > cond > queen1 > cond >
queen1 > cond > queen1 > cond >
queen1 > cond > queen1 > cond >
queen1 > cond > queen1 > cond >
queen1 > cond > queen1 > cond >
queen1 > cond > queen1 > cond >
queen1 > cond > queen1 > cond >
queen1 > cond > queen1 > cond >
```

```
queen1 > cond > queen1 > cond >
queen1 > cond > queen1 > cond >
queen1 > cond > queen1 > cond >
queen1 > cond > queen1 > cond >
queen1 > cond > PRINT-SOLUTION
```

`>>:p`	; to check the value of a variable,
`Broken at COND.`	; set the environment to one before
	; cond
`>>:v`	; to check local variables

```
Local variables: right,left,column,
                 j, i, and n.
```

`>>n`   ; check the value of n
`8`

`>>i`
`8`

`>>j`
`0`

`>>column`
`(4 1 3 6 7 5 2 0)`

`>>left`
`(11 7 8 10 10 7 3 0)`   ; find an error,
                             ; i+j=8 is in left
`>>right`
`(3 5 2 -2 -4 -3 -1 0)`

`>>:r`   ; get out of the break

```
. . . . . Q . . .
. Q . . . . . . .
. . . Q . . . . .
. . . . . . Q .
. . . . . . . Q
. . . . . Q . .
. . Q . . . . .
Q . . . . . . .
```
                             ; error must be in left

`Break.`   ; call break again

`>>:q`   ; back to top level

```
Top level.
>(ed 'qp.lsp)
```

;; add (1)

```
Loading QP.LSP
Finished loading QP.LSP
t
```

```
>(queen 8)                          ; reexecution
```

```
Break.
```

```
>>:r
```

```
. . . Q . . . .
. Q . . . . . .
. . . . . Q .
. . Q . . . . .
. . . . . Q . .
. . . . . . . Q
. . . . Q . . .
Q . . . . . .                      ; succeeded!
```

```
Break.
```

```
>>:q
```

Symbol Index

=, 30, 98
/=, >, >=, <=, 30
+, -, *, /, 188
1+, 1-, 188

~a, ~A, 230
~b, ~B, 230
~d, ~D, 230
~e, ~E, 230
~o, ~O, 230
~s, ~S, 230
~x, ~X, 230
~%, 230

#\, 196, 228
#|, 228
#=, 213, 228
#-, 241
#+, 239
#(, 193, 229
#., 228
#', 122
#:, 34, 84, 228
##, 213, 228
#a, #A, 194, 229
#b, #B, 228
#c, 187
#o, #O, 228
#r, #R, 228
#s, #S, 205, 229
#x, #X, 228

&allow-other-keys, 108
&aux, 108
&key, 108
&optional, 108
&rest, 108

features, 238
load-verbose, 233

modules, 237
package, 73
print-array, 210
print-base, 210, 216
print-case, 71, 210
print-circle, 210, 213
print-escape, 210
print-gensym, 210
print-length, 210
print-level, 210
print-pretty, 210
print-radix, 210
read-base, 217
readtable, 217
standard-input, 208
standard-output, 209
terminal-io, 209

:allow-other-keys, 114
:append, 222
:array, 215
:base, 211
:capitalize, 215
:case, 214
:circle, 212, 228
:count, 157
:direction, 221
:downcase, 215
:element-type, 195
:escape, 209
:external, 80
:from-end, 157
:gensym, 215
:if-exists, 222
:inherited, 80
:initial-element, 153, 193, 199
:input, 221
:internal, 80

General Index